W9-ACP-188

SIX
BILLION
SHOPPERS

ALSO BY PORTER ERISMAN

Alibaba's World:
How a Remarkable Chinese Company Is
Changing the Face of Global Business

SIX
BILLION
SHOPPERS

THE COMPANIES
WINNING THE GLOBAL
E-COMMERCE BOOM

PORTER ERISMAN

ST. MARTIN'S PRESS ☒ NEW YORK

www.stmartins.com

Library of Congress Cataloging-in-Publication Data

Names: Erisman, Porter, author.
Title: Six billion shoppers : the companies winning the global e-commerce boom / Porter Erisman.
Description: First edition. | New York, N.Y. : St. Martin's Press, [2017] | Includes bibliographical references and index.
Identifiers: LCCN 2017010839| ISBN 9781250088673 (hardcover) | ISBN 9781250088680 (e-book)
Subjects: LCSH: Electronic commerce—Developing countries. | Consumers—Developing countries. | Entrepreneurship—Developing countries. | Developing countries—Commerce.
Classification: LCC HF5548.325.D44 E75 2017 | DDC 381/.142091724—dc23
LC record available at https://lccn.loc.gov/2017010839

ISBN 978-1-250-08867-3 (hardcover)
ISBN 978-1-250-16496-4 (international, sold outside the U.S., subject to rights availability)
ISBN 978-1-250-08868-0 (ebook)

Our books may be purchased in bulk for promotional, educational, or business use. Please contact your local bookseller or the Macmillan Corporate and Premium Sales Department at 1-800-221-7945, extension 5442, or by email at MacmillanSpecialMarkets@macmillan.com.

First U.S. Edition: September 2017

First International Edition: September 2017

10 9 8 7 6 5 4 3 2 1

For Melanie, Lindsay, and Jacob, with love

CONTENTS

ACKNOWLEDGMENTS

I'd like to offer my deepest gratitude to all of the entrepreneurs who shared their stories for this book.

Thanks also to Jason Overdorf for his help on the India chapter. Jason drew on his experience as a journalist in both China and India to help me connect the dots between the two countries.

I'd also like to thank the team at St. Martin's Press for their support in making this book happen. A special thanks to Emily Carleton, whose help and support on my first book, *Alibaba's World*, helped lead to *Six Billion Shoppers*, in which she also played an important role. I'd also like to thank the others at St. Martin's Press who helped with the book: George Witte, Annabella Hochschild, Donna Cherry, Sara Thwaite, Gabrielle Gantz, Karlyn Hixson, Paul Hochman, Rowen Davis, Sally Richardson, and Jennifer Enderlin.

Thanks also to my mother, who helped me recall the scenes we encountered when visiting the floating markets of Bangkok when we traveled there in 1985 (a trip that first sparked my interest in emerging markets). And finally, a special thanks to Mayumi, little Aili, my father, and the rest of my family for giving me the support and sense of purpose required to undertake a project like this.

SIX
BILLION
SHOPPERS

INTRODUCTION

A SHOPPING MALL IN EVERY POCKET

MY EYES LOCKED ON THE KNIFE BLADE, NOW WITHIN INCHES OF my throat. My attacker's three accomplices held my arms behind my back, exposing my chest. For a moment, e-commerce was the last thing on my mind. The more important question was, *Am I going to die here, in broad daylight, in a Bogotá alleyway?*

"*Barrio! . . . barrio! . . . barrio!*" Even with my *Sesame Street* Spanish, I recognized that word. *Neighborhood.* Clearly, I had entered the wrong one.

My first trip to South America was off to a bad start. I had arrived in Bogotá the night before to kick off a five-city speaking tour, during which I would share my experience of working at Alibaba and observing the e-commerce boom in China. I played it safe at first, crashing in my hotel room despite the tempting salsa music emanating from the bar across the street.

When daylight came, I ventured out along the avenue to the Plaza de Bolívar, a wide-open square lined by Spanish colonial buildings. The entire city seemed to be outside, with kids playing freely in the streets, which were closed to traffic. *Maybe Colombia*

*is much safer than what was depicted in all the drug movies I
watched when I was growing up,* I thought.

The only signs of Colombia's violent past were the police,
dressed in military fatigues and toting rifles over their shoulders.
Stationed at regular intervals along the avenue, they were clearly
in place to keep the peace and allow pedestrians to enjoy their
Sunday morning.

Emboldened by the added security, and eschewing old stereo-
types, I ventured outside the city center to see if I could find a path to
the top of a nearby mountain to get a view. I passed a yellow church
and could hear people singing hymns. From behind the church I
walked up a cobblestone path in the direction of the mountain.
That's where I met my teenage attackers.

As their angry yells got louder, the ringleader fumbled to lock
his folding knife in place, as if preparing to stab me. I began to
panic. "Please! Please! *No comprende. No comprende!*" I pleaded. I
pulled my wallet from my back pocket and dropped it on the
ground in front of me. I reached into my front pocket and handed
over my iPhone. Although they didn't seem to actually want my
money, I was offering everything I had.

Finally, the attackers let go of my arms and took a step back.
The leader scowled at me and motioned with his hand, shooing me
away. The message in his eyes was clear—don't come back. I ran
down the hill as fast as I could, cursing my naiveté.

"You must have crossed one of the barrio's invisible lines," a
local told me later. "There is a lot of drug and gang activity up there,
and people know where the boundaries are. People can be killed
for just walking into the wrong neighborhood. You're lucky you
didn't fight back."

I couldn't believe how naive I'd been. Personal safety was something I'd never had to worry about in China. This was a much-
needed reminder that in most developing countries, poverty comes
with a fair degree of violence.

Once I shook off the nerves, I realized I might have a bigger
problem. The Colombian government had sponsored my trip to

spread the gospel of e-commerce and entrepreneurship by drawing upon what I had learned in China. In a country where safety and security were such a concern, could those lessons apply? Just a few years earlier, Colombia was considered a failed state. Narcotrafficking had done huge damage to the country, destroying the economy and trust in government institutions.

But at that moment I finally understood the true role of e-commerce in emerging markets: e-commerce had succeeded in China precisely *because* the economic and legal infrastructure of the country was weak when the Internet was introduced. China lacked the economic, political, and legal institutions necessary for commerce to thrive, and Internet companies and their online communities had stepped in to fill the void.

And why wouldn't that be true elsewhere? From Bogotá to Shanghai, from Mumbai to Lagos, the weaker the institutions, the greater the opportunity for e-commerce to take root. And just as e-commerce entrepreneurs in China had faced and solved logistical, payment, and trust issues, Colombian entrepreneurs could use the Internet to address local concerns, including safety and security. And as a business community addresses these issues, e-commerce blossoms, creating new opportunities for entrepreneurs, multinationals, and customers alike.

Does this notion seem Pollyannaish? Absent the example of China, it might. But I had a front-row seat during China's e-commerce revolution, so it's clear to me that other countries are following suit, transforming both their economies and the way retail is conducted around the world. The boom will affect brands, retailers, providers of logistics, and financial institutions in highly disruptive ways that will become fully apparent only over time.

Just look at where China is today. In 2000, when I joined Alibaba, just as it moved out of founder Jack Ma's apartment, skeptics told me that e-commerce would never work in China. The reasons they cited were many: Payment infrastructure was inefficient. Credit card use was nearly nonexistent. Logistics infrastructure was poor. Engineering and management talent was concentrated in Silicon Valley. And, most important, they said, Chinese shoppers would never trust online merchants enough to buy products online.

Fast-forward less than twenty years, and the figures are staggering:

- China has now become the largest e-commerce market in the world.
- In 2016, in a single twenty-four-hour period, Alibaba's consumer websites alone handled more than $17.8 billion in transactions, more than the total combined online sales of Black Friday and Cyber Monday in the United States.
- E-commerce in China now represents 14 percent of total retail sales in the country, compared to 8 percent in the United States. By 2020, e-commerce in China will reach an estimated 21.5 percent of total retail sales in the country.[1]

And this is with only half of China's population online. We can only imagine how big the market will become as the rest of China moves online.

Since Alibaba's $25 billion[2] initial public offering (IPO) in 2014—the largest in history for *any* company—China has received most of the headlines about e-commerce. But the China experience has triggered an investment wave in e-commerce in India, Southeast Asia, Latin America, and Africa. This book will take you through these emerging mega-markets to show where they started, where they stand now, and where they likely are going.

To give the discussion historical context, I will begin in the United States, at the American frontier of the 1800s, when retail took root in the great emerging market of its time. Part of the story is how retail's gradual evolution in the United States made for a relatively smooth transition from traditional commerce to e-commerce, which the giants eBay and Amazon dominated in the early days. The other reason to start with the United States is that the early history of e-commerce in today's emerging markets has been one of failed attempts to apply US business models to developing countries. Understanding how the US experience skewed early attempts to introduce e-commerce to emerging markets can help us understand why e-commerce in the developing world—and brands and companies there—is growing in a different direction.

In Chapter Two we head to China, the biggest e-commerce market of all. To understand how China's deep cultural roots have led to a more social approach to e-commerce, we will visit some of China's remote villages. Then I'll explain how, after years of Maoism, the opening of China's economy triggered the conditions that enabled China's e-commerce to leapfrog beyond that of the West and play a much more important role in China than its counterparts did in North America and western Europe. In tracing this evolution, I will discuss some of the key players, including Tencent, Jingdong, and my former employer, Alibaba.

Chapter Three will cover China's current state of e-commerce and its likely future direction. China's market has matured into a more structured one than India's and Southeast Asia's, so it provides an excellent window to the future of e-commerce in emerging markets. I will describe how China's main platforms for e-commerce differ from those of eBay and Amazon. I also will show how Chinese businesses are making the most of the e-commerce opportunity and discuss some of the bigger trends and lessons of the Chinese experience.

In Chapters Four and Five we travel to India, the world's next mega-market. Mumbai's *dabbawallas* (lunchbox deliverymen) provide a great example of how innovative companies are overcoming one of India's biggest challenges, logistics. When I interviewed the key pioneers of e-commerce in India, they generously discussed their mistakes and their successes, India's unique challenges, and where its e-commerce may be headed. All the global e-commerce leaders, from eBay to Amazon to Softbank to Alibaba, have made India the center of a proxy war for global dominance of e-commerce, investing billions of dollars in a mad scramble for "the next China." What they are doing provides a sense of how businesses should be positioning themselves for India's e-commerce boom.

In Chapter Six we focus on Southeast Asia, which, after India and China, offers the greatest potential for e-commerce to flourish. But not all the new e-commerce companies in emerging markets are working in their own backyard. Rocket Internet, the company pioneering e-commerce in Southeast Asia, and the one most aggressive in its efforts to do e-commerce business there, is based in, of all places, Berlin. Although Rocket is not nearly as well known as Amazon, eBay, or Alibaba, it has been rolling out an e-commerce empire that spreads well beyond Southeast Asia to Nigeria, Pakistan, and Mexico City. It's known as a clone factory for starting small companies modeled on Amazon and Alibaba in more than one hundred countries and relentlessly building, through much trial and error, some of the leading e-commerce companies in their markets. But Rocket has also burned through cash and stirred controversy among investors, who are wondering when the payoff will come. Has Rocket pioneered a new model for the Internet as a "venture builder" that quickly and profitably adapts successful US business models for the developing world? Or has it simply led investors astray with salesmanship and a cynical business model based on copying the hard work of others? My interview with a senior Rocket executive provides some insights.

Indeed, e-commerce is booming in Southeast Asia. Indonesia has been the magnet for investors' money: Tokopedia alone has reportedly raised nearly $250 million to take on Lazada, a company started by Berlin's Rocket Internet. When I interviewed Tokopedia's founder, he described how he expects his company to battle Lazada, whose new controlling shareholder is Alibaba. Can Tokopedia, the self-proclaimed "komodo in the jungle," beat Alibaba's crocodile in the Yangtze at its own game? And what will the lessons be for other Southeast Asian markets?

In Chapter Seven we travel to Latin America, where e-commerce is beginning to take off after a somewhat slow start. Some of the early pioneers of Mercado Libre, the e-commerce leader in the region, have interesting ideas about why e-commerce expansion in Latin America has trailed growth in China—and why that may be about to change. In Mexico City, executives at Linio, Mercado Libre's Rocket-backed challenger, think they are poised to win the market in Latin America.

In Chapter Eight we travel to e-commerce's final frontier, Africa. There we meet Africa's largest homegrown e-commerce company, Konga.com, based in Lagos, Nigeria. One of the most formidable business assets of Nigeria, Africa's most populous nation, is its optimistic entrepreneurial spirit, quite a powerful force when attempting to overcome political instability and widespread corruption in order to do business.

Much of this book is written like a travelogue, and I want to explain why. In my eight years at Alibaba, I saw a common reaction from investors and Western companies that were entering the China market. They'd spend a lot of time discussing numbers, market potential, and the "what?" of the market. But they spent remarkably little time asking "why?" the market is how it is. I am hoping that by providing some additional texture—of places, the people who live there, and their culture—readers will get a better understanding of the context in which e-commerce is unfolding. It's not enough to know that China has 1.3 billion people and nearly 500 million of them shop online.[3] I want to help explain *how* they shop online and *why* they shop the way they do. That may help you avoid some of the pitfalls that have literally cost businesses billions of dollars as they attempted to crack e-commerce in emerging markets.

You'll see that I cover some markets, like China, in extensive detail, whereas my discussion of others, such as Southeast Asia, is broader. My goal is not to discuss every detail of every emerging market. Plenty of detailed analyses do that quite well. Rather, my goal is to focus on certain markets or companies to find the broad themes that tell the story of how e-commerce is developing.

You'll also notice that I'm focusing on e-retail of physical products, not other areas that are often included in e-commerce, such as travel and other services. That's because e-retail represents the biggest segment of consumer commerce. Once the market for physical products is transformed into e-commerce, other markets, such as online media and digital products, tend to follow.

A quick word about conflicts of interest. Although I have previously been employed by, or served as a consultant for, some of the companies I discuss in this book, I am no longer affiliated with any of them. With the exception of privately held Flipkart, in which I hold a small number of shares, I do not have a financial interest in any of the companies mentioned in this book.

For some of the entrepreneurs in the book who share a last name, such as Jack Ma and Pony Ma, or Binny Bansal and Sachin Bansal, I often use their first name, rather than last, so that readers can keep clear which Ma or Bansal I'm referring to.

Although I began this book with the idea of sharing what I had learned about breaking into e-commerce in emerging markets, I realized after my unfortunate encounter in that alley in Bogotá that those teenagers were precisely the people who could most benefit from e-commerce. In China I'd seen how e-commerce empowered struggling villagers by allowing them to sell their products online. And it offered those villagers who ventured to the city entry-level jobs as couriers. E-commerce has provided young students and recent graduates, who might otherwise have been destined to work in creaky state-owned enterprises, an outlet to pursue their dreams, create their own brands, and earn enough money to think about life and ideas beyond the need to put food on the table. It has also absorbed unemployed or displaced workers, giving them a foothold from which to rebuild their careers.

E-commerce has proved to be more creative than disruptive in emerging markets, creating opportunities that otherwise would not have existed, not simply killing old retail incumbents, as it did in the West. I hope that explaining how e-commerce is growing in emerging markets will help accelerate its adoption.

To be sure, creating opportunities for people to more easily buy and sell more stuff won't save the world. But e-commerce can arguably play a larger role than any other industry in lifting emerging markets out of poverty. The smartphone has done more than put a shopping mall in every consumer's pocket: it has also put a retail storefront in every entrepreneur's pocket. Plugging more small entrepreneurs from emerging markets into the global economy will help them escape poverty. Perhaps those successful entrepreneurs will include my attackers in Bogotá.

The story of the first twenty years of e-commerce was about the scramble to serve the developed world's one billion shoppers. The story of the next twenty years will be even more fascinating, as e-commerce marketplaces from China to India to Africa give entrepreneurs access to an even bigger prize—the emerging world's six billion shoppers.

HOW THE WEST WAS WON

O-ho the Wells Fargo Wagon is a'comin' down the street,
Oh please let it be for me!
—*The Music Man*

BEFORE YOU CAN TRULY UNDERSTAND E-COMMERCE IN EMERGING markets—and the mistakes it's already made—it's helpful to remember how e-commerce evolved in the United States. So I want to go back in time, to the American frontier—an open market if ever there was one.

IT'S 1875 ON the Nebraska plains, and as you watch the summer sun rise over your wheat fields, things are looking up. It should be a bumper year on the 160 acres that you occupied for five years and finally acquired from the US government. *Thank goodness for the Homestead Act*, you think to yourself. It's harvest time, and from now on, all profits from every harvest will be yours.

A rooster crows, telling you it's time to get the day started. You head outside and secure your horses to a mechanical reaper. You take a seat atop the reaper and grab the reins. With a strong whip and a loud *"Yaaarrr!"* you set the horses in motion. But before the squeaky wheel behind you has made a full revolution, you hear a loud *snap!* The horses veer off to the side, and the reaper spins out of control before finally wobbling to a standstill.

Darn it, you think. The leather on that brittle old harness must have broken. You dismount the reaper, examine the harness, and realize the leather is beyond repair. You'll need a new harness. So you unhitch the horses, take off the harness, saddle up your strongest horse and put the other in a field, and head off on the hourlong trip to town to visit the general store.

The dusty road takes you past neighboring homesteaders. Some are out in the fields. Spread across the countryside are a mix of wooden homes and wheat fields, some still occupied and some abandoned by homesteaders who found living off the land too hard or too lonely compared with the bigger towns and cities they came from.

After clomping along a dusty road for an hour, you arrive in town, which is not much more than a small cluster of wooden buildings. You head straight to the general store, a two-story log structure that also hosts the town's church. After tying up your horse, you walk in through the swinging doors, pleased to see some familiar faces.

"Well, look who's here!" announces the shop owner, Lee Addison, as you enter the room. You make the rounds, shaking hands with the other farmers, and take a seat in a rocking chair next to an empty barrel that doubles as a table. Gina Addison, who is married to Lee, soon puts a glass of lemonade on the table for you. "This will help you cool down," she says. "There's more where that came from."

"So what brings you to town?" asks Lee.

"Broke my harness this morning. I'm hoping you've got one here I can buy."

"I think I've got one in the storeroom. It runs fifty dollars. Let me go check."

Lee heads to the back of the store and you turn to your friend John Moore, who lives down the road. "Fifty dollars?" you whisper. "I love old Lee, but that's a lot of money for a harness. Farming is a good living, but in my next life I'm going to run a general store. That's where the real money is."

"I know what you mean," John replies. "Lee's a good man. But while we're out there sweatin' in the fields, he's sitting pretty here, sippin' lemonade and making a handsome profit. But ever since I got that Montgomery Ward catalog, I buy my big-ticket items there."

"Montgomery Ward? What the heck is that?"

John cranes his neck to make sure that Lee's not within earshot, lowers his voice to a whisper, and pulls out a small booklet with *Montgomery Ward Catalog* at the top. "Here, take a look," he says. "I'll bet you can find that same harness in here for half the price of what old Lee's sellin' it for."

Curiosity piqued, you flip through the book until you come across a selection of harnesses. You're amazed by the variety: double-buggy harnesses, single-strap harnesses, long-tug harnesses, plow harnesses, and even goat harnesses.

Running your finger along the page, you come to a double harness. It's only $25!

"Told you so," says John. "It'll only take a few weeks to get here, and I've got a harness I can lend you in the meantime. And if you don't like the new one, you can send it back for a full refund."

"But do you trust these fellas with your money?" you ask. "There are a lot of hucksters out there."

"I pay it cash on delivery. When you get to the American Express office, take a look at the harness. If you don't like it, you can send it back. Satisfaction guaranteed."

"No penalty?"

"Not even a dime. In fact, the wife and I are putting in an order next week. If you'd like, you can put your order in with ours."

You take John up on his offer and put in an order. And because you are saving money, you decide to add a couple items—a new hand mirror for your wife and a harmonica for your son.

"Keep the catalog," John says. "I'll get a new one with the order."

You hear old Lee's footsteps and quickly slip the catalog into your satchel. "Let's just keep this between us for now," John says.

"I don't want old Lee gettin' upset. I have to see him at church every Sunday."

Lee comes back into the room with the harness. "I found what you're looking for," Lee announces. "Why don't you come have a look?"

"Thanks, Lee. It looks nice. But I think I may have found a solution. What do I owe you for the lemonade?"

"All right, sir, as you wish," Lee says with a puzzled look. "Don't worry—the lemonade is on me."

You slap a penny on the counter and shake Lee's hand. He deserves something for the fresh lemonade, after all. "Thanks, Lee. Always a pleasure."

You walk out the swinging doors, untie your horse, and climb into the saddle. As you ride away, Lee scratches his head and turns to his wife. "He's a nice fellow. But that sure is a long way to ride for some lemonade."

THE EVOLUTION OF RETAIL

When we think of the first e-commerce innovators, several names come to mind. Amazon's Jeff Bezos. EBay's Pierre Omidyar. Even my former boss at Alibaba, Jack Ma. But few people would put Aaron Montgomery Ward on their list. In fact, what I remember of Montgomery Ward from my childhood is a crumbling old department store in a nearby shopping mall.

But Montgomery Ward was the Jeff Bezos of his time. If a Tech-Crunch Disrupt conference had been held in 1875, Montgomery Ward would surely have been the headliner. His business model was both innovative and disruptive, changing the way people shopped in the American West.

In 1872, the year Montgomery Ward was founded, the United States was the great emerging market of the world. The Civil War was nearly seven years in the past, and the peace accelerated a huge migration from East to West. The original spark for this migration was the Homestead Act, which Lincoln signed in 1862, thirteen months after the start of the Civil War, to encourage western migration by offering settlers 160 acres of public land. To earn the land homesteaders had to pay a nominal fee and live on the property for five years. After that it was theirs.

Before the Homestead Act, only 14 percent of Americans lived west of the Mississippi River. By 1890 that figure had nearly doubled.[1] About 70 percent of the population still lived in rural areas,[2] but the westward expansion helped make Chicago a major hub for the growing railway system. And where the railroads didn't go, express delivery services such as Wells Fargo and American Express served the western settlements with horse-drawn wagons.

The settlement of the West created an agricultural boom as the value of agricultural products tripled during the last five decades of the nineteenth century.[3] During this period manufacturing became increasingly important, and by 1900 the United States led the world in manufacturing, producing twice as much as England and half of all of Europe combined.[4] Although the diversity and availability of products quickly increased in the coastal cities, such goods had not yet found their way to the homes of customers scattered throughout the American West.

Residents of rural areas typically shopped at the local general store, which played an important part in the social lives of its customers, who had few other gathering spots. The general store was where the shopkeeper dispensed the latest crop intelligence and gossip about neighbors, and men might throw back some whiskey while complaining about the latest goings-on in Washington.

Yet farmers often resented store owners, who captured sizable margins on the products they sold. At the general store flour might be twice the wholesale price. The markup on shoes was 60 to 200 percent. Wool suits cost three times the wholesale price. And if customers purchased products on credit, they typically paid a punishing interest rate of 12.5 percent.[5]

Against this backdrop came Aaron Montgomery Ward, a former general store manager and traveling salesman. Ward had worked and lived among farmers and was familiar with their problems. He came up with a catalog business so he could sell directly to them. With $2,400 and his brother as a partner, Ward's first catalog was a single sheet of paper, just a price list for a handful of products. By 1874 it had grown to a seventy-two-page catalog with images, prices, and product descriptions.[6]

The Montgomery Ward catalog was the first general-item mail-order catalog to be published and shipped to farmers. Ward told his customers they would receive "the lowest wholesale prices. . . . By purchasing with us you save from 40 to 100 percent which are the profits of the middleman. . . . Don't waste your money by paying $35.00 for an article which you can get for $20.00." Throughout the catalog were small nudges for skeptical shoppers to take a leap of faith: "Never let good opportunities go by. If you do, you will never be rich."[7]

Ward knew westerners would be skeptical, so he encouraged buyers to check his references, saying, "We do not wish to be classed with the numerous swindlers of our city, and particularly desire every person to make inquiry about us before giving us an order. If this plan is always followed, honest men will be supported and swindlers will die out."[8] He encouraged his customers to tour Montgomery Ward's warehouse in Chicago. He also encouraged customers to contact his team, saying, "We cheerfully answer inquiries" and "We have 25 typewriters always ready to wait on you."[9]

If you didn't want to pay COD, you could send payment by US Post Office money order, American Express money order, or cash at a local Express office (and "express" at the time meant package deliveries done by horse and wagon). Where these services were not available, customers could pay with postage stamps. And anyone who examined their order upon delivery and found it not to their liking could simply return it for a refund.[10]

Before long, the Montgomery Ward catalog was available throughout rural America. By 1904 Ward was mailing more than three million of his six-hundred-page catalogs. While his catalogs did not replace the general store, they certainly challenged and disrupted it. Long trips to the growing cities to buy hard-to-find items were not as necessary. Montgomery Ward had brought Chicago's Michigan Avenue to shoppers on the frontier. With his catalog he'd put a well-stocked store on every kitchen table.

THE RISE OF BIG RETAIL

Had the Internet come along in Montgomery Ward's time, the majority of retail might have leapfrogged online, with Ward pioneering the way. But, as we know, this didn't happen, and America's physical retail infrastructure began its slow and steady evolution.

While catalogs battled general stores for retail dominance in rural America, cities gave rise to department stores, America's new "palaces of consumption." In 1878, when Macy's opened for business, a *New York Times* headline announced "The Great Sixth-Avenue Bazaar; Opening Day at Macy's & Co.'s—A Place Where Almost Anything May Be Bought." Other department stores appeared, including Marshall Field's in Chicago and Hudson's in Detroit. These glistening department stores, with their festive lighting and attractive window displays, became entertainment destinations, attracting city dwellers and visitors alike to spend an entire Saturday browsing the wide selections while dining at the stores' restaurants and tea rooms.[11]

The industrial revolution gave rise to a growing middle class hungry for new products. Seeing this trend, Ward and his rival, Richard Sears, extended their businesses beyond the catalogs, starting and aggressively growing their own retail stores. Ward had no stores in 1926 but had five hundred just three years later.[12] Sears rapidly grew his retail empire as well, building not just department stores but, after 1950, entire shopping malls, with Sears stores serving as the anchor tenant. J.C. Penney appeared in the western United States and built a large chain of department stores.[13]

America's growing culture of consumption survived the Great Depression and World War II, only to explode during the postwar boom. With the Depression and two wars behind them, Americans were more than ready to shop. When they turned on their television sets for the first time, they were exposed to a steady stream of product propaganda created by Madison Avenue. With the winds of national media at their backs, regional brands sailed outside their traditional boundaries and grew into national brands.

During the 1950s the demographics of the United States were changing along with its geography. The growing interstate highway system, combined with white flight from the cities, encouraged the growth of suburbs. When the white middle class moved to the 'burbs, retailers followed, and American shoppers drifted away from downtown department stores and into the enclosed malls, strip centers, and mass retailers that took their dollars from the 1950s into the 1990s. In the suburbs retailers faced lower costs of doing business and less expensive land, which helped them cut prices. Increasing car ownership meant shoppers could not only get to the malls but also stock up on products, filling the huge trunks of their cars with a month's worth of supplies.[14]

Retailers' consolidation into regional chains gave them even greater economies of scale. But it took a former general store owner named Sam Walton to recognize that American retail was ripe for yet another dramatic step.

THE WALMART EVOLUTION

If Montgomery Ward was the great retail disruptor of the nineteenth century, Sam Walton was his twentieth-century counterpart. His Walmart took physical retail to the limits of efficiency in a pre-Internet world. Combining scale with technology to bring down prices dramatically, he laid the groundwork and provided the inspiration for Jeff Bezos and Amazon. Walton's journey is worth exploring, because it helps explain the critical evolutionary step that emerging markets missed out on.

In 1945, when Sam Walton opened his first general store, a Ben Franklin franchise, retail in rural America was still fragmented and inefficient, with few chains that reached beyond their home markets. As Walton writes in his autobiography, "Our [Ben Franklin] store was a typical old variety store, 50 feet wide and 100 feet deep, facing Front Street, in the heart of town, looking out on the railroad tracks. Back then, those stores had cash registers and clerk aisles behind each counter throughout the store, and the clerks would wait on the customers. Self-service hadn't been thought of yet."[15]

Having clerks fetch products off the shelf might have helped prevent shoplifting, but customers found the process slow and annoying. But more significant than the slow service was that shoppers in rural America still had the same primary complaint they'd had for a hundred years—high prices. Retailers' margins ran from 30 to 45 percent, yet they offered little selection.

Walton pioneered the idea of accepting lower margins in exchange for higher volumes. Women's panties gave Walton his eureka moment: he saw that discounting prices on women's underwear at prices well below those charged by his competitor across the street led to much higher sales volumes. In what seems like common sense now, Walton explained his insight by saying:

> Here's the simple lesson we learned—which others were learning at the same time and eventually changed the way retailers sell and customers buy all across America: say I bought an item for 80 cents. I found that by pricing it at $1.00 I could sell three times more of it than by pricing it at $1.20. I might make only half the profit per item, but because I was selling three times as many, the overall profit was much greater. Simple enough. But this was really the essence of discounting.[16]

Selling high volumes of discounted products was the founding principle of the first Walmart, which opened in 1962 in Rogers, Arkansas. Walton was not the only one who figured this out. The same year, several other major discount chains opened, including Woolco, Kmart, and Target. Backed by parent companies that were goliaths of retail, like F.W. Woolworth, S.S. Kresge, and Dayton-Hudson, Walmart's discount competitors enjoyed strong financing and decades of experience. Yet Walmart would eventually best its competitors and emerge as the titan.

So what made Walmart succeed where others struggled?

In Walton's own words, it was necessity: "The things that we were forced to learn and do, because we started out underfinanced and undercapitalized in these remote, small communities, contributed mightily to the way we've grown as a company."[17] Indeed, an inefficient rural retail infrastructure meant that Walmart was able to leapfrog past its competitors and establish an entirely new way of doing business.

Walmart's explosive growth was an all-American tale of entrepreneurship. In the eight years after Walton opened that first store in Rogers, Walmart went on to build thirty-two stores with combined annual sales of $31 million. The strategy was to saturate rural markets: "Each store had to be within a day's drive of a distribution center. So we would go as far as we could from a warehouse and put in a store. Then we would fill in the map of that territory, state by state, county seat by county seat, until we had saturated that market area."[18]

An avid pilot, Walton scouted for locations from the cockpit of his two-seat turboprop airplane, which he originally bought as a way to get from one store to another. "But once we started really rolling out the stores, the airplane turned into a great tool for scouting real estate. . . . From up in the air we could check out traffic flows, see which way cities and towns were growing, and evaluate the location of the competition—if there was any. Then we would develop our real estate strategy for that market."[19]

One important factor helped propel Walmart beyond its competitors—Walton's early embrace of the computer. In 1966 Walton enrolled in an IBM school for retailers and saw the potential of using computers to capture sales information and manage inventory and logistics. He recruited a techie from among his classmates to help put together a computerized warehouse and distribution system. "We were forced to be ahead of our time in distribution and in communication," he wrote, "because our stores were sitting out there in tiny little towns and we had to stay in touch and keep them supplied."[20]

By 1980 Walmart had 276 stores that were generating $1.2 billion in revenue. With its distribution centers serving as the hub, routes to the stores serving as the spokes, and computer systems seamlessly linking them, Walmart was able to saturate retail in rural America. Walmart's expansion ultimately defeated the inefficient variety stores out on the frontier. "They were so accustomed to getting their 45 percent markup, they never let go," Walton later explained. "It was hard for them to take a blouse they'd been selling at $8.00 and sell it for $5.00, and only make 30 percent. With our low costs, our low expense structures and our low prices, we were ending an era in the heartland. We shut the door on variety store thinking."[21]

Walmart's explosive growth continued and the company seemed unstoppable. As Walmart entered the 1990s, it was the largest retailer in the United States. By 1992 it had 371,000 employees. The early 1990s saw Walmart begin to expand globally, and by the summer of 1995, it had nearly 2,500 stores.[22] Inspired by Walmart's successful business model, big-box retailers and category killers emerged, such as Toys "R" Us, Circuit City, and Barnes & Noble. One by one, these retail chains sucked up the business of smaller retailers, courting customers—and controversy—along the way. They pushed down prices, squeezing the margins of local retailers who couldn't compete with the scale and efficiency of their discount competitors.

By 1995 the efficiency of US retail seemed to have reached its upper limits. Virtually any product a consumer needed was within arm's reach and at a reasonable price. Want a Coke? Just stroll down to the local 7–Eleven or reach out to a vending machine. Want a new dress? Head to the nearby air-conditioned mall to shop in a wide variety of department stores and specialty retailers. Need groceries? The local supermarket has everything you could want. Want a book? Head to Barnes & Noble.

Indeed, by 1995 the US retail market was about as efficient and convenient as one could imagine. Products were readily available and prices were reasonable.

The American retail landscape had evolved from independent general stores and mom-and-pop shops to glossy air-conditioned stores with nationally recognized names in neon. Payment was easy: by credit card, debit card, or personal check. Shipping was convenient, reliable, and inexpensive.

Not sure about a product's quality? Just read *Consumer Reports*. Not sure about a retailer's integrity? Call the Better Business Bureau to find out if anyone has lodged complaints against that business. There seemed to be no new frontiers for retail.

Of course, as everyone now knows, the opposite was true—1995 was the start of a new era, when Netscape's IPO triggered the Internet revolution, with retail taking center stage. But when the Internet age arrived, it built on an efficient and mature physical retail infrastructure that had already embraced computers and data analysis. This perfect confluence of developments set the cogs of invention in motion for a young financial analyst in New York . . .

THE AMAZON REVOLUTION

For about fifty years Sam Walton carried the retail baton, pioneering the discount retailer business model. His folksy personality, sense of showmanship, and understanding of rural retail had made Walmart the king of the hill. But the advent of the Internet ushered in a new, more data-driven era, requiring a different set of skills. And a quant jock from Wall Street—Jeff Bezos—would take the baton from Walton and carry retail into the era of e-commerce.

Bezos got his initial inspiration for Amazon while working for a New York financial firm with a strong belief in quantitative analysis as the Internet began to take off. Analyzing the market, Bezos decided that books represented the best product category from which to start his "Everything Store." So he headed to tax-friendly Seattle, Washington, and started Amazon in his garage.

Although he and Walton approached retail with different personalities and from different angles, Bezos drew a great deal of inspiration from Sam Walton and Walmart. Walmart was an incredibly efficient, data-driven company that used technology to keep costs down. But Bezos did not need twenty-five hundred storefronts and addresses from which to sell his products. By bypassing physical storefronts and selling directly through his website from his garage, Bezos was able to squeeze a few more crucial drops of efficiency out of the Walmart model.

Amazon took advantage of the systems and processes that Walmart had helped create. Bezos poached some key logistics managers from Walmart, built on Walmart's expertise, and applied it to an online model. The basic science and technology of managing inventory in an efficient market was already there—it just needed a simple upgrade.

Bezos also benefited from other established links in the e-commerce chain. Customers could easily pay for their purchases with credit cards. The US Postal Service (USPS), although the butt of many jokes, was reliable enough for e-commerce: the mail-order catalog industry had already trained the postal service. And if the USPS proved too slow and bureaucratic, consumers could choose from a variety of reliable express shipping services that could deliver products overnight. Most important, Amazon's system could easily track its products.

Bezos also benefited from the world's best Internet infrastructure at the time. The US population was quick to adopt the Internet, and dial-up speeds were at least fast enough to upload product images before customers gave up.

By the dawn of the twenty-first century, Bezos had a firm grip on the baton that had been handed from Montgomery Ward to Sam Walton. The success of Bezos's inventory-led model landed him on the cover of *Time* as the Person of the Year in December 2000. Amazon was on its way to becoming the dominant online store for everything. But while Amazon focused on new items, the Internet had no equivalent for used items and collectibles, which gave rise to the other e-commerce giant of its day.

EBAY: THE EVERYTHING ELSE STORE

Bezos pioneered the inventory-led model, but he was not the only one riding the e-commerce wave. In the San Francisco Bay Area, Pierre Omidyar, a software programmer, was experimenting with a site called AuctionWeb. When the first item Omidyar listed on the site, a broken laser pointer, sold to an electronics enthusiast in Canada, Omidyar realized that the Internet might be a great way to connect buyers and sellers of used items and collectibles. His marketplace quickly attracted people trading in all sorts of odd goods and collectibles. Within a year AuctionWeb's sales reached $7.2 million. One year later, driven partly by the Beanie Baby frenzy, AuctionWeb's sales reached $95 million.[23]

As his website grew massively popular, Omidyar changed AuctionWeb's name to eBay in 1997. A year later he hired a seasoned MBA, Meg Whitman, as CEO. Six months after that Whitman led eBay to a highly successful IPO on Nasdaq. Using the IPO money, Whitman helped power eBay's international expansion and extended eBay's auction model to western Europe, where it proved to be a hit. EBay's business model worked because it allowed sellers to empty out their basements and attics and find buyers for items that would otherwise not have found a market. EBay's model proved that strangers in the United States and western Europe could trust each other to do business online. EBay argued that its success had proved that, when it came to e-commerce, "People are basically good."

By 1999 eBay had joined Amazon atop the list of e-commerce media darlings, with Whitman and Bezos gracing *Business Week*'s cover, under the headline "eBay vs. Amazon."[24] Amazon grew into the leading everything store for new products. EBay grew into the leading store for everything else: used goods, collectibles, and one-of-a-kind products. The only remaining question was, which of these companies would ultimately dominate global e-commerce?

THE AMERICAN INDEPENDENTS

While the e-commerce whales eBay and Amazon captured most of the imagination and media attention, a number of other sizable fish were swimming in the same ocean. Existing retailers and individual brands began to build their own online retail stores. They moved more slowly than their purely Internet counterparts but still represented the majority of e-commerce sales in the United States. Operating their own websites offered several advantages over selling on a platform like Amazon. With their own websites they could control the branding, service, and overall customer experience. And they could direct their existing customers to their websites through their offline marketing efforts. In addition, many of these merchants offered catalogs from which their customers had been ordering products by telephone for many years. These merchants knew how to fulfill orders remotely through an efficient shipping and delivery infrastructure in the United States.

But one factor above all others allowed e-commerce by independent retailers to flourish in the United States—a high-trust environment, something that most residents of industrialized countries take for granted. Indeed, the fundamental requirement for e-commerce is trust. One element is trust between the merchant and the customer. Because brands and retailers in the United States had a history with consumers, they found this trust relatively easy to transplant from an offline environment to an online one. For example, customers knew that J.Crew would honor its return policy online, just as it did offline.

A second component of trust is more abstract—trust in institutions that protect customers in case of fraud or a dispute between a buyer and seller. Customers knew that credit agencies, media, and nonprofits like the Better Business Bureau held vendors accountable. They also knew that, in the event a dispute couldn't be resolved, they could turn to the courts for protection. Most online shoppers assumed that, so long as they were dealing with a merchant based in the United States, reasonable protections were in place, and merchants would honor and fulfill their online purchases.

These factors allowed thousands of retailers to emerge online, coexisting with eBay and Amazon. Retailers could simply create their own online storefront, plug in to the existing logistics and payment infrastructure, and be up and running on the Internet. Combined, these retailers constituted the majority of the e-commerce market. To bring traffic to their online stores, they could simply market their URL to existing customers or place banner ads on other websites. Later, when Google pioneered search advertising, retailers had even more cost-effective ways to bring traffic to their websites.

THE END OF AN ERA AND DAWN OF A NEW ONE

In December 2000, just one year after *Time* named Jeff Bezos Person of the Year, Montgomery Ward announced it was closing its doors after 128 years, shutting 250 stores and dismissing its 28,000 associates. The retailer cited a disappointing holiday season, no doubt influenced by the growing influence of e-commerce. Ward's collapse was a strong reminder that today's disruptors can become tomorrow's fallen giants.

Montgomery Ward had abandoned its catalog in 1985, the same year that the first dot-com domain name was registered.[25] It's easy to see what Aaron Montgomery Ward's retail revolution might have looked like if it had happened in the Internet era. All it takes is a look westward from his base in Chicago, past the wheat fields of America's frontier, across the Pacific Ocean, and into the heartland of China.

2

THE RISE OF E-COMMERCE IN CHINA

Share of e-commerce in China is likely to be the defining
measure of business success on the Net.

— *Meg Whitman, 2005*

BACK IN 2000, WHILE HEADLINES ABOUT EBAY AND AMAZON DOM-
inated the business media, it was hard to imagine that China would
soon overtake the United States as the world's e-commerce leader.

But in 2016, China's online transaction volumes surpassed
those of the United States, with more than 450 million online shoppers generating $750 billion for the year.[1] And while the market is
already huge, the next few years' growth could be staggering. The
revolution that Alibaba pioneered has given way to a genuine
boom, led by hungry e-commerce entrepreneurs who have followed
in Alibaba's wake, building innovative business models with no
Western equivalent. This momentum seems only to be accelerating.
Just consider the following retail projections by eMarketer for
2020[2]:

- China will spend nearly $2.5 trillion online, 3.5 times as
  much as the United States.
- China's 575 million online shoppers will account for 60 percent
  of the world's online sales.
- These 575 million customers will account for only half of

China's population, which means the room for growth remains huge.

- China's online sales will continue to grow at 24 percent, the fastest rate in the world.

How did this all happen, and what does it mean for businesses worldwide? And what is it about China's evolution that has made e-commerce follow a different path than that of the West? Behind these astounding numbers lies a set of historic, economic, social, cultural, and political factors. To fully understand the context, it is helpful to travel beyond the gleaming skyscrapers of China's modern cities to the villages and rice paddies of rural China.

THE VILLAGES: THE HEART OF CHINESE CULTURE

The gravel under my bicycle tires ground and popped as I rolled down the winding mountain road into the tiny village in the heart of Guizhou Province. I was on a solo bicycle journey, loosely retracing the route of the Red Army's Long March. It was 2002, the depth of China's Internet bust years, and Jack Ma and I had agreed that I'd take a year off from Alibaba until he needed someone with my international skill set again. I took advantage of my sabbatical to revisit one of my favorite places—China's rural interior.

This was my fourth visit to Guizhou, China's least developed province. It was not a popular vacation spot for China's city dwellers, but I kept coming back, lured by the rural scenery and traditional life that offered a window on the roots of Chinese culture. Even in 2002, life in Guizhou was much as it had been for thousands of years. Farmers with pointy straw hats waded through water as they used compliant water buffalo to plow the terraced rice paddies.

The cooperation of villagers was apparent at every turn. To irrigate the fields, families with adjoining plots worked together to allow water to flow in a controlled manner from one rice paddy to the next, making sure that each interconnected plot received ample water for the rice to grow and thrive. Unlike the wheat farming of the American West, this was no individualist pursuit. Sorting out the irrigation routes, resolving any disputes, and ensuring social harmony required the coordination of the entire village.

Villages composed of tightly clustered wooden homes sat at the base of the hills, separated only by narrow winding footpaths. The villages offered a strong sense of community but little privacy. It was often hard to know where one family's property ended and the neighbor's began. During the day the villagers worked together, helping each other when machinery broke down. At night they drank rice wine together, celebrated festivals, and—no doubt—quietly gossiped with each other about other residents who perhaps were not carrying their weight in the community.

Market days were often announced by the early morning wail of pigs being slaughtered, a sound so loud that I at first thought an airplane was landing. Villagers would fill baskets with their goods, tie them to opposite ends of a bamboo pole, sling the cargo over their shoulders, and walk slowly down the hillsides, the baskets bouncing with their steps.

The markets rotated from village to village depending on the day of the week. Early on market days villagers would stake out a good position along the roadside, setting up their baskets and scales. Meat sellers clustered at one end of the market, with prospective buyers inspecting and weighing live chickens, ducks, fish, snakes, and—yes—even dogs. At another end of the market farmers sold produce and grains, negotiating with buyers over the prices of their bok choy, mushrooms, chili peppers, and cabbage. Buyers often frequented sellers from whom they'd bought for years, and the price they settled on depended on their relationship.

I always enjoyed my time in the villages, even if the hospitality could be a bit smothering. But each time I left a village, people warned me about the folks in the next place I was pedaling to: "You're safe in our village here. But be careful when you get to the next town. There are some shady characters over there." I'd toss my saddlebags onto the back of my bike, pedal to the next village, and find myself smothered in hospitality again. When it was time to leave, I got the same warning. Their repetition of this advice made it clear to me that trust within the tight-knit social circles in China did not extend to strangers from other groups.

Did Rice Cultivation Put the Social in China's Social Commerce?

I didn't know it then, but my visits to China's villages would help me answer one question that always bugged me—*why* is commerce so much more social in China than in the United States? The answers may lie in an unexpected place—a 2014 study about the effect of rice cultivation on culture.

For years studies by cross-cultural psychologists have shown that Westerners tend to be more individualistic in their worldview and East Asians more interdependent and group oriented. While long observed, these differences had never been convincingly explained. Before 2014 the prevailing explanation for this was a theory of modernization—that as countries modernize, people become more individualistic. But this didn't explain why individuals in wealthy modern societies like Japan and Korea still maintained a strong sense of shared collective identity.

But a 2014 study published in the journal *Science* laid out a persuasive hypothesis—that a tradition of rice cultivation is a stronger predictor of interdependent thinking than modernization. The researchers offered a "rice theory of culture" that argues that because rice paddies need standing water, farmers in rice regions need to closely cooperate to build elaborate irrigation systems. Wheat farming simply requires rain, making it less important for neighboring farmers to work together. On the other hand, the study explained, "paddy rice makes cooperation more valuable. This encourages rice farmers to cooperate intensely, form tight relationships based on reciprocity and avoid behaviors that create conflict."[3]

The researchers had asked study participants to sketch diagrams of their social networks using circles to represent themselves in relation to their friends. To measure the differences in outlooks, the researchers simply measured the sizes of the circles and found that

Westerners drew themselves significantly larger in relation to the others in their networks than did their East Asian counterparts. The researchers found that Americans are likely to draw the circle representing themselves about 6 millimeters larger than the circles for others in their network, while Europeans draw themselves 3.5 millimeters larger. In contrast, Japanese draw themselves smaller than the others in their network.

Researchers found cultural differences even within China between rice-farming and wheat-farming regions. In the wheat-farming north, participants were likely to have a more individualistic worldview. In the rice-farming south, participants had a more collectivist view. An important finding is that this difference persisted among city dwellers, who had acquired their cultural traits from ancestors over centuries, suggesting that this tendency toward tight social networks survives modernization.

Could rice cultivation explain this major difference between Chinese and Western culture? To me, it seems as likely as anything I've heard so far. During my fifteen years in China, it became clear that group associations were much deeper there than in the United States. I didn't need to look any further than Alibaba, where my Chinese colleagues were much more excited about and willing to go along with group activities than their Silicon Valley counterparts. Company celebrations might end with all in attendance holding hands and singing songs. At annual meetings my colleagues and their teams would gladly dress up in costumes and do cheers. One annual event for Alibaba employees and their spouses even evolved into a mass wedding celebration, complete with Jack Ma leading an exchange of vows between couples. In the United States, Silicon Valley companies come under criticism for being cultlike. But you'd be hard-pressed to find a Silicon Valley start-up where employees gather at company events to hold hands and sing about rainbows—a not-unusual occurrence at Alibaba and other Chinese tech companies.

Groups in China simply have a much greater sense of shared identity than do groups in the West. This is evident even in the leadership of some tech giants in China. In the United States, tech founders seem to come in pairs. Steve Jobs and Steve Wozniak. Bill Gates and Steve Ballmer. Sergey Brin and Larry Page. But in China, the founders come in groups. Alibaba had eighteen cofounders. Baidu had seven knights. Ctrip had Four Tigers. Even today Alibaba's corporate control is in the hands of the twenty-seven members of the Alibaba Partnership. This structure has been controversial in the West, drawing criticism for taking control of the company from average investors and putting it in the hands of a large committee. But it makes sense, given the strong group orientation in China.

Why am I discussing China's cultural roots at such length? Because Western companies that didn't understand the role of culture in China's e-commerce landscape have wasted billions of investment dollars. As I will show, this group orientation explains how merchants and buyers do business online, how trust flows through e-commerce in China, why Chinese consumers are more likely to rate and recommend products than their Western counterparts, and why new e-commerce models are upending traditional product development cycles by using online communities to help create products for the brands that serve those shoppers.

But before I get to these revolutionary new models, let me trace the evolution of e-commerce in China.

THE GREAT LEAP BACKWARD: CHINA'S RETAIL IN MAO'S DARK AGES

In the 1930s no shopping street in China was more famous than Nanjing Road. It ran through the heart of Shanghai's international settlement and stretched about 1.5 miles from the Bund to the racetrack. Visitors from China's countryside would have walked down the wide boulevard as trams, double-decker buses, rickshaws, cars, and pedestrians all vied for space in the bustling street, which was lined with a unique blend of colonial architecture, Art Deco buildings, and Chinese shophouses adorned with elaborate wooden carvings. And no shopping trip to Nanjing Road would have been complete without a visit to the Dai Sun department store—China's largest—where shoppers could find a variety of goods unavailable elsewhere in China, including Cuban cigars, Swiss watches, and German fountain pens. To make their city experience complete, shoppers at Dai Sun would line up to ride on China's first and only escalator.[4]

But the consumer paradise abruptly came to an end when Mao's Red Army captured Shanghai and communist soldiers marched down Nanjing Road in May 1949. Just five months later Mao stood in Beijing's Tiananmen Square to proclaim the founding of the People's Republic of China. Soon thereafter China's private businesses were nationalized as "whole people enterprises," plunging China's retail into an ice age.

Under Mao, China's wholesalers and retailers were organized into hierarchical, state-run entities, transforming their function from profit-making enterprises to simple storage facilities that managed the flow of products from state-owned factories to central distribution centers and then to local wholesalers and finally to retailers and end users. The state set prices and issued citizens commodity ration coupons for daily necessities such as food, fuel, and even bicycles. Rations were distributed equally to ensure that everyone in the collective system would receive their fair share. The government creatively rebranded the Dai Sun department store as the "No. 1 Shanghai Department Store," and its former competitors became known as the "No. 2," "No. 3," and "No. 4 Shanghai Department Stores" (if only branding today were so easy). For the next thirty years, while Walmart and the US retail chains were busy consolidating and modernizing retail in the United States, China's economy and retail infrastructure were locked in a deep freeze.

OPENING AND REFORM: THE CHINESE CONSUMER COMES BACK TO LIFE

Mao's planned economy failed to provide the paradise it promised, and nearly thirty years later Deng Xiaoping brought about the reforms that gradually thawed China's economy out of its ice age and returned China to a market economy. Buyers and sellers could once again haggle over prices, and going through state-owned wholesale channels was no longer mandatory. But as China's economy opened up, the reform of retail was particularly slow, because of the Communist Party's sensitivity about private property ownership and its desire to preserve stability in the prices and supplies of basic goods.

Thus, even as China opened up, its retail remained stodgy, slumbering, and slow to adopt technology. When I arrived in Beijing as a student in 1994, I had to take a forty-five-minute cab ride across town just to find imported products at the state-run Friendship Store. Long counters separated shoppers from the products for sale. Getting a product from the shelves required catching the attention of a sleepy clerk who would write down your order on a flimsy piece of paper you took to the cashier. Once you paid, the cashier would stamp the paper, and you had to return to the counter to present your stamped receipt to claim your product. The concept of self-service—or even shopping carts—hadn't quite caught on yet. Want another product in another category? Then repeat the process a second time in the section of the store devoted to that product's particular category. Want another? Repeat it a third time. By the time I got the Pringles and electric razor I'd come for, I felt as if I'd applied for citizenship.

The introduction of international retail management, expertise, and technology no doubt would have made China's retail channels more efficient overnight and brought down prices for consumers. But rather than embrace international retailers, China's leaders decided to play it safe and took baby steps instead. From 1978 to 1991, they forbade foreign investments in retail and wholesale. Starting in 1992, they allowed some foreign investment but largely limited it to special economic zones. Even then, government rules required that Chinese partners had to own 51 percent of all retail businesses, and imported products could not make up more than 30 percent of the items on offer. For the next few years foreign investment in retail operated in a regulatory gray area, with local government policies and national policies often unclear and at odds. Regional chain stores began to grow in the more sophisticated cities but usually were locally operated and lacked modern international retailing techniques.

The turning point came in 2001, when China became a member of the World Trade Organization, which required that retail be fully liberalized. In 2004 China lifted most restrictions on foreign investment in retail. Walmart, the French department store Carrefour, and others began to aggressively expand from their bases in the major cities and into the second-, third-, and fourth-tier cities. But what started as a race between offline retailers took an unexpected twist when the Internet hit China's shores.

EARLY E-COMMERCE IN CHINA:
US MODELS AND OTHER FALSE STARTS

The "Amazons of China"

For those of us in China in 1995, the Netscape IPO that sparked the US tech boom seemed a world away. Except for a few expats and academics who used the Internet to stay connected with overseas colleagues and friends, the Internet was slow to catch on in China. But as the US dot-com boom reached a crescendo in 1999, US investors began to look beyond the United States, and China was suddenly in their crosshairs, even though fewer than ten million Chinese were online.

The highly successful Nasdaq IPO of Yahoo!-style portal China .com in July 1999 was the catalyst that China's Internet needed, and venture capitalists soon were on planes to China in search of the next big things. They were attracted by the familiar—companies modeled after Amazon, with its business-to-consumer (B2C) model, and eBay, with its consumer-to-consumer (C2C) auction model. They assumed that these business models would soon dominate e-commerce. For investors eager to see Chinese counterparts to the US success stories, there were a number of e-commerce companies following the Amazon and eBay playbooks.

The most commonly replicated approach was Amazon's B2C

model, which embraced the notion of building large central warehouses, stocking a variety of goods across many categories, and using the Internet as a storefront. In China the most visible and prominent of these Amazon clones was 8848, started by a former software retailer, Wang Juntao. Wang started 8848 in March 1999 with the goal of making the company as well known as the origin of its name, Mount Everest and its altitude of 8,848 meters. Wang was quickly dubbed the "father of China's e-commerce" and graced the covers of business magazines around the country.

Other Amazon clones followed Wang Juntao into B2C. The husband-and-wife duo Li Guoqing and Peggy Yu opened Dangdang.com in November 2009, entering the market, like Amazon did, as an online bookseller. Yu, an MBA grad of New York University, had worked on Wall Street after graduation and observed the rise of Amazon. Her husband, a book publisher in China, became her partner in the start-up, bringing book industry expertise. Together they created China's largest online bookstore. Not far behind Dangdang was another online bookseller, Joyo.com, which had financial backing from the software maker Kingsoft in late 1999.

Despite lots of media buzz, complete with dot-com essentials such as workers who roller-skated around warehouses (Segways were not invented till 2001), these B2C businesses gained neither traction nor profits. The Amazons of China soon realized that not enough shoppers were online to drive the sales volumes required to justify their asset-heavy business models. Even as the number of netizens grew in China, the overall infrastructure for commerce was too inefficient to allow these businesses to realize sufficient profits. Amazon had been successful in the United States because its business model built on an efficient infrastructure for managing inventory, shipping, logistics, and payment. But in China everything had to be built from scratch, making it simply too expensive to squeeze out any profits. Credit card penetration was negligible, so companies had to rely on cash on delivery, a more expensive option. Logistics were costly because China's logistics players were fragmented, regional, and didn't communicate with each other, raising the costs—and time—for getting a product from warehouse to doorstep. Reverse logistics to manage returns were even more complicated. China had no history of a thriving mail-order catalog industry, and delivery there was traditionally one way, providing no easy way for customers to return products. Worse, companies and customers had no technology that would allow them to track the delivery of a product through the fulfillment process.

The mounting costs made the Amazon B2C model unworkable in China. Two years after he was dubbed the father of e-commerce in China, Wang Juntao was forced out of 8848. Internal divisions and disputes between Wang and his board ultimately led to their divorce. Not long thereafter, 8848 shut down.[5]

The other Amazon clones, Dangdang and Joyo.com, managed to survive the bursting of the Internet bubble and limped through the next few years as more and more Chinese came online. But their businesses never became significant to the overall e-commerce market in China. Amazon bought Joyo for $75 million in 2004, a purchase that returned little value to the investors who had invested more than $52 million in the company just before the sale. Dangdang fared better, managing to go public on the New York Stock Exchange in 2010. Although Dangdang is a success story in its own right, its market share has hovered around 1 percent of China's total e-commerce market, never quite making the impact that its investors had hoped for and certainly not the impact its counterpart, Amazon, has made in the US market.[6]

The eBay of China

Although Amazon's inventory-led model failed to drive China's e-commerce forward, eBay's marketplace model did slightly better. EBay's successful 1998 IPO inspired several eBay clones in China, led by entrepreneurs hoping to replicate eBay's success. Rising to the top was EachNet, founded in 1999 by Shao Yibo, a mathematics whiz who was one of the first students from mainland China to receive a full scholarship to Harvard. Shao worked at Boston Consulting Group for two years, returned to Harvard for business school, and headed back to China after graduation to join the Internet gold rush. He raised $7 million in angel funds and venture capital and was soon on his way with EachNet.[7]

Shao quickly learned that China faced unique obstacles to making a success of the auction model, chief among them the lack of trust between buyers and sellers who had no previous relationship. Whereas eBay in the United States had concluded that "people are basically good" in their e-commerce dealings, Shao was finding the China market tougher, lamenting that "in the U.S., if you place a bid, it's a contract, and by law you need to fulfill that bid if you win the auction. That's very clear. People would be afraid of getting sued if they did not abide by that contract. In China people don't care." He described the attitude of early EachNet users as "'I place a bid, I don't want it anymore, tough luck.'"[8]

To help address the issue of trust, EachNet limited its auctions to Shanghai and set up trading posts where customers could meet sellers in person after connecting online. At the trading posts customers would inspect the goods to their satisfaction and then pay cash. But by 2001 Shao had found these trading posts too expensive to use nationally and shut them down.

It became apparent that eBay's auction model was not suitable for the China market. EBay's auction model had succeeded in the United States because it provided a marketplace where one-of-a-kind items could find a price. Whether it was a collectible, like a hard-to-find Pez dispenser, or a used item, like a slightly faded oriental rug, the only way to determine the market price was to put it online and allow people to bid on it. Instead of putting the items on the front lawn for a yard sale that might attract only nearby neighbors, eBay created a nationwide yard sale where sellers had a better chance of finding the specific item they were looking for. And with its auction model, prices would start low and escalate with the bidding until they reached the market price.

Chinese, on the other hand, did not have basements or garages full of consumer goods that had accumulated for years. They had relatively few possessions and an aversion to buying used goods.

And forget about collectibles. Outside of a few antiques, the one collectible item that everyone had was the one they were hoping to get rid of—Mao's *Little Red Book* and its ideology.

It turned out that a marketplace for new, standardized products had a better chance of success than one designed for used items and collectibles, so EachNet acquired a distributor in its hottest category, mobile phones, and began to focus more on mobile phones and accessories.

But EachNet still faced challenges, especially with payment and logistics, because of the big gaps in China's commercial infrastructure. To address the payment issue, EachNet encouraged customers to apply for credit cards, which had been allowed only since 1999, but their participation was slow. And credit card usage still didn't solve the chicken-and-egg problem of settlement risk—a merchant hesitant to send the product before receiving payment, and a buyer hesitant to send money before receiving the product. To resolve this issue EachNet set up its own escrow service to hold customers' payments and release them only after they confirmed satisfactory delivery of the product. EachNet took a 3 percent commission on each transaction. But the service never took off and was sidelined in favor of developing a direct payment system like PayPal, which had been a key driver of eBay's growth in the United States.

In 2002 EachNet reached about three million registered users, generating a transaction volume of about $2 million per month—big for the China market but a drop in the bucket for its US counterpart, eBay. But EachNet's prospects received a sizable boost when Shao's sister Harvard Business School alum Meg Whitman led eBay to invest $30 million for a 33 percent stake in EachNet. EBay had already become one of the most valuable Internet companies in the world, and Wall Street's confidence in Whitman and her company's business model were at an all-time high. EBay's investment provided Shao with the funds that would allow his business to take a quantum leap. In return eBay got a compelling story to tell Wall Street about eBay's growth in China at about the time the US company suffered a resounding defeat in Japan at the hands of Softbank and Yahoo. Fifteen months after its initial investment, eBay exercised an option to take full control of EachNet and invested an additional $150 million.

In 2003, back at eBay's home in San Jose, California, the prospects for EachNet must have seemed bright. And on Wall Street they must have seemed even brighter. In eBay's reach for global domination, it had never failed to win a market in which it was the market leader. The network effects of a marketplace had simply proved too great for any challengers to overcome. But eBay soon found itself in battle with a competitor it hadn't anticipated.

Enter Alibaba and the B2B Marketplaces

The rise of my former boss, Jack Ma, and my former employer, Alibaba, has been well documented by now, but it's worth revisiting just how Alibaba became China's e-commerce leader and, in particular, how Alibaba's business model evolved differently from that of eBay, Amazon, and their Chinese counterparts. The Alibaba story helps explain e-commerce in China and illuminates how e-commerce might develop in other emerging markets that share the characteristics of China.

Jack Ma was born in Hangzhou in 1964 and came of age just as China was opening up to the world. He took an interest in English and befriended foreign tourists who visited his hometown; he would walk them around Hangzhou's famous West Lake at a time when few cities in China were open for tourism. His love of English led him to become an English teacher, and, after twice failing the math portion of his college entrance exams, Jack finally enrolled in a teacher's college. After graduation he spent five years as an English teacher before striking out on his own to start the Hope translation company in 1994.

The translation business grew in parallel with the export boom on China's east coast, with small exporters seeking his help in translating their marketing materials into English. Over time he could see that one of the biggest challenges these small exporters faced was finding buyers for their products. The traditional methods of trade shows and printed catalogs were expensive, and catalogs were out of date almost as soon as they were printed.

While on a trip to the United States in 1994, Jack was introduced to the Internet by a friend, and he was struck by an idea—he would build a website to connect Chinese companies and customers overseas. Upon returning to China, he created China Pages, an online English directory of Chinese companies and information that is still regarded as China's first Internet company. As the company grew, China Pages caught the attention of a local government-backed telecom company, which pressured Jack into a partnership. But he quickly realized that he and his new partners had different visions for the Internet, so he left China Pages to join a government department in Beijing that was helping China's smaller businesses use the Internet.

In Beijing Jack soon realized that the government officials he worked with wanted to use the Internet to control, rather than empower, China's small enterprises. He decided to leave Beijing, and in 1999, just as the Internet boom was beginning to reach China, he gathered seventeen friends in his Hangzhou apartment to start Alibaba.com. He hoped that the website would help businesses around the world find new business opportunities and share in the treasures of e-commerce.

While EachNet, Dangdang, Joyo, and 8848 were focused on making it possible for consumers to buy items online, Alibaba was focused purely on building a business-to-business (B2B) marketplace. Alibaba wasn't alone in the B2B space as Internet start-ups, such as MeetChina.com, and traditional catalog businesses, such as Global Sources, were transitioning to an online business model.

When I joined Alibaba in 2000, most Americans, including me, were not familiar with import-export as a sector for small and medium-sized businesses. I had no idea where the metal springs in our ballpoint pens came from. And those plastic knobs on our backyard sprinkler systems? They somehow just showed up. But along China's east coast, tens of thousands of manufacturers of all sizes were busy producing the widgets, components, textiles, and general "stuff" that went into the items people used each day.

Back in 2000, the common refrain among Wall Street investors and analysts was that the "holy grail" for any B2B marketplace was to build an end-to-end transaction platform that would allow importers to make wholesale purchases with the click of a button, just as someone could instantly buy a book from Amazon online. "Just think," went the argument. "If you can capture just a one percent commission on the $6.8 trillion of world trade, a B2B marketplace could grow as large as a hundred Amazons."

But when Alibaba made a brief attempt to build an end-to-end transaction platform, we quickly learned that this argument had a central flaw. Sure, the Amazon model worked well when the only real variable in the purchase process was price, and everything else—such as delivery and payment terms—was largely constant. But import and export of items in wholesale volumes often have variables more important to businesses and that businesses want to negotiate. Product quantities, payment terms, shipping terms, production timing, and quality control were all important variables that they needed to negotiate. With large orders worth hundreds of thousands of dollars, importers and exporters were in a constant battle to push their risks to the other party. If you were purchasing a thousand champagne glasses for a hotel, price might be the most important variable. But if you were purchasing a thousand champagne glasses with "Welcome to the 2001 U.S. Open" emblazoned on them, timing might be the more important term. After all, if the exporter missed the event deadline, the glasses no longer had value. And what if glasses broke in shipment? Who would bear the risk?

We quickly abandoned the idea of building an end-to-end transaction platform for business and realized that the main value we could provide was what Jack Ma had observed about the exporters who were his translation clients—help in finding a business partner. So we adopted a completely open marketplace, where we did not try to lock buyers and sellers into an end-to-end transaction platform. Rather, Alibaba served as an interactive trade show: we would provide a booth for sellers, give them the tools to decorate their booth and display their products in any way they wanted, and leave the rest up to them. Rather than taking a commission from each transaction—which they would have done anything to get around—we would simply charge an annual subscription fee for their online booth and then sell them additional services, such as sponsored keyword listings, prominent display in their product category, and certification as a "Gold Supplier" if they met certain standards.

Our competitors, meanwhile, stubbornly pursued the closed marketplace strategy, hoping to corral the world's importers and exporters in their enclosure and regularly tax them for a percentage of sales through the platform. Naturally, the entrepreneurial and independent-minded customers resisted this, and our competitors soon either went out of business or disappeared. After a long struggle Alibaba achieved profitability in 2002, emerging as the last marketplace standing in the B2B domain, and—more important— cemented a strong belief in an open marketplace model that would *empower* sellers with customizable storefronts rather than *control* sellers in closed end-to-end platforms. This part of Alibaba's corporate DNA served us well when it came time to battle our biggest competitor yet—eBay.

C2C: An E-Commerce Ecosystem Built by an Army of Ants

Many thought Alibaba's entry in the consumer e-commerce market in 2003, Taobao.com, was not a smart move. When Jack told a group of outside investors about his vision for Taobao, one stood up in the middle of the meeting, walked out the door, and said on his way out, "Jack, eBay will win." Even within Alibaba, some in senior management resisted the idea of competing with eBay. After all, Alibaba had just turned the corner. The company had survived China's SARS (severe acute respiratory syndrome) scare despite four hundred Alibaba staffers having been quarantined. Alibaba's B2B business had reached profitability and was growing quickly. But just as the company's future seemed secure, Jack made a "bet the company" kind of decision—to enter the C2C e-commerce market and go head to head with eBay's EachNet. The eBay-Taobao battle turned out to be a turning point in e-commerce, marking the shift of e-commerce's center of gravity from the United States to China.

When he started Taobao, Jack Ma explained his reasons for the move: "In the world today there are only two companies that understand how to build and run an online marketplace—eBay and Alibaba. Today, eBay is focused on consumers in China. But sooner or later they are going to start coming after our customers—small businesses. And when they do, our B2B business is going to come under threat."

On Taobao's first day it was essentially a clone of eBay. But in the months that followed, it evolved and morphed into an entirely new sort of animal—one that better fit the China market. Western analysts often assume that Taobao must have beaten eBay in China because of government favoritism. But I believe that the main reason Alibaba succeeded was that it adapted to the particular needs of local markets instead of aping the models of eBay and Amazon.

Amazon's approach in the United States was essentially to move the "Walmart economy" online, creating a large retailer based on a high-volume, low-cost model that relied on massive scale and technology to create cost savings. EBay's approach was to move the yard sale economy online, creating a market for used goods and collectibles. But Taobao's was to move the mom-and-pop economy online, where small retailers could open stores to sell new products. This better fit China's retail environment, which had more in common with the one Montgomery Ward first faced than the one Amazon or eBay had faced in the United States.

Why did this focus on mom-and-pop shops and small entrepreneurs better fit the China market? The large retail chains were too focused on building traditional retail stores to take a serious interest in e-commerce. And the large brands weren't interested in e-commerce, because it represented a proportion of overall sales too insignificant to justify the cost and investment of trying to build an online operation. So getting e-commerce off the ground required one company (Alibaba) that would take the lead and resolve all the inefficiencies of China's e-commerce infrastructure on behalf of all of China's small businesses. Only then would the larger companies notice.

At Alibaba we had learned that small retail entrepreneurs who were signing up for Taobao had something in common with the small manufacturers who were Alibaba's customers—their initial need was for a storefront from which they could find and attract buyers. They didn't want to add a middleman who might limit their freedom and skim commissions from their razor-thin margins. If they could get leads about potential buyers online, they could hustle to close a deal with them and find a creative way to fulfill the purchase, just as they did in the offline world.

For example, let's say a shopper found a sweater she liked but had a few questions about the material, whether it would shrink when washed, and whether she might be able to receive a discount if she bought two additional sweaters for her friends. On Taobao's platform she could communicate directly with the seller by phone or instant message, negotiate some of the terms, and either head to the vendor's online boutique or, if they were in the same city, have the vendor send an assistant to the buyer's neighborhood so she could touch and feel the product before making a final decision. Sure, this was inefficient. But it was worth it for these small vendors who made only a few sales a day. And, most important, it worked because of its similarity to the way Chinese shoppers were already accustomed to doing business.

In addition to providing a marketplace that the Chinese user was more comfortable with, Taobao announced that its services would be free to buyers and sellers for the first three years. EBay publicly derided this policy, responding that "free is not a business model." But in the context of China, where businesses didn't yet believe in the power of e-commerce, the policy helped reassure sellers that they didn't have to take risks to get started with an online shop. "Only after our customers make money using Taobao will we try to take money," Jack Ma would say. EBay, on the other hand, charged product listing fees and transaction fees that discouraged sellers from giving the platform a try.

EBay's biggest mistake was migrating EachNet's platform to eBay's global technical platform. It had the effect of "de-localizing" the website: it lost the localized look, feel, and functions that Chinese users liked. It also had the effect of slowing down EachNet's ability to introduce new features, because the home office in San Josc had to approve every decision.

Within a few years of Jack Ma declaring war on eBay in China, Taobao went from a 7 percent market share of the C2C market to an 83 percent market share. In 2006 eBay shut down its China site and effectively withdrew from the market. Although it has enjoyed many successes before and since its experience in China, eBay's loss of the China market is now a classic case study of how not to approach the China market.

THE TAOBAO APPROACH—WHY IT WORKED IN CHINA

To understand how e-commerce works in China, it's worth taking a closer look at what made Taobao so different from eBay. Doing so reveals a lot about China's e-commerce landscape and offers insight into how e-commerce may evolve in other emerging markets that share many of the China market's characteristics.

Merchant Focus

Amazon and eBay are *product-focused* websites, and their customer is the shopper. They provide little space for third-party sellers to brand their stores, and they offer merchants a text link or, at most, a simple banner graphic to personalize their store. Customers who want to learn more about a third-party merchant who is selling on Amazon or eBay need to visit other websites.

Taobao took a different approach. Our primary customer was not the shopper; it was the third-party merchant who was selling on our site. We realized that retail in China began with trust between the buyer and seller and that the seller needed tools to build a business in the Taobao marketplace. We recognized that if we could make merchants happy, over time they would make their customers happy.

Customizable Storefronts

To make our merchants happy, we allowed them to create dynamic, exciting, and interactive online storefronts within the Taobao marketplace. Just as Alibaba provided exporters with online trade show "booths," Taobao gave small retailers in China a place where they could express themselves and differentiate their shops from others'. These merchants didn't yet have the tools or expertise to build effective websites on their own. So we allowed them to build what was essentially their own website—it just happened to be on Taobao rather than lost in the vast Internet sea. The storefronts we offered were so customizable that these merchants saw no need to build their own websites. Many used their Taobao URL on their business cards, so whenever they promoted their Taobao shop, they brought traffic to our marketplace, essentially doing our advertising for us.

A Look and Feel That Fit China

Designers in the West accept as religious tenet that website usability depends on a clean, crisp, minimalist design that blocks out noise and directs users to buy something online. When they come to China, these same designers usually are shocked to find local websites that favor bright colors, flashy animations, and a more cluttered design.

My theory is that the daily life of a typical web user in Shanghai is so different from that of someone in, say, Sweden that it affects the way Chinese approach an online interface. Shoppers in China are used to the busy shopping environment typified by Nanjing Road. But in rural Sweden, a shopper might spend an hour driving along a quiet country road, enjoying the serenity of farmland punctuated by a few red homes and cows, to get to a store.

Yes, this example is somewhat exaggerated. But research backs up the idea that Chinese Internet users expect more visual stimulation than their Western counterparts. I once attended a talk by Kaifu Lee, then the head of Google China. He discussed how Google had used laboratory studies to track the eye movements of Internet users in China and compared them with the eye movements of Internet users in the United States. They found that when US Internet users visit Google, their eyes go straight to the search box. But when Chinese Internet users visit Google China, their eyes skip around the website, as if looking for surprises, stimulation, and new experiences.

We observed this phenomenon among Taobao's users, although in less scientific ways. Shoppers responded positively to flashy promotions that leaped out at them. Largely because Taobao was offering the more exciting website, eBay China shoppers quickly migrated to Taobao, describing it as having more *renxinghua*, or human feel. To eBay's Western managers, Taobao probably appeared to be too cute and flashy, no doubt stepping well outside the bounds of eBay's graphic design standards. But Chinese shoppers were drawn to Taobao's more colorful and visually stimulating marketplace.

Extensive Ratings

EBay and Amazon pioneered the use of online ratings as a way for shoppers to compare merchants and products. These ratings helped buyers evaluate sellers, and they provided a powerful incentive for sellers to give a high level of service. We learned the importance of online ratings from Amazon and eBay, but Taobao took them to an entirely new level.

We realized that, in a low-trust society like China's, buyers would need more ratings variables than those offered by US e-commerce sites. After all, China didn't have credit reports, Better

Business Bureaus, or effective small-claims courts to resolve disputes. So we had to create detailed ratings systems to bridge the trust gap and allow buyers to better evaluate the merchants with whom they were doing business.

The rating systems on Taobao have evolved over time and now serve as comprehensive online reputations for the small businesses that sell on the site. Shoppers rate merchants on their service attitude, accuracy of product descriptions, and shipping performance. This system is both lighthearted and user friendly, inviting customers to award points with Red Roses (good), Yellow Roses (so-so), and Black Roses (poor). Taobao encourages buyers to add text comments to explain their rating and even upload photos of products to show how what they received compares with the images posted online.

Buyers can view the rose point totals of a seller as well as the seller's historical trends to see whether the merchant's performance is improving or declining. Finally, Taobao uses the points from the roses to provide an additional layer of ratings that displays the seller's overall trust record according to a scale of hearts, diamonds, blue crowns, and red crowns.

Buyers are held accountable as well. After each successful transaction, sellers have a chance to rate buyers, who also build up "trust records," starting with red hearts and ascending to diamonds, blue crowns, and red crowns. And because so many Taobao sellers are also buyers, their trust records for each role are displayed separately online for all to see.

Seem confusing? Yes, it does to me, too. But to a web population crazy about online games, this "gamification" of ratings makes participating in ratings more fun while giving buyers and sellers much-needed information about each other.

Unfortunately the participants in the game aren't all good actors. The importance of having high ratings has also led to the widespread practice of "brushing," whereby shop owners conspire with third parties who make fake orders online in order to enhance a merchant's ratings. Instead of shipping a product, merchants send their co-conspirators empty boxes and, in exchange for a service fee, the fake customers will write positive ratings as if they had made an actual purchase. The practice has resulted in a cat-and-mouse game between Taobao and the "brushers" in an attempt to combat the practice.

Despite the problem of brushing, a highly engaged online population supports the ratings system, with an estimated 80 percent of Chinese netizens rating and reviewing products and sellers online. This makes for an extensive and dynamic system that has allowed Taobao to bridge the trust gap between buyer and seller in China, where it is so much wider than in the United States.

Communication Tools

When I first came to China as a student in 1994, before e-commerce had transformed the traditional way of doing business, I noticed immediately how human commerce was. If I wanted a basic bicycle in the United States, I had to drive to Target and pick one off the shelves. But the process in China was entirely different. There, if I mentioned to a friend that I wanted a bicycle, he would refer me to a relative who knew somebody who knew somebody who had a bicycle shop. At the shop I'd be offered a cup of tea and chat with the owner in my limited Chinese. We'd discuss the price, the owner would knock a few percentage points off the price, and then I'd walk out of the store with my new bicycle.

Going through a network of friends provided assurance that I would get a reasonable deal and that the bicycle would be new, not an old, broken bicycle refurbished and packaged in a new box. The personal reference offered the seller a customer who might go on to refer other students to his bicycle shop, now that the seller and I had forged a personal connection. And friends who made the introduction earned some social capital: the seller might reciprocate somewhere down the line.

I had to learn about this social nature of commerce in China through trial and error, but it came naturally to my Chinese colleagues. So it's not surprising that they felt that integrating live chat tools in Taobao was critically important to replicate this offline approach. We had seen that China's netizens were crazy about staying in touch with friends, family, and business partners through instant messenger tools such as MSN and QQ. To us, preventing buyers and sellers from communicating with each other—as eBay did—was simply unthinkable.

So we introduced an online chat function called AliWangWang. Users downloaded it to their computers and later to their smartphones, and it allowed them to communicate in real time. Because it was an integral part of the seller's online storefront, it was like a merchant who welcomes shoppers to the store. First-time visitors to a merchant's Taobao shop could ask questions and get to know the seller a little better in order to judge his or her professionalism. Sellers could better understand the needs of shoppers and make recommendations that might lead shoppers to put more items in their baskets. And, in Chinese tradition, the buyer usually could get the seller to reduce the price a bit—or even a lot if the seller was buying in volume, by perhaps getting several friends to join in on the purchase.

Our Silicon Valley counterparts pursued an entirely different approach. EBay's thinking was that if buyers and sellers could communicate in real time, they might take their transaction offline and avoid paying eBay commissions. Besides, the thinking went, the beauty of technology is that it can automate customer service so effectively that human interactions are unnecessary. But allowing shop owners in China to communicate with buyers was about more than customer service. It was about sales and relationship building, which could lead to stronger buyer-seller relationships.

Over time AliWangWang provided additional tools; one allows merchants to have several service people chatting with customers simultaneously as they shop in larger numbers. It was, in effect, like having a live sales staff at a physical retail store, except that sales personnel were working remotely in customer service centers, saving costs for the retailers as sales staff grew to keep up with the growing online demand.

Community

When Jack Ma addressed his Alibaba cofounders, he discussed why his first venture, China Pages, had failed and how Alibaba would be positioned differently. The main difference was that Alibaba would not be just a website or a marketplace but a *community*, he said.

EBay also understood community, as evidenced by the passion that eBay's early US merchants exhibited in organizing events and get-togethers that culminated in eBay's annual, arena-filling eBay Live! events. But what eBay didn't understand was that the Chinese online community was like the US online community on steroids.

Chinese are passionate about their online communities in a way that Westerners have to see to believe. China's culture is, as I discussed earlier, more group-oriented, while Westerners tend to be more individualistic. To a typical online community member in China, the community is far more than an online forum and becomes part of their identity.

So when we designed our online communities for Taobao, eBay's simple online forums and message boards were not enough for China's customers. We built bright, colorful online channels dedicated to bringing together Taobao members with common interests. We highlighted the success stories and key information or skills that sellers had acquired by using Taobao. We gave Taobao sellers tools for organizing their own meet-ups and clubs. We allowed people to post lengthy blogs dedicated to their businesses.

As the forums grew in popularity, they became more democratized and took on a life of their own. We allowed community members to elect forum moderators who would engage those community members in active discussions. We created a series of awards for which Alibaba members could nominate sellers, and then the whole community would vote on the nominees. We established arbitration panels with elected members who would have final say in disputes between buyers and sellers. And Jack Ma would regularly communicate with community members to explain new policies or solicit feedback. This community of the members, by the members, and for the members filled the role of a virtual government institution, something the offline world lacked in most respects.

For further proof of just how engaged community members were with each other, consider that marriages coming out of the Taobao community were so numerous that we even established a channel to celebrate them. In China you wouldn't be surprised to hear someone say that she met her husband through Taobao. But you would be hard-pressed to find a woman who met her husband on Amazon.com. That's how human Taobao is.

THE REST OF THE ECOSYSTEM

Creating a marketplace where buyers could meet sellers was the core service of Taobao, but two other gaps in the e-commerce chain still needed to be addressed—payment and logistics. Slight tweaks to the US model were enough to complete the loop.

Payments

The ubiquity of credit cards in the United States fueled the early growth of both Amazon and eBay. Consumers were used to using credit cards for catalog purchases over the phone, and persuading them to use a credit card online was simply an incremental step.

For Amazon the transition was almost seamless, as early media reports about Amazon quickly made it a trusted brand. EBay faced a slightly more difficult challenge, because shoppers didn't need to pay eBay—they needed to pay eBay's merchants. So eBay had to facilitate payments between buyers and its many small sellers. EBay did this fairly easily by acquiring PayPal and encouraging its use. For the most part, buyers trusted eBay's sellers and needed only a way to send the money to the seller. Because setting up systems for each seller to accept credit card payments was too difficult, PayPal provided the answer by making it easy for eBay's shoppers to create and fund their PayPal accounts online, whether with credit cards or electronic bank transfers.

In China, on the other hand, credit cards had been made legal only in 1999, and their adoption by consumers was slow to take off. So when Alibaba's payment system, Alipay, was launched in 2004, persuading customers to visit their banks and fund their Alipay accounts was a significant challenge. Of course, every challenge creates an opportunity. And we realized that if we could make it easy for people to get their bank accounts connected to Alipay, we could establish a deeper relationship with users. This deeper relationship even left open the possibility that Alipay could eventually evolve into a bank.

The good deals on Taobao gave Chinese shoppers the incentive to take the time to fund Alipay. A critical difference between Alipay and PayPal helped set us apart—Alipay was an escrow-based payment system. It would release a buyer's funds to the seller only after the buyer gave notice that he'd received the goods and they met his expectations. This simple tweak helped make Alipay a much more attractive payment system than PayPal, because buyers and sellers were assured that Alipay would assume the risk if one side of the transaction did not live up to its obligations.

Logistics

Compared with other emerging markets, China's logistics were good enough to get e-commerce off the ground. History may have helped. From the earliest Chinese empires to the establishment of the People's Republic, China had nearly always maintained a centralized administration that kept track of who was where in the country. This centralized administration also built a national postal system that, although slow and inefficient, could still deliver packages reliably. In addition, in the years since China had opened up to the world, entrepreneurs had founded courier companies that, although fragmented across the country, could handle the vast majority of deliveries. It wasn't a great logistics infrastructure, but buyers were willing to wait a few days to get a bargain online or a product they could not find in their hometown.

A SHOPPING MALL IS BORN: TMALL

Scrappy buyers and sellers on Taobao built China's e-commerce ecosystem at a time when the larger players were more focused on selling through physical retail channels. By 2008 Taobao had become China's largest shopping destination in terms of transaction volumes, forcing major retailers and brands to notice, especially because their own e-commerce initiatives had largely failed to attract online traffic.

Major brands and distributors did not want to sell on Taobao because they didn't want their products to appear next to those of small and medium-sized merchants whose reliability might be uneven and whose products might be of questionable authenticity. The risk to their brands was just too great. To serve these sellers, Taobao opened Taobao Mall, which allowed larger and more qualified sellers to set up branded storefronts inside a premium channel within the Taobao marketplace. This differentiated them from the typical small Taobao retailers.

Shoppers on Taobao now were becoming more sophisticated and had growing expectations for the products and sellers they found on the marketplace. Buyers still were filled with uncertainty about the quality and origin of goods offered by Taobao vendors. Although seller ratings helped, shoppers still had nagging questions. Will this really be an authentic Nike shoe? Were these L'Oréal cosmetics properly stored in transit? Is this really a *new* iPhone?

Taobao Mall gave buyers assurances that they were buying authentic goods from authorized dealers. No longer were they buying from the virtual flea market on the city's outskirts. Rather, they were shopping at the virtual equivalent of the glossy shopping mall in the center of the city. Sure, the prices were slightly higher. But the shopping experience was better. And it came with the guarantee that

Taobao Mall had certified the sellers, taken hefty deposits from them, and would use those deposits to guarantee transactions if the seller attempted to cheat the buyer.

Taobao Mall gained enough sellers to be spun off into its own marketplace, Tmall, and brands from around the world soon flocked to it to sell their goods. Although Tmall is a separate website from Taobao, its listings were integrated in Taobao search results, clearly marked as Tmall listings, and they diverted Taobao shoppers to Tmall. Tmall proved to be the cash cow of Alibaba's consumer marketplaces. Tmall sellers paid for listings, keyword advertisements, and promotions and agreed to transaction commissions of about 5 percent, depending on the product category.

Alibaba found it much easier to make money from Tmall than from Taobao. Taobao sellers were accustomed to free services and resisted any attempt by Taobao to charge fees. Tmall sellers, on the other hand, were more than happy to pay these fees because the costs of operating a Tmall store were much lower than those for a store in the offline world.

Alibaba gave Tmall several of the key features that had made Taobao so successful. Shoppers could use AliWangWang to chat in real time with salespeople through instant messaging. Storefronts were entirely customizable, so brand owners could truly personalize their Tmall shop, using all the graphics, images, video, and brand identity elements they would use on their own websites. Extensive ratings played a key role, keeping both buyers and sellers accountable. Encouraged to share links to new products they liked, shoppers formed a strong sense of community online. And Alibaba's preferred partners could handle fulfillment while Alipay processed payments.

One constituency was not thrilled by Tmall—Taobao merchants. Tmall put them in direct competition with the larger brands, which were now selling identical products alongside those offered by the little guys. As Tmall continued to raise the qualifications for Tmall sellers, many small entrepreneurs didn't make the cut and found themselves sitting on thousands of dollars' worth of inventory.

The tension hit a peak when, after a Tmall rule change, hundreds of Tmall users staged a protest at Alibaba headquarters, forcing the government to intervene and handing Jack Ma and Alibaba a public rebuke for not giving sellers enough time to prepare for the new policy. These protests died down over time as Alibaba made the case that Tmall was creating a safer and more reliable shopping environment by raising the qualifications of sellers.

With the widespread use of Taobao and Tmall, online shopping in China gained mainstream acceptance. The question for China's shoppers was no longer whether shopping online was safe but rather where they would shop. Because Taobao and Tmall had made the online retail ecosystem much more mature and efficient, B2C models would be able to thrive in China. Logistics had improved greatly. Online payment platforms found widespread adoption. Thus ten years after the first "Amazons of China" appeared, the B2C model made a comeback. But it wasn't early entrants like Dang-dang or Amazon (which now owned Joyo) that rose to prominence. Rather, it was a company that was born in the unlikeliest of times— during the SARS crisis.

RETURN OF THE AMAZON MODEL AND THE RISE OF JINGDONG

When eBay withdrew from the China market in 2005, Alibaba seemed to have no serious challengers for dominance of the market. But the gradual rise of Jingdong Mall, or JD.com, gave Alibaba its first post-eBay challenge and created a sort of battle of the business models. The Alibaba-Jingdong battle is more than a battle of websites. It has set up a battle between the two online ecosystems, a battle that has important implications for the future of e-commerce not only in China but worldwide, as it will help predict which business model is more likely to succeed in other emerging markets.

Richard Liu, a Chinese entrepreneur born in 1974 to a family of businesspeople in the coastal province of Jiangsu, started Jingdong as a retail company in Beijing in 1998. Liu came to Beijing initially to study social sciences and bought a restaurant as a way to support himself through college. When his staff ran off with his money, he lost the restaurant and was forced to borrow $31,000 from his father, which was deeply embarrassing but taught him an important lesson. "I gradually understood that the restaurant bankruptcy was my fault," he said, "because I had not established management structures, done oversight, or established financial systems and procedures."[9]

Several years later he redeemed himself by setting up Jingdong, a successful consumer electronics shop in Beijing's Zhongguancun IT district. Within five years he had twelve stores that brought in more than $1.45 million a year. But when SARS hit China in 2003, customers stayed home, and Liu realized the only way to run his business was to sell online. So he opened an online version of his store, 360buy. "I wouldn't have entered e-commerce if hadn't it been for SARS," Liu later remarked.[10]

Since then Jingdong has expanded aggressively, blazing past its B2C rivals, DangDang and Amazon China. While Jingdong is known for electronics, it has expanded into books, clothing, accessories, and general merchandise. When customers complained about unreliable deliveries by China's inefficient patchwork of couriers and delivery services, Jingdong rolled out its own nationwide delivery fleet. It has used this to differentiate itself from Taobao/Tmall by selling Jingdong as a place that manages the entire consumer experience. Because it has its own delivery fleet, it can track and manage product deliveries and returns more seamlessly. This of course has come with a cost, and by 2016 Jingdong was employing more than 100,000 people, the vast majority in delivery.

Over the years Jingdong has expanded its offerings to include a marketplace model, allowing outside merchants to plug in to the Jingdong distribution platform and putting Jingdong in head-to-head combat with Alibaba's Tmall. This has allowed Jingdong to further increase its product variety and support its big investments in its national distribution infrastructure. As cross-border trade has increased, the company has also worked hard to attract international brands to sell on its global platform.

Jingdong's increasing competition with Alibaba and their different business models has also led to a public spat between Liu and Jack Ma. Ma's well-known prediction that Jingdong's asset-heavy business model "[will] end in disaster" only fueled the animosity. Liu has frequently taken to the media to counter that Taobao and Tmall were huge sources of counterfeit goods and only a business model such as Jingdong's can help weed out fakes.

Whose Business Model Will Prevail?

The biggest question about Jingdong remains its decision to own and operate its logistics and delivery infrastructure. It is what investors either most love or most hate about Jingdong's business model. Even Amazon has left deliveries and last-mile delivery up to third parties. Alibaba's approach has been to create a consortium—the Cainiao Network—that connects the existing logistics providers in China. Cainiao has 1,200 employees and handles 33 million packages a day. Jingdong, on the other hand, has 100,000 employees handling 3.4 million packages a day. To reach Alibaba's delivery-to-employee ratio, Alibaba argues, Jingdong would need 1 million employees.

Which model will win? No one seems sure. Jingdong defenders say that as China's e-commerce infrastructure becomes increasingly efficient, the full-service model will win—because greater scale can keep a lid on the costs across the entire ecosystem of an inventory-led model. Alibaba defenders argue that managing inventory across multiple categories is simply too difficult a job for any one player to handle. Seasonal trends and changing fashions make it important for specialized category managers to be close to their customers and know when to stock the right inventory. This, they say, is better done by specialized merchants than large, cross-category retailers.

Alibaba's partisans also argue that a marketplace model made up of diverse smaller sellers creates a greater sense of community, which leads to a more effective system of ratings. This social power of community gives Alibaba an advantage but one that Jingdong was able to counter in part by teaming up with another Chinese Internet goliath—Tencent.

TENCENT—A COMMUNITY ON STEROIDS

In 2004 I attended a small dinner with Jack Ma and a roundtable of Morgan Stanley executives. One turned to Jack and asked, "What Internet company in China, besides Alibaba, do you think we should be looking to invest in?" Jack didn't hesitate: "Tencent. What they've created is really valuable. But people don't seem to realize it yet."

I wish I'd taken Jack's investment advice. When Jack made his recommendation, Tencent's share price on the Hong Kong Stock Exchange hovered around HK$1 per share. By April 2017 its stock price had increased to HK$230, making the company worth $279 billion, ranking it among the ten most valuable companies in the world.

Tencent is a household name in China but largely unknown outside the country. This owes to the quiet leadership style of its plodding founder, Pony Ma, who has eschewed the media limelight while building one of the world's largest tech companies.

Indeed Pony's style could not be more different from Jack Ma's (no relation). Jack Ma's extroverted, attention-grabbing style has attracted international media coverage and made him the face of China, Inc. Pony has largely remained enigmatic and notoriously averse to media attention. But the social media empire Pony has built is no less impressive than Alibaba's e-commerce empire.

Pony was born in 1971 in southern China, where he studied computer science at Shenzhen University. After graduation he worked at a telecom company but left to found Tencent in 1998. His first product to catch on, in early 1999, was a near clone of ICQ, the Israeli instant messaging product for desktops. Even as he named his product OICQ, Pony brushed off criticism that his creation was simply a copy of the Israeli product, claiming "[To] copy is not evil."[11] But, under pressure, he ultimately changed the name to QQ and adopted a penguin as its mascot.

QQ quickly became a hit with young Chinese netizens, who proved to be crazy about connecting with others online, making friends, and expanding their social networks through QQ's platform. QQ quickly expanded well beyond instant messaging, allowing users to form groups, post photos, and personalize their profiles online. What was once a clone of ICQ soon morphed into a dynamic social network that, one could argue, was a Facebook for China before Facebook existed.

In April 2000 the success of QQ helped Pony attract a $2.2 million investment from IDG, the tech-oriented US publishing company, and Richard Li, son of the Hong Kong tycoon Li Ka-shing. But one year later, when Tencent's large community failed to produce a model for making money, Li and IDG sold their 47 percent stake to the South African media company Naspers for $32 million. (Naspers' investment would prove to be one of the greatest investments of all time, rivaled only by Softbank's investment in Alibaba.)

Tencent had its own struggles in the early 2000s and nearly ran out of money. The company had millions of customers but no clear way to make money from its free services. After some trial and error, the company found it could charge users microfees for sending QQ messages. Tencent next started several value-added services that brought in enough revenue for the company to list on the Hong Kong Stock Exchange in 2004.

When it first went public, investors had questions about how QQ could grow its revenue base. Tencent's stock gradually rose as it found new ways to make money from its platform, offering users a chance to buy emoticons, ringtones, and storage space. But Tencent found its golden goose when it expanded into online games. It bought the rights to popular games from around the world, adapted them for China, and made money on the sale of virtual weapons and other virtual items, pulling in millions of dollars from transactions that generated one penny at a time. By the end of 2016 the revenues from these game-related value-added services hit $10.2 billion.

As Tencent's community grew, e-commerce seemed to offer an attractive opportunity, so it established Paipai in direct competition with Taobao. Like Taobao's users, Paipai's could create online shops and sell items online. But Paipai's market share never exceeded 10 percent, and it eventually gave up on the market.

Despite the failure of Paipai, Tencent solidified its place in China as the dominant social networking player when it moved the power of its community from the desktop to the smartphone with the introduction of WeChat, known in Chinese as Weixin, in 2011. As smartphones became the primary method Chinese use to access the web, Tencent's aggressive move to mobile allowed it to quickly build an ecosystem much more dominant than that of any of its Western counterparts.

WeChat has essentially taken the interconnectedness and tight-knit community of the rice fields and villages to the smartphone, making it an even bigger part of people's lives in China than the smartphone is in the West. To compare WeChat with Facebook simply doesn't do it justice. WeChat is much more than an app or a social network. It is an entire ecosystem, putting content, community, and commerce under one roof. Think Facebook plus Whats-App plus Zynga plus LinkedIn plus just about everything else you might want to use to organize your life. By March 2016, more than 700 million Chinese used WeChat religiously, with three fifths of these users using it more than ten times a day.[12]

In addition to chatting with friends in their contact list, users can search for nearby WeChat users, browse their public newsfeed "moments," form new friendships and connections, and—yes—even find dates. Users can browse news, content, and product recommendations from celebrities. Users shop online at WeChat's brand stores. And they can pay offline merchants with Tenpay by scanning QR codes at point-of-sale terminals or even send money to others using Tenpay's "Lucky Packet" feature.

WeChat is even replacing the previously all-important custom of exchanging business cards in China. On a recent trip to China I noticed that business meetings ended by connecting on WeChat rather than by exchanging business cards. And for group meetings, it's not uncommon for attendees to take advantage of WeChat's "shake" feature to simultaneously connect with others nearby who are shaking their mobile phones, especially convenient when an entire group in a room wants to connect and form a group at the same time.

Perhaps one of the most surprising aspects about WeChat is just how quickly new acquaintances or business associates are willing to connect with each other on the service. People using social networks in China make fewer distinctions between the professional and the personal than Westerners do. This blurring of worlds has made a service like LinkedIn much less important, because friends and colleagues alike are using WeChat contact lists.

WeChat's dominance in social networking did not go unchallenged, especially by one of Pony Ma's biggest admirers, Jack Ma. Alarmed that WeChat might pull away Alibaba's shoppers, Jack introduced his own mobile messaging platform, Laiwang, and declared war on WeChat in 2012. In his drive to gain more adopters for Laiwang, Jack called on each of Alibaba's employees to recruit one hundred new Laiwang users, reportedly withholding the bonus of anyone who failed to meet the quota. Despite Jack's exhortations and threats, Laiwang was never able to catch up, and WeChat became the dominant player in social networking and instant messaging.

Undeterred, in 2013 Alibaba began acquiring shares in Sina Weibo, China's early social networking pioneer, which is regarded as the Twitter of China. In contrast to WeChat, which allows only connections to have access to a user's private posts, Weibo is a public platform where individuals and celebrities post public blogs and commentary. Over the years government crackdowns on political content have put Weibo at odds with officials, and this has stifled its growth. Although Weibo is still a force in China, it did not allow Alibaba to catch up with Tencent in social networking.

With his company's position firmly in place, Pony once again turned his attention to e-commerce and entered a partnership with Alibaba's biggest rival, Jingdong. In 2014, Tencent invested $215 million for an initial 15 percent equity stake in Jingdong and teamed up to redirect WeChat traffic to Jingdong's platform. The deal gave Tencent yet another way to monetize its user traffic. In exchange, Jingdong got the traffic it needed to maintain its growth and scale. And it set the stage for the battle for the future of China's e-commerce market.

3

THE GREAT MALL OF CHINA

BACK TO THE FUTURE

China is changing so quickly that if you blink, you miss something. This really hit home when I returned to Shanghai in 2016 after just one year away from the city. When I arrived at my apartment building, I found forty cardboard boxes full of packages streaming down the entrance stairs. They flowed through the lobby and into the previously sleepy management office, where two workers now sat at their desks, surrounded by towers of even more boxes addressed to residents of the building. When I visited the convenience store around the corner, it was similarly inundated. "We hold deliveries here for customers next door to pick up," the clerk told me.

A bit later I headed across the street for lunch at a glossy new noodle shop. There was no wait staff, just three touch screens on which to place an order. I made my selection, pressed Pay, and was offered a choice of Alipay or Tencent's WePay. Since I had neither on my phone, I opted for cash. After a receipt printed out, I walked across the room to find a bored restaurant worker playing games on her iPhone, clearly not used to customers who could not use their cell phone for payment. I handed her my receipt, and she rang up the bill on the cash register.

"These touch screens are a great ordering system," I remarked. "But do customers ever have problems using it?" "Just the older ones," she replied, revealing what a dinosaur I'd suddenly become. "The young people all pay with their phones. In fact, many just download our restaurant's app to their phones, order, and pay from that."

Later, I met George Godula, founder and head of Web2Asia, for coffee. His company started as a digital advertising firm, but it has morphed into an e-commerce service provider, helping Western companies sell on Tmall, Jingdong, and other online platforms. George opened his empty wallet and explained, "This is normal in China. I don't even use cash anymore. Everything I do, from [hailing] taxi[s] to dining out to paying bills, can all be done on Alipay or WePay. I have friends who haven't even set foot in a grocery store in three years—they buy all of their groceries on their smartphones and have them delivered."

On my next trip to China, in 2017, I discovered that it was not just the consumers who were going cashless, but the retailers as well. When I visited the local Starbucks, a long line of customers quickly moved through past the cash registers, with all the local customers presenting their mobile phones to charge their purchases to WePay or Alipay. The movement of the line came to an abrupt halt when I tried to pay with a 100-yuan note. The cashier stopped to examine the bill, holding it up to the light and inspecting it for authenticity. For a moment, it felt like she'd never seen cash before. A few blocks away, I saw a small gourmet coffee shop with the words written on the wall above the ordering window "Scan code. No cash acceptable."

It was becoming clear that dinosaurs like me would either have to get up to speed or find themselves extinct. When it came to e-commerce, China had at last reached the point that many had long predicted—it had leapfrogged past the West.

THE WORLD'S LARGEST E-COMMERCE MARKET

If there's one number that drives home the scale of e-commerce in China today, it's $17.8 billion—the value of transactions on Alibaba's websites in one twenty-four-hour period in 2016—specifically, Singles' Day. Singles' Day is a shopping festival Alibaba invented in 2009 and tied to a sort of "anti-Valentine's Day" holiday that China's singles already celebrated. In 2016 Alibaba's sales on the day once again exceeded the combined total of online sales for Black Friday and Cyber Monday in the United States, and the figure is even more astounding when you realize it doesn't even include what happened on all the other e-commerce websites in China that day.

But of course Chinese don't shop online only on Singles' Day. Drive through any city in China, and you will see couriers weaving in and out of traffic on their motorcycles and electric bicycles and carrying loads of packages stacked high atop one another. The sea of cardboard boxes seems to be ever on the rise, but the way Chinese consumers are buying their products is shifting. While consumer-to-consumer (C2C) transactions accounted for nearly 100 percent of e-commerce in China in 2005, that figure has shrunk by about half as shoppers increasingly buy online from large, reputable retailers rather than the scrappy, smaller retailers. The C2C market, still almost entirely dominated by Taobao, is slowly evolving into a place where shoppers go to find deals on unbranded goods or "long tail" products—unique and specialized products that sell one at a time to individual consumers yet as a whole account for a significant volume of transactions.

The business-to-consumer (B2C) sector is where the bulk of the growth is and where competition is heating up. The vast majority of B2C sales in China still occur on platforms rather than on discrete branded websites. According to estimates by iResearch for 2016, Tmall (57 percent) and Jingdong (25 percent) were dominating the B2C market—together they accounted for four-fifths of the total B2C market. Sharing the rest of the B2C market was a fragmented collection of players, led by the electronics retailers

Suning (4 percent) and Gome (1 percent), discount brand retailer VIP.com (4 percent), and online grocer Yihaodian (1 percent). Amazon China and its original local imitator, Dangdang, each captured less than 1 percent of the total B2C market.[1]

MOBILE

As cell phones proliferated in China, the big question was whether consumers would use their phones as often as their desktops to shop online. The answer is an indisputable yes. According to the Boston Consulting Group, mobile phones are already the primary means by which China's online shoppers make their purchases; by 2015 Chinese made 51 percent of their online purchases with their cell phone, whereas only 35 percent of shoppers worldwide did so.[2] On Singles' Day 2016, Chinese shoppers made 82 percent of their transactions at Alibaba by cell phone.[3] And for all of 2016, the total number of Chinese mobile payments (to online and offline merchants) was almost fifty times greater than in the United States.[4]

As mobile commerce increases, what is important for brands to know is that Chinese smartphone users opt for larger screens than their Western counterparts, giving brands more space in which to display their products and brand identity. It also means that more Chinese are watching videos on their viewer-friendly smartphones, and because videos allow marketers to deliver richer content, burgeoning cell phone use is a bonus for them. Data download speeds have increased while prices have come down. Mobile data in China are less expensive than in many other developing markets.

SOCIAL COMMERCE AT AN ENTIRELY NEW LEVEL

People in the West talk about social commerce a lot. The discussion is usually about how social networks such as Facebook, Twitter, and Instagram are increasingly referring shoppers to e-commerce platforms. The path for a consumer is usually from one specific platform for social networking to another platform, such as Amazon or a manufacturer's website, for the actual purchase.

But social commerce in China is an entirely different phenomenon. While these social and shopping platforms operate independently in the West, in China they are all merged together, making the *social* entirely indistinguishable from *commerce*. Nowhere is this more clear than on Taobao, which has been a highly social platform from the start and enjoys much more consumer engagement than its Western counterparts. Individual shoppers might use Amazon's mobile app a few times a week. And when they do visit the website, they spend an average of nine minutes there. Shoppers' behavior is simple—they visit Amazon to buy something and then get on with their day. But Taobao shoppers use its mobile app an average of seven times per day, for a total of twenty-five minutes.[5] That's even more than the sixteen minutes Twitter's users spend on its service worldwide. And Twitter's entire reason for being is for users to socialize and share ideas.

So what are Taobao users doing when they use the Taobao app? They are socializing in one of Taobao's one thousand special interest groups, which range from wedding planning to fishing. Or they are livestreaming merchants' events. Or reading and commenting on blogs by community experts. Or meeting and chatting with new friends with common interests in the group forums.

Much of this community development is organic, made up of the millions of amateur bloggers and shoppers for whom Taobao has created a platform. But it is also assisted by a few nudges from Alibaba, which gives bloggers and community experts an incentive to write about and recommend products by offering them a commission on sales. Taobao also organizes livestreams and blogs that Chinese celebrities might use to introduce a product, such as a new line of makeup.

An important aspect of all this socializing is the creation of social networks around special interests. This is encouraging people to make new connections rather than depend on their existing networks of friends. As Alibaba cofounder and vice chairman Joe Tsai explains,

"On Facebook, you're friending all of your friends because you already know each other. In our case, we start with strangers but then use data to find a commonality of interest and create a community around that interest."[6] As the growing Chinese middle class finds new hobbies and pursuits, a Taobao community might provide a new car owner with a place to find other BMW owners, who subsequently will meet in person at Sunday driving clubs. Taobao might give anglers a place to discuss which fishing lures work best in their local area. All this activity can lead to sales on the Taobao platform.

So what explains this passion for social commerce in China? Some of it is a pent-up interest in leisure pursuits, after decades when simply getting by was a struggle. Some of it is China's new cult of consumption. But I would argue that the primary factor is an underlying culture that is highly social, going back thousands of years to life in the rice-growing regions of China. Chinese love to connect and feel a part of something larger than themselves. The packets and switches that run along the pipes of the Internet have replaced the irrigation canals that fed the rice terraces and China's social fabric.

ALIBABA VERSUS TENCENT: THE BATTLE OF THE ECOSYSTEMS

The social nature of e-commerce in China has blurred the lines between platforms that have remained highly distinct in the West. This has increased the importance of reaching customers at all points of contact and led to a different kind of battle for online shoppers. The battle for e-commerce in China is best thought of as a battle of two competing ecosystems. Each ecosystem consists of an alliance of companies defined by many intertwined investments and exclusive partnerships. The first, led by Alibaba, accounted for approximately 75 percent of the total online retail sales in China in 2016. The second, led by the alliance of Tencent and Jingdong, accounted for approximately 15 to 20 percent of total online sales in the same year but is steadily chipping away at Alibaba's market dominance.

The driving factor behind the emergence of ecosystems is that

China is a low-trust society, where consumers are more comfortable shopping in environments where a trusted player, such as Alibaba or Tencent, has endorsed the merchant and offers guarantees in case a transaction goes awry. By overseeing their ecosystems, Alibaba and Tencent help ensure that all players are held accountable for their commercial activities. They reward merchants for good behavior and, based on their rankings, award them more prominent locations in the ecosystem. Bad players can be ejected from the ecosystem and their business prospects closed off.

In an offline environment shoppers can usually—but not always—ascertain whether a retailer is legitimate. But even then it's not always easy, as evidenced by the many fake physical Apple stores that have cropped up in China, copying everything from store design to employee attire. Ascertaining who online is legitimate is even harder. Sure, an online brand store looks real, but who's to say that it is not just an imitation? A retailer's presence on Tmall or Jingdong Mall assures customers that they will be buying real products from real brands or their authorized dealers.

Another reason that platforms play a larger role in China is that inefficiencies in the market are too difficult for an individual retailer to iron out. Instead, platforms take care of logistics and payment on behalf of all the merchants. This has led Alibaba and Tencent to operate as conglomerates, with partnerships sealed in blood by equity stakes, and this creates stronger links in the e-commerce chain.

Much like the battle between Microsoft and Apple for primacy in desktop operating systems, Alibaba and Tencent are battling for the operating system of e-commerce in China. Here's where their two ecosystems stand and the advantages and disadvantages of each.

The Alibaba Ecosystem

Since its record-breaking $25 billion IPO in September 2014, Alibaba has used the money it raised to acquire, and invest in, companies from a vast array of industries. To the outside observer, why Alibaba bought some of what it did is not clear (the most striking of these investments is its $192 million stake in the Guangzhou Evergrande soccer team).

In an attempt to clarify Alibaba's vision, the company convened its first-ever investors' day in June 2016 to explain how all the pieces fit together. In addressing attendees, Jack Ma, Alibaba's chair, noted that investors often ask him two questions. The first is "Can you explain Alibaba in one sentence?" The second: "Are there any Western companies that can explain Alibaba?" The answer to both, he said, is no. CEO David Zhang followed Jack on stage and explained that Alibaba is building an "e-commerce media ecosystem" that uses digital channels to reach far more consumers than the more than 400 million who frequent Alibaba's retail marketplaces. The components of this ecosystem in China include:

Core E-Commerce Properties
- Alibaba China (wholesale Chinese-language marketplace)
- Alibaba International (international wholesale marketplace)
- Taobao (C2C marketplace)
- Tmall (B2C marketplace)
- Taobao Rural (services for rural buyers and sellers)
- AliExpress (international consumer retail)
- Tmall Global (cross-border sales)

Mobile Media and Entertainment
- Youku (a YouTube-like video site)
- Tudou (an additional video site)
- Tmall TV (Alibaba's answer to Netflix)
- UC Browser (a mobile phone browser strong in search functions)
- Alibaba Pictures (a film and video content producer)

Local Services
- AliTravel (travel services)
- Koubei (classified ads)
- Elema (a dining and food marketplace/community)

Payment
- Alipay (online payments)
- Ant Financial (Alibaba's financial arm)

Logistics
- Cainiao (extensive logistic network and marketplace bringing together many of China's logistics providers)

Advertising
- Alimama (an advertising marketplace)

Data and Cloud
- Alibaba Cloud (Alibaba's answer to Amazon's cloud services)

Offline Retail
- Sunning (a large electronics retailer into which Alibaba invested $4.6 billion for a 20 percent stake in 2015)
- Intime Retail (a large retail and mall operator that Alibaba acquired in 2017)

Zhang's argument for this large web of related companies is that it creates synergies across all the platforms. In the United States, he explained, separate platforms, such as YouTube, Facebook, and Twitter, independently handle the functions of branding, sales, and broadcasting. This makes it hard to provide a 360-degree branding experience for companies. And US privacy laws often prevent sharing of user data across different platforms and companies.

In China, on the other hand, Alibaba has stitched together a more seamless ecosystem that can track users across platforms by using a unified identification system. For example, consumers can follow a link from Alibaba's Weibo (a Twitter-like social media community) to Alibaba's Youku (the video site), and a click of a video advertisement will redirect them to Tmall, where a consumer buys something. Alibaba has used about 20 percent of its market capitalization to build this ecosystem, and the company claims it touches 95 percent of Chinese Internet users. The end result, according to Alibaba's vision, is a retail-tainment ecosystem where companies can build their brand, manage their customers, expand their marketing channels, and introduce new products under one roof.

The Tencent Ecosystem
Tencent has aggressively created its own ecosystem for e-commerce by stitching together a number of investments and partnerships to take on Alibaba. The core components of its e-commerce ecosystem include:

Social Networking
- WeChat (Tencent's dominant mobile messaging service)

Commerce
- Jingdong (Tencent's online retail partner; 25 percent of Jingdong's new customers are referred by links from Tencent's gateway.[7])
- Yihaodian (online grocery store)
- Weidian (online storefront service connecting micro-retailers to buyers)
- "Service Accounts": brand stores for large retailers (Tencent's answer to Tmall)
- "Subscription Accounts": value-added services for small and individual retailers

Payment and Finance
- WePay (Tencent's payment platform and answer to Alipay)
- Webank (Tencent's financial arm and answer to Ant Financial)

Media
- WeChat video/Weishi (Tencent's equivalent to YouTube)
- Sougou (online search)

Alliances

- Didichuxing (Uber-like mobile car-booking service, unique because it is partially owned by Tencent, Alibaba, and Baidu)
- Dianping (marketplace and community for food delivery)

The heart of Tencent's ecosystem is WeChat. With 700 million WeChat users in China, 25 percent of whom check their WeChat accounts more than thirty times a day, Tencent has begun to marry the power of China's online community with commerce, giving rise to entirely new business models.

An example of this is Luojisiwei (Logical Thinking), which has more than 3.5 million followers on WeChat. Every day WeChat subscribers receive a sixty-second voice message about historical, social, or business issues. Best described as a sort of in-depth "thought of the day," the content often draws on books and other products available for sale in Luojisiwei's WeChat store. Appearing alongside these daily voice message reminders are links to the store, where community members can buy books, calendars, stationery, and tickets to seminars by speakers on a wide range of topics.

Another example is Kidsbookmama, a WeChat account and store run by a publisher of children's books. Parents with young children subscribe to the account for free to gain access to articles and parenting advice from experts and other parents in the community. Integrated with the content is a WeChat merchant's store that sells books, toys, and food items for families.

In addition to housing these niche stores, WeChat allows larger brands to set up brand pages to which users can subscribe, as well as "service accounts," which are full-service storefronts for merchants that can include an increasing number of functions, such as customer service, sales, payments, and bookings. For actual sales of products, companies still usually use WeChat for building their brand but send customers to WeChat's partner, Jingdong, for making purchases. Tencent does prohibit companies from including links to Tmall and Taobao in their WeChat presence, but brands have found creative ways around this, technical loopholes that disguise the Tmall link as a link to another location. This has led to a rigorous game of cat and mouse between WeChat and sellers that are trying to promote their stores on Taobao and Tmall.

The attempt by Alibaba and Tencent to wall off their systems from each other has intensified their competition as they scramble to establish their own services, such as WeChat or Alipay, as the industry standard. The fight to have the industry standard has often occurred in other domains, such as taxi-booking apps, with their investments in rival companies losing millions of dollars in an attempt to capture market share. In some cases Alibaba and Tencent have decided to team up to defeat outside competitors, such as the merger of their taxi-hailing apps to defend against foreign invader Uber, which the company Alibaba and Tencent formed ultimately went on to acquire. But their truces have an on-again, off-again feel to them, often surviving while convenient, only to fall apart again.

THE LITTLE DRAGONS: NEW ENTRANTS AND INNOVATORS

While the big dragons Alibaba, Tencent, and Jingdong battle it out, a number of little dragons, with offerings ranging from cross-border retail to specialty retailers, are making inroads. These little dragons often have the backing of the big dragons. One such retailer, the online grocery shopping platform Yihaodian, with which Tencent and Jingdong are allied, has figured out new ways to drive grocery sales by taking advantage of virtual storefronts. Instead of operating physical grocery stores, Yihaodian has built wall displays at subway stations with product images and codes that shoppers can scan with their mobile phone to add products to their shopping basket. By the time they get home, their groceries are on their way. In what is likely to be a trend, Yihaodian was swallowed up by the Tencent-Jingdong universe in a deal that saw Yihaodian's owner, Walmart, hand the company over to Jingdong in exchange for 5 percent of Jingdong's stock.

Another innovative start-up, Little Red Book, has created a

mobile shopping and media platform focused on cross-border goods. To gauge customer demand for products, the company posts Pinterest-like images of foreign products and counts the number of "likes" that each receives. If a product reaches a certain threshold, Little Red Book will add the product to its inventory and alert the customers who "liked" it that the product is available. The app attracted 15 million users in two years and now generates $200 million in sales, helping Little Red Book raise $100 million from Tencent and other investors in 2016 at a reported $1 billion valuation.[8]

The mobile phone maker Xiaomi has even blurred the lines between manufacturer and e-commerce retailer, making online sales its core retail channel from the start. More than just a smart phone manufacturer, Xiaomi views itself as an Internet company or software company. Its rival, Apple, operates in relative secrecy, keeping every detail of its new products under tight wraps. Xiaomi, on the other hand, has created a massive online fan club of loyal customers who suggest product ideas and give instant feedback on new product designs.

OPPORTUNITIES FOR INTERNATIONAL BRANDS

Despite its slowing growth, China's is still the fastest-growing and second-largest consumer economy in the world. And at the same time, e-commerce is growing faster in China than anywhere in the world. Together these two trends create unprecedented opportunities for international brands to sell in China.

For years many of the big brands and retailers, such as Nike, Gap, Sony, Coca-Cola, Adidas, Mango, Uniqlo, Lacoste, and Toys "R" Us, have been selling on China's marketplaces. But the e-commerce boom in China has made the market accessible to more than just the large multinationals. Niche brands and vendors selling everything from live Maine lobster to bottled fruit juice from Slovenia are using e-commerce to sell in China.

As more Western companies look to tap the potential of the

China e-commerce market, third-party consultants and solution providers have sprung up to ease their entry to the market. One of the leading consulting companies is Export Now, started by Frank Lavin, a former White House aide to Ronald Reagan who later served, among other roles, as an ambassador to Singapore. Lavin founded Export Now in 2010 to help consumer brands sell products in China. I spoke with Lavin, Export Now's CEO, to get a sense of the issues international brands need to consider when looking at the China market. Many of the same lessons are applicable to other emerging markets.

Lavin thinks macroeconomic statistics tend to understate the opportunity for e-commerce in China. "The one thing that really gets people," Lavin explained, "is that they look at an average GDP [gross domestic product] or purchase power parity [relative consumer buying power] number, and they say, 'You know what? This is a poor country, this is a developing country.' In the US, if you are Nike, you might be speaking to 60 percent of the population. In China you might only be speaking to 10 percent of the population. But that 10 percent is 140 million people. That's bigger than any European country. That's a pretty nice market segment for you—and, by the way, if it's 10 percent this year, it will be [much larger] next year. In China you are only talking to a segment of the population, so that's a real adjustment for a lot of multinationals to take if they've never been in a developing market before."[9]

China also represents a potentially exciting opportunity for smaller brands. "The base is so large," Lavin said. In smaller countries, "the ability to experiment is just more limited, whereas China is just so massive that you can have an initiative that has only very niche appeal, but you're still quite comfortable with it because the numbers are OK."

Where e-commerce makes the difference is that, in the past, it would not have been economical to serve niche markets through physical retail, because the consumers with the financial wherewithal to buy premium products were too scattered geographically. But the Internet allows brands to reach these consumers without the consumer density the brands would require in developed markets.

"What's interesting about China is that it is so massive," Lavin explained, adding that the development of retail offline is going to take longer. "You're not going to solve offline [retail] in two or three years. You look at companies like Nike or Procter & Gamble, and they say, 'We've been doing this about thirty years and we're only 75 percent done.' Some companies really get that and say, 'If 20 percent or 30 percent of my total sales in China would be e-commerce anyway, let me just get that started now, and then I can spend the next five years building out offline. Some companies get that, but some companies just don't." Lavin tells potential clients that e-commerce as a "channel is so powerful, so cost-effective, it's really where you need to start."

He said the hardest part for companies to understand "is that you can have an e-commerce strategy independent of your offline strategy. In no place in the world could you say that, until about two to three years ago in [regard to] China. . . . Until about three years ago no one had ever said, 'Let's get e-commerce going first.' Everybody in the world had said, 'Once your brand is established and your distribution is there, and you're doing everything right, e-commerce will give you a lift. E-commerce will help you get [an additional] 5 percent or 7 percent lift on your base.' . . . What you had viewed in your home market as simply a strategy to augment success might just be" the primary or sole channel for selling online.

It's not always easy to convince Western brands, which have a history of building their brands offline, that e-commerce is the place to focus on. According to Lavin, "Some companies are very dogmatic about what they do overseas and how they do it, and some companies are market rationalists who say, 'Let's think this through.' And so, really, it's almost like asking them what's their religion. If [selling offline] is their religion, that's their religion. And so a lot of our work is leading a horse to water. All we can say is, 'When you are ready to go online, we will be ready to work with you and, by the way, you might be ready to go online today.'"

Leading horses to water often involves demonstrating that demand for their products already exists in China. "Sometimes all you need to do is show [brands] their competitors," he said, or tell the client that brands with similar price points, appeal, and customer behavior are already selling online in China. Other times, "we say, 'Your brand is already in the market—it's all over Taobao, and you might as well bring that transaction back in-house and get full value for it and not let the gray-market people define your brand in the market.'"[10]

In many ways, "parallel imports" were one of the greatest drivers of Taobao. Scrappy entrepreneurs would head overseas and before heading home would load up their bags with foreign products unavailable in China that they then would sell to Chinese customers. Indeed, the sale of parallel imports on Taobao is what has accelerated the growth of Tmall, by giving authorized dealers and brands themselves a place to sell products.

Brands have reacted to these parallel imports in different ways, Lavin said. "Every company has a different philosophy. Some companies say frankly, 'We don't mind—a sale is a sale, and if someone wants to go to Bangkok every month with a duffel bag, fill it up with cosmetics, and resell it, I guess that's OK.' And other guys say, 'That's not OK—we lose quality control, pricing leverage in the market, [and] brand definition, and we can't introduce the right products in the right way, and we don't like that. We are sort of outsourcing our distribution inadvertently to a third party.'"

Lavin makes the case to brands that "there is brand activity in this market and it behooves you sooner or later to get control of that because there are risks of adulteration. It's only one step to go from parallel imports to counterfeit." Someone who goes to Bangkok every month to buy a thousand jars of face cream eventually figures out that he can make those jars. Or maybe the guy in Bangkok is selling face cream that has expired or that he stores improperly, Lavin tells clients. "You are really beating up your product and not taking care of it," Lavin noted. "There's a million reasons why companies need to get into that supply chain and not just be indifferent to it."

A key driver of parallel imports was that many brands put higher prices on their products in China than elsewhere, and importers undercut those prices. But this is an antiquated concern in the Internet era, Lavin said. "In the old days there were national prices due to lack of transparency. You could have [a] 30 to 50 percent difference by market. Now you have easy price discovery and easy parallel import arbitrage, so the customer fights back. I tell the brands to be very careful about price discrimination. The Chinese customer will look online and say, 'Why in the world should I give you a few hundred renminbi for this face cream if I can get it in the United States for twenty bucks?' You risk hurting your brand image if you are viewed as price gouging."[11]

Setting up an online shop in China will cause some of these conflicts with traditions or business models in a brand's home country, but being able to sell to Chinese consumers is leading brands and retailers to ignore the risks and dive in. So what should brands consider when approaching the online market in China? Here are some steps to take:

1. **Research the demand.** See if the thousands of scrappy entrepreneurs selling parallel imports on Taobao are already selling your products online in China. Lavin also advises looking at competitors and similar products in the market to see if they already have a presence in China.

2. **Determine your mode of entry.** The key question here is, "Should I sell into China purely through cross-border sales or should I establish a China-based team?" Many companies already have business operations in China, which automatically answers this question. But those without a team in China don't need one: they can start selling in China by setting up an online shop.

Tmall pioneered this practice through Tmall Global, whose sellers can operate their businesses from their home country, hold the inventory outside China, and then fulfill orders by shipping from their home country to the customer in China. Operating a Tmall storefront is a lot like operating a company's own B2C website, and sellers have full control of design, operations, fulfillment, and logistics.

By testing the waters on Tmall before setting up local operations in China, international brands are able to minimize the risk of storing inventory locally that may fail to sell and the up-front costs that a larger commitment might require. If companies find a demand for their product on Tmall, they can increase their investment. But the days of having to build a multimillion-dollar factory to do business in China and then finding out that local customers don't like your product are now over.

Nevertheless, you still have to make some financial commitment. To weed out the smaller or less-committed international retailers, Tmall has instituted a number of up-front deposits for sellers. Tmall uses the deposit to help guarantee a seller's transactions as well provide an incentive for sellers to make the most of their investment. Tmall reimburses many of the up-front charges over time, if a seller meets certain benchmarks for customer satisfaction and sales volumes. In addition, once a seller's store is on the platform, the owner will have to spend promotional dollars on Tmall, for example, to pay for keyword ads that drive traffic. Finally, Tmall's commissions range from 0.5 percent to 5 percent, depending on the product category. That's not an insignificant sum, but most brands consider it a small price to pay, given the savings of selling online versus through a brick storefront.

Jingdong and WeChat have also rushed to embrace this cross-border trend, offering similar services to global retailers. Tmall has a head start, and offshore companies regard it as easier to work with. But Jingdong and WeChat are sure to grow this area of their business and do their best to challenge Tmall. Despite some back-and-forth on policies governing customs duties for cross-border purchases, the Chinese government has for the most part been encouraging cross-border trade.

Is it possible to go it alone and simply open your own storefront for your brand independent of the Alibaba, Tencent, or Jingdong malls? Of course, anything is possible, but in this case you are unlikely to be successful. It is simply too hard to generate traffic for your store if it is not on some or all of the major platforms. Many brands have tried, only to decide to move their stores to the major platforms.

3. **Select third-party partners.** The rise of e-commerce platforms in China has created a huge ecosystem of service providers who help local and foreign brands start and manage their e-commerce stores in China. These players are known in the industry as TP partners (a now-generic term in the industry believed to have derived from an abbreviation of "Taobao Partners") and are certified by Alibaba and Tmall. TP partners approach the business from different starting points and bring different strengths. Some, such as Web2 Asia, started as digital marketing agencies and followed their customers into e-commerce. Others, such as Baozun, whose operations became so huge it had an IPO in 2015, are more focused on logistics and cater to large, high-volume clients like Nike that require massive logistics and warehousing capabilities. Others, like Export Now, are one-stop shops that help larger brands with every aspect of the process. TP partners can also help you determine which platforms are best for your products. For example, "JD has some real strengths in personal electronics and appliances, but Tmall really rules most of the rest. There are specialty verticals but I would

say, in general, Tmall is going to be the platform of preference for most [international] brands," Lavin said.

4. **Determine the resources you need to allocate.** How much
   investment does it take for a brand to start selling in China?
   Less than a physical retail operation but more than simply
   building a website. There really is no one-size-fits-all answer.
   Several costs are involved in the effort to stand out from
   competitors, such as buying online promotions and paying
   for keyword ads so that a brand's products appear more
   prominently in the marketplace's search results. Brands need
   to provide more product photos and videos than they would
   in the West, because China's online shoppers expect more
   virtual "touch and feel" from their online experiences. In
   addition, most shops will need to provide live sales and customer service through online messaging, which requires hiring and training staff to serve shoppers online.

5. **Launch, revise, grow.** The benefit of starting an online retail
   operation in China is that it can grow as the business grows,
   with the ability to limit risks along the way. Sellers can start
   selling into China as cross-border sellers, outsourcing most
   of the operation to third-party TP partners. Then, as sales
   grow and customer response comes in, the business can be
   expanded and local teams added. Over time, brands can decide which components of their operation to outsource and
   which to take in-house. It is important to note that most
   brand building can be done digitally, meaning you can experiment and refine your campaigns online, rather than in
   the more expensive physical world. "How your brand is
   received and defined [in China] is overwhelmingly digital,"
   Lavin said. Through blogs on Weibo, conversations on We-
   Chat, and videos on Youku, "the consumer is absorbing all
   this information online," he noted. "Online is not just a revenue channel: it defines the brand."[12]

COUNTERFEITS

A European brand manager once said to me, "We want to sell online in China but are worried about exposing ourselves to the risk of counterfeits. What should we do to protect our brand?" The fact is, the risk of counterfeits is ever present in China, even if you are not already selling there. But I think that e-commerce platforms are now more a part of the solution than the problem.

The headlines might make you think otherwise. Alibaba, the largest e-commerce company and easiest target, has taken a lot of heat for the number of counterfeits merchants sell on its sites. But that's changing. The emergence of B2C malls like Tmall and Jingdong Mall have effectively created "counterfeit-free zones" where both brands and shoppers know that the products being bought and sold are real.

It's now the rare exception for a buyer on Tmall to find that the product she ordered is a fake. And when this happens, she is guaranteed compensation above and beyond the product's value. Now the biggest challenge arises when both buyer and seller know they are dealing in fake products. I believe that this problem won't be fixed until the Chinese government gets serious about enforcing its laws and sending violators to jail. So far it has lacked the political will to do so, but in 2017 Alibaba began to call on the Chinese government to add more bite to its enforcement of counterfeits. But in the meantime Alibaba has begun to sue merchants—its customers—when it finds them selling counterfeits on Alibaba's platforms. This is one way to help deter sellers of fake goods.

KEY TAKEAWAYS

China's evolving e-commerce landscape is dynamic and complex. To help clarify where things seem to be headed, I've brought together what I think are the key takeaways.

China's online retail has already leapfrogged past the West. For years analysts imagined that China's retail infrastructure might skip the evolutionary steps of growth, consolidation, and maturation that took hundreds of years in the West and jump straight to online sales. And that's what happened: China now has the world's largest e-commerce market, expected to constitute anywhere from 21.5 to 25.5 percent of all retail in China by 2020.[13] This requires businesses to suspend what they know about the history of retail in the United States and western Europe and accept that China's e-commerce has entered an entirely new phase and the old rules simply don't apply. Online retail is no longer an additional channel through which to sell products. It is becoming central to how companies research, develop, brand, and market their products. A mind open to entirely new ideas is crucial for addressing the market.

E-commerce in China is more *creative* than *disruptive*. *Creative disruption* is the phrase du jour, with tech entrepreneurs taking great pride in—and being celebrated for—how much they are disrupting traditional ways of doing things, often with little sympathy for those who are being disrupted. Uber is a great example, with a bold and brash CEO who is building a great service that customers love but often with little outward sympathy for the millions of taxi drivers whose lives are being upended.

Online retail in the West was in many ways no different. Jeff Bezos has had little sympathy for the small independent booksellers, not to mention the large book chains, that shuttered their doors as Amazon blew up their business models. "Amazon is not happening to book selling, the future is happening to book selling," Bezos says in his defense.[14]

In the case of China, and emerging markets in general, the online retail boom is more creative than disruptive. It is creating opportunities and driving consumption where they didn't exist rather than simply blowing up old business models.

In 2013, when e-commerce was becoming a norm in China,

McKinsey & Co. found that online retail purchases were not simply replacing purchases that would otherwise take place offline. Rather, the firm found that e-commerce "actually seems to spur incremental consumption in China, especially in lower-tier cities where there is pent-up demand for choice in merchandise that physical retail stores have not yet managed to deliver." In looking at 266 cities, McKinsey found that in China nationally, 61 percent of e-commerce transactions were substitutions for online spending but a whopping 39 percent were new consumption that would not have occurred otherwise. In third- and fourth-tier cities, the effect was even more pronounced: 57 percent of the online consumption was additional spending, and only 43 percent replaced offline spending. And, McKinsey estimated, e-commerce boosted China's private consumption by 2 percent, supporting the government's goal of shifting China's economy from one reliant on exports to a model more driven by domestic consumption.

In addition, McKinsey estimated that e-commerce had given rise to an entirely new $13 billion industry of service providers made up of online advertising and payment systems, warehousing, express delivery, and IT services that online retailers use to support their online stores.[15] The lesson is that e-commerce builds more than it destroys in an economy.

E-commerce in China is dominated by marketplaces. Roughly 90 percent of online retail in China is conducted on marketplace platforms, compared with about 24 percent in the West. The lesson? It's fine to have your own brand store or retail website, but if you want to reach buyers, you also have to have a presence on the marketplaces.

China's e-commerce ecosystem is producing innovative business models. Try to forget everything you know about Amazon, eBay, and top retailers in the West. The storefronts of China's online retailers offer a potent cocktail of community, social features, celebrities, and media. It's never clear where one feature begins or another ends.

These business models are likely to catch on in other emerging markets, such as India and Southeast Asia.

Cross-border e-commerce is a huge and growing opportunity. Industrious entrepreneurs who bought products overseas and sold them through their own shops on Taobao accounted for much of Taobao's early success. Two factors drove this phenomenon. First, China often taxed imported goods—especially luxury goods—at rates as high as 100 percent. So, to avoid those taxes, small dealers would pack their suitcases with goods they bought in Hong Kong or on overseas trips. Second, Taobao offered access to products that Chinese consumers simply could not find in their country. Thus a Chinese student studying overseas might stumble upon a product that might appeal in China and set up an online shop, selling from outside of China but below the radar of customs officials. Retailers sometimes realized that a large proportion of their online sales in the US market were for products that were being diverted to online sales to China.

These gray-market goods and parallel imports often gave brands headaches, and often their first reaction was to try to stamp out products they found online in China, acting on the assumption the goods were fakes or illegal imports. But such sales also can be a sign that a company's brand already has a market in China. Indeed, Chinese consumers are hungry for imported products that come direct from the source, which they view as authentic and a better guarantee of quality than locally bought goods. This is especially pronounced in the case of food and health safety, such as infant formula, because several food safety scandals have driven Chinese consumers to look overseas for sources of safe food products.

The consulting firm Bain & Company predicts that cross-border retail sales in China will grow by 30 percent annually in the future, reaching a value of RMB1 trillion by 2020.[16] Without ever setting foot in China, retailers can build customized Chinese-language websites and sell directly into China through their own virtual stores stocking their own brands. But until they establish their brand in China, they are probably better served by plugging into marketplaces such as Tmall Global and Jingdong, which offer brands an effective way to reach the Chinese consumer without having to build local distribution capabilities.

FUTURE TRENDS

E-commerce will grow even during an economic slowdown in China. The growth of China's gross domestic product may be slowing, but its consumers' purchasing power is still on the rise. Boston Consulting Group estimates that by 2020, Chinese consumption will have grown by $2.3 trillion, even if GDP growth slows to 5.5 percent. It also predicts that e-commerce will drive 42 percent of that consumption growth, with 90 percent of that growth coming from mobile e-commerce. Private online consumption will grow by 20 percent annually through 2020, compared with 6 percent annual growth in offline sales.[17]

"Online to Offline" will be more important to China than in the West. The love of the smartphone in China will make online to offline (O2O) a bigger part of retail in China than it is in the United States and Europe. Marketing tied to physical stores will spark impulse purchases and allow retailers to lure groups of friends to make deals together. Imagine a group of friends who are connected online, and all like a certain restaurant that has a WeChat page. As they are strolling down a street of restaurants, they receive notification of a 20 percent discount if they bring a party of six or more to the nearest restaurant in the chain. Or a retailer might offer a buy-one, get-one-free deal if a shopper brings in a friend to buy shoes. The combination of social media and mobile phones will make O2O sales a more powerful relationship in China than elsewhere.

Lower-tier cities in China remain a rich source of opportunity for e-commerce players. McKinsey predicts that by 2025, China will have more than 220 cities with more than one million inhabitants.

Yet China's physical retailers have only begun to open stores outside the first-tier cities on China's east coast. The number of middle-class shoppers in these lower-tier cities is growing, but they have no place to spend their new wealth locally. No wonder they are using online shopping to find the products they want or need. In fact, consumers in China's fourth-tier cities direct 27 percent of their disposable income to e-commerce purchases, compared to 18 percent in first-tier cities.[18]

Traditional retail stores in China will be designed around online retail, not vice versa. On a recent trip to China I walked into a new mall on a busy shopping street and expected to find several specialty retailers. What I saw astounded me. A luxury car sat in a ground-floor window near the entrance, but small restaurants and food courts dominated the five-story mall. I could hardly find a retailer. Clearly, the e-commerce boom was not apparent years earlier when the owners reviewed the initial blueprints for their mall.

In fact, China's e-commerce boom is having a stronger effect on traditional retail than it did in the West. In the West, big-box retailers like Borders and Best Buy learned that having a massive retail footprint doesn't work in the e-commerce era. But retailers in China still have time to build with e-commerce in mind, providing small storefront showrooms where shoppers can touch and feel items, as well as pick up products they ordered online if, for example, they want to pick up a surprise gift for a loved one at the store on the way home from work rather than have it arrive at home in an ugly cardboard box.

Counterfeits will become less of a problem over time. Long before e-commerce, China had a huge problem with counterfeit goods. But the Internet made its counterfeit problem all the more visible as merchants and counterfeiters alike used Taobao and other marketplaces to sell their goods online. And as the largest publicly listed Chinese e-commerce company, Alibaba has taken most of the heat from brand owners and international critics. Although Taobao has two thousand employees dedicated to rooting out fakes among its merchants' product listings, it takes only a few seconds of browsing Taobao to find Gucci or Balenciaga handbags listed at the suspiciously low price of $30.

The bottom line is that counterfeits are big problem. But even without a solution, brands can run highly profitable businesses in China.

The Chinese government and key stakeholders will continue to embrace e-commerce. For the reasons I have already mentioned, public stakeholders in China, especially the national and local governments, will offer few roadblocks to e-commerce. Because of the national government's largely supportive view of e-commerce, China has fewer roadblocks than more mature retail markets, such as Europe or the United States. Delivery jobs are soaking up unemployed migrant workers; entrepreneurs are building shops online, hiring staff as they grow; and e-commerce is generating new consumption. These important tailwinds will propel Chinese e-commerce.

This of course could all be challenged if a Trump-led trade war were to break out. Averting such a trade war was no doubt the reason Jack Ma met with Donald Trump less than two weeks before Trump took office. Outside of Trump Tower, Ma and Trump declared their intention to work together to create one million jobs in the United States by encouraging export of US products to Chinese consumers through Alibaba's shopping websites. If the United States and China enter into a trade war, the Chinese government may begin to impose stricter controls on e-commerce, particularly cross-border. But at least for now, the trend appears to be toward greater acceptance of rather than resistance to cross-border purchases.

Luxury brands will increasingly have a presence online in China. In my travels through Europe I hear a common refrain from executives at companies that sell luxury brands: "We don't sell online—especially on marketplaces—because it dilutes our brand value." It's easy to understand why they feel this way. In the West the primary motivation for many to buy online is lower price or convenience, and retailers built websites with these customers' priorities in mind. Particularly on marketplaces like Amazon or eBay, selling Hermès scarfs in the same marketplace where one can find used Pez dispensers is difficult.

But the brand experience in China is entirely different. Consumers first hear about, learn about, and then experience brands online. So it's only logical that they should be able to buy online as well. Look no further than the many homegrown fashion brands in China that started as a Taobao store and grew to become standalone brands generating millions of dollars in sales. If someone can start a new brand from scratch online and realize that much success, surely a famous brand can find ways to tell its story online without diluting its appeal.

Online shoppers are becoming increasingly brand conscious, moving up the ladder from lower-cost unbranded goods to branded goods. Saving money by shopping online is no longer their main motivation—and this bodes well for brands.

The used goods market will become a significant online market in China. Yes, that old eBay auction model may now be worth a fresh look. The primary reason that the auction model failed to take off in China was the low supply of secondhand goods. But with products from several years of shopping binges accumulating in China's small homes, it's easy to imagine that the market for used goods will reemerge.

E-commerce will continue to transform rural China. The opening of China to foreign businesses in 1978 and subsequent reforms made its farmers the first to get rich. But China's rural areas soon lagged behind their urban counterparts. Skyscrapers went up in China's cities, whose infrastructure improved, while rural areas remained trapped in the dark ages. When the Internet first started to boom in China, it looked like the country might experience a digital divide as wide as the offline divide.

But e-commerce has proved to be transformative for rural economies by connecting China's far-flung rural areas. The first effects of e-commerce that rural areas felt came from the sellers' side, often driven by fresh college graduates who were returning to their home villages and setting up online stores offering agricultural products, crafts, and other small-industry products. This led to the emergence of "Taobao Villages," villages that Alibaba designated as having at least 10 percent of village households engaged in e-commerce or at least 100 active online shops opened by villagers. By 2015 China had more than 780 Taobao Villages.[19]

But rural China is also hosting increasing numbers of rural distribution centers, built by Alibaba, Jingdong, and others, for all those goods ordered by urban consumers. Alibaba has pledged to invest $1.6 billion to build 100,000 service centers in rural China in three to five years and by mid-2016 had already set up 16,000 Alibaba Centers in rural villages in 29 provinces. Operated by independent local entrepreneurs, these service centers are not the same as Amazon's distribution centers in the United States. Alibaba's rural service centers provide Internet access and training to consumers and businesses, extending e-commerce to those with no Internet access and helping them to buy and sell through Alibaba's marketplaces. According to Alibaba, orders placed by or with rural sellers generated 7 billion packages in 2015, which represented an increase of more than 55 percent from 2014. Not surprisingly, those rural users who do have Internet access use mobile devices to go online; as a result, 60 percent of China's total transaction volume is generated by shoppers using mobile devices.[20]

Other emerging markets can duplicate the experience of rural China and help lift rural areas out of poverty. By using service centers and sales agents, even areas where Internet access or illiteracy is an issue can reap the economic benefits of e-commerce.

Same-day delivery may soon be a reality in China. The battle between Jingdong and Alibaba is pushing logistics even further. Alibaba has a goal to ensure twenty-four-hour delivery to virtually anywhere in China. Jingdong has the same goal. This is not only possible but will also be affordable, as the labor costs for delivery are exceptionally low in China. The nation's 1.18 million delivery couriers are typically male, between twenty and thirty years of age, and from rural areas; they make a median salary of about $20 per day. Yes, exceedingly low wages by Western standards. But for many it still represents a step up from the meager opportunities in the countryside and an entry-level job for a rural migrant who has just moved to the city. One thing is certain—until wages of delivery couriers increase, the idea of using drones for e-commerce deliveries in China is nothing but a publicity stunt.

China's e-commerce ecosystem has created a virtuous circle in which product and brand innovation can thrive. The combination of e-commerce penetration, seamless e-commerce infrastructure, a highly social and involved consumer base, and low-cost manufacturing has built a virtuous circle that will incubate new brands and products online that will spread nationally and even internationally. Domestic brands like Xiaomi (cell phones) are increasingly using the power of the online community to solicit production suggestions from its user base. They are using their core online fans for consumer surveys, discussion forums, and prototype testing, then modifying the resulting products and quickly rolling them out. China's role as factory to the world gives brands a strong advantage because they can conceive of products, then design, test, manufacture, and sell them within the country's borders.

This virtuous circle will give China a comparative advantage over other Asian countries. Gone are the days when online retail was just another channel. It is now a driver of innovation that will power China ahead. It's an important example for other emerging markets—embrace e-commerce to your own country's benefit or resist e-commerce at your country's peril. Beyond establishing a solid Internet backbone that allows for fast, reliable, and inexpensive Internet connections, policy makers should consider laws and regulations that accelerate the adoption of e-commerce rather than hamper it. Sure, physical retailers and government officials seeking rents from players will resist it. But a smooth, integrated e-commerce ecosystem is essential for an effective economy. China's e-commerce system is already sophisticated, whereas other emerging markets are still running on DOS.

4

INDIA—THE NEXT MEGA-MARKET

E-commerce in the West is just the dessert. In China it's the main course.

—*Jack Ma*

E-commerce in China is the main course. In India, it's a seven-course meal.

—*Sandeep Aggarwal, founder of India's ShopClues*

JUST WHEN IT SEEMED OUR DELIVERIES WERE GETTING OFF TO A good start, a monkey jumped atop our *dabbas*, or lunch boxes. The furry intruder grabbed their handles and attempted to pry open the lids to get to the food. Our efforts to coax him down were fruitless, and he jumped up and down atop the lunch boxes and swiped at anyone who came near. Finally, after we pleaded with the woman panhandler accompanying him, the monkey jumped off the dabbas, leaving our lunches intact. Our lunch deliveries to nearby offices could finally get under way.

I had decided to spend the afternoon shadowing Mumbai's famous *dabbawalla* deliverymen to learn more about what Indians cited as the greatest hurdle to e-commerce on the subcontinent—logistics. Without fail, Mumbai's dabbawallas deliver 130,000 meals to workers across the city every day so that everyone gets a home-cooked lunch that meets the dietary restrictions of their caste and creed.

Dabbawalla derives from the words *dabba*, a box containing a meal, and *walla*, which means "the man who carries." For more than one hundred years the dabbawallas have been shuttling food from the homes of office workers on the city's outskirts to their desks and offices in central Mumbai. Dabbawallas are such an institution that India's largest e-commerce player, Flipkart, partnered with a dabbawalla union for last-mile delivery in 2015.[1]

Mumbai's dabbawallas meet a need: people in India have many religions, each with its own dietary restrictions. Mumbai's Muslims avoid pork, Hindus avoid beef, Jains avoid meat altogether, even avoiding onions, potatoes, and garlic. Meanwhile, everyone is concerned about the cleanliness and cost of so-called outside food—that is, anything not cooked at home. So, for about $10 per month, the dabbawallas pick up home-cooked meals from their customers' houses and deliver them to their worksites.

The scheme is remarkably efficient.

The five thousand dabbawallas operate a hub-and-spoke delivery system, passing lunch boxes like relay batons between deliverymen. The lunches are marked with color-coded symbols, numbers and letters denoting the point of origin and destination of the delivery. The delivery network has received worldwide attention for its efficiency and low error rate, studied by everyone from Richard Branson to the faculty of the Harvard Business School.

I'd started my day at one of the main hubs, Christchurch railway station. Just before lunchtime the dabbawallas pushed their way through the crowd to scramble onto the platform. Dressed in crisp white shirts and the traditional Gandhi cap, some were carrying as many as thirty lunch boxes balanced precariously on their heads.

From the Christchurch station I followed one crew to a patch of pavement a block away, where they dropped off and sorted the lunch boxes.

My tour guide and interpreter, Viren de Sá, arranged for me to shadow Anil Bagwhat, a career dabbawalla. I asked Bagwhat about the monkey encounter. "Does that kind of thing happen often?" He seemed unfazed. "In this job, there is always some new thing happening," he replied. "Given a chance, I could write a book about all of my stories."

Each of us slung a few bags of lunch boxes over our shoulders and walked to the neighboring offices. The markings on the lunch boxes told Bagwhat exactly where to go, and he walked into the nearby office buildings and dropped them off at the front desk or outside the office doors. Office workers immediately snapped up the deliveries. "Dabbawallas are the only people in the city that follow official IST—Indian Standard Time," Viren de Sá explained to me. "Everyone else in the city follows a different IST—Indian stretchable time."

Our sunny afternoon was fairly relaxed, and I could see the appeal of life as a dabbawalla in contrast to that of the officer workers behind the desks. "I've been working here twenty-eight years, and this is my life," Bagwhat told me. "My father was a farmer, and when I came to Mumbai as a boy, I didn't know what to do. My older brother was a dabbawalla, so when I was fifteen, I just started to emulate him. There is joy in this work. Every day you are outside with your friends. Even in the monsoon we still work. All I have to do is put on a raincoat. This is my life and this is my family."

Still, it is a hard life, and he didn't want it for his kids. Although Bagwhat enjoys job security and respect, dabbawallas earn only about $200 a month. "My daughter is studying pharmacology. I enjoy this life but it is too much labor," he told me.

What does all this have to do with e-commerce? The success of the dabbawallas shows that it's possible to solve India's logistics problems. It's an issue complicated by many factors, especially the lack of accurate addresses.

I first noticed this when I was trying to send packages in India. Addresses often read more like descriptions, with phrases like "behind the temple" or "close to the baobab tree." "Street names in India are very complicated," Viren de Sá told me. Some cities have several streets with the same name. Every city in India has a

Mahatma Gandhi Road, and some have as many as five. Street names seem to change as frequently as the elected officials. Many names are difficult to spell, and quite often nobody knows the official name of a given street. "If I say Marine Drive, everyone will know this place," he said. "But if I use the official name, Netaji Subhash Chandra Bose Road, nobody knows it. So people realize that it is better to use landmarks. Landmarks remain constant."

The issue of addresses is even more complicated in India's countryside. Unlike growth in centrally administered China, India's has been largely unplanned, and as a result many people do not have addresses at all.

Indeed, India faces all the problems China had to solve and a long list of other challenges. Here, e-commerce is indeed a seven-course meal, not just the main course that it is in China. To make e-commerce work in India, every link in the e-commerce chain needs either the solution to a problem or an improvement—logistics first and foremost. But, as in China, the bigger the challenge, the greater the opportunity. And that has made India the central battleground in global e-commerce.

THE SCRAMBLE FOR INDIA

In February 2016, as I was eating a breakfast *dosa* (pancake) in Mumbai, all I needed was the front page of the local newspaper to tell me that I was sitting at the global epicenter of e-commerce. The whole thing was dedicated to stories about what it called "The Great Indian E-commerce Liftoff." Snapdeal had just raised $200 million at a $7 billion valuation. The mobile payment provider Paytm was preparing to invest heavily in its own expansion into a smartphone-based marketplace. Headlines declared that India's largest e-commerce retailer, Flipkart, "Wants to Do an Alibaba" to take on the global giants. EBay, too, was pumping money into India.

But the frenzy was not limited to the headlines. Full-page newspaper ads touted upcoming online sales by the leading e-commerce sites. Billboards for Amazon India littered the highway from the airport into Mumbai. Even fans of *kabaddi* (an Indian form of tag) could not escape e-commerce ads, as Flipkart sponsored televised professional kabaddi tournaments. When it came to using investors' money to pay for splashy ad campaigns, India's e-commerce players were partying like it was 1999.

Clearly, India had become the central battleground market for the big players in global e-commerce. By 2016, anyone who was anyone was there. Amazon, eBay, and Alibaba all were backing local proxies. And the investors who had funded e-commerce in other emerging markets, including Naspers, Softbank, and Rocket Internet, were pouring money into India. By 2017, Facebook, Microsoft, and Tencent were joining the Indian e-commerce fray. China had proved that e-commerce could work in developing markets, and no one wanted to miss out on "the next China."

ON THE FACE of it, they had good reason to swarm India. The country had not only the hottest emerging market but also the hottest e-commerce market in the world. While growth was slowing in the other members of BRICS (Brazil, Russia, India, China, and South Africa) or even heading toward recession, India was powering along, growing faster than ever. That much was clear from the Mumbai skyline, where cranes rose above unfinished skyscrapers far as the eye could see. Mumbai of early 2016 reminded me of Shanghai in the 1990s.

Optimism was in the air. People sensed this was India's time. India's prime minister, Narendra Modi, had learned from China's export boom and was busy promoting India as a new manufacturing hub that could challenge China and potentially lift India's workers out of poverty. The entire city of Mumbai was blazing with banners and billboards for Make in India Week, a week designed to celebrate innovation and encourage foreign investment.

Indians were tantalized by the possibility that, after years of being closed off from the world economically, their country might finally live up to its full potential. And nowhere was their excitement more evident than in e-commerce. Just one year earlier Modi had announced his Digital India campaign to accelerate India's entry into the Internet era. Affordable smartphones were bringing the Internet to the pockets of millions of Indians each month, and Internet access was spreading to the hinterlands.

But while the technology was advanced, traditional ways of doing business were shaping technology's application in the Indian market, which had formed over hundreds of years.

FROM BOMBAY'S BAZAARS TO BAAZEE: THE HISTORICAL CONTEXT OF E-COMMERCE IN INDIA

Walking through Mumbai's teeming bazaars can feel as if the entire population of the country has squeezed into a few narrow lanes. Merchants and shoppers balance rugs, clothing, toys, and large bags full of goods on their heads as they zigzag through the crowds. Motorcycles and cars weave in and out, horns blaring, as drivers fight for space with the sea of pedestrians, who are dressed in brightly colored saris, black burkas, and even skinny jeans. Here and there cows loll lazily in the shade, nibbling at a patch of grass or browsing in the garbage.

Nearly two thousand years ago the area now known as Mumbai was simply a collection of seven islands inhabited by fishers. From about 200 B.C. through the fourteenth century, various Hindu dynasties controlled the islands until Muslim traders from Gujarat took control of them. In 1534 the Portuguese took over because they needed a port to facilitate the spice trade, only to cede control to the British as part of the dowry of Catherine de Braganza when she married Charles II in 1661. Charles II leased the islands to the East India Company in 1668, and the seabeds around the islands were filled in over time as Mumbai grew into an important international trading port.[2]

That lease marked the beginning of a period of about 250 years when a corporation—the East India Company—ruled India.

Following the Indian Rebellion of 1857, the British Crown assumed direct control of the country. For the next several decades Britain solidified its hold on India, building roads and railways, establishing cotton mills and other commercial infrastructure, and creating a class of English-speaking local administrators.

But the start of the twentieth century saw increasing resistance to British rule. Indians began fighting for greater participation in their own government. Mohandas K. Gandhi—popularly known as the Mahatma, or great soul—led a nonviolent movement to compel Britain to quit India that began in 1942. A central part of the Quit India campaign was a boycott of British cloth, which Gandhi regarded as a symbol of colonial oppression, in favor of homespun cotton, or *khadi*, instead.

When India finally won its independence in 1947, ending the long colonial era, the focus on self-reliance and *swadeshi*—Indian-made products—continued.

The economic policies of Jawaharlal Nehru, India's first prime minister, emphasized local production and the protection of the small producer. From 1947 to 1991 India's economic policy was a combination of protectionism and central planning. The idea was to ensure that India—whose resources Britain had exploited—could be economically self-sustaining.

Strong government intervention in business typified the era, and high prices and taxes dominated. India nationalized its pillar industries such as steel, power, telecommunications, and banks. The government discouraged multinationals that were thinking about setting up shop in India, and for the most part they stayed out.

In some respects the plan was a success. By protecting local industries Nehru laid the foundations for several of today's multi-billion-dollar conglomerates—including the Aditya Birla Group, Tata Group, Bajaj Group, and many others. But the system of manufacturing quotas was prone to abuses. The so-called License Raj (also known as the Permit Raj) gave bureaucrats virtually unlimited power to demand payoffs to allow companies to make their products. And the command-and-control system in turn facilitated crony capitalism.

The strict controls meant that preliberalization India was known for its deprivations. "It was a world where the absence of things—Wrigley's Juicy Fruit, Seiko watches, Parker pens—was experienced not just as scarcity but as a superior form of austerity," writes Mukul Kesavan, a history teacher and author. Homes and cars had no air-conditioning. The only cosmetics available were made by Lakmé, a brand name made up by the Tata Group—it's a faux French version of the name of the Indian goddess Lakshmi. And people traveling abroad were allowed to convert only a small sum in foreign exchange—not enough for dinner in most of the developed world.[3]

India had ejected both IBM and Coca-Cola for refusing to comply with a foreign exchange provision that required foreign firms to dilute their stakes in local outfits to 40 percent. As a result, a generation of thirsty youngsters grew up envying wide-open Pakistan, of all places, as they sipped the medicinal-tasting Campa Cola. And every business trip abroad became an opportunity to stock up on essential supplies, ad executive Shovon Chowdhury recalled in a recent essay, writing, "Very few people have purchased Pampers from as many countries" as he has.[4]

No amount of foreign exchange controls could avert disaster, however. Irresponsible government spending in the late 1980s, combined with an ever-increasing oil import bill, sent India spiraling into a balance-of-payments crisis in 1991. Government debt soared to 50 percent of GDP, and the country's foreign exchange reserves fell to a paltry $600 million—barely enough to cover two weeks of imports. With default imminent, the Reserve Bank of India airlifted sixty-seven tons of gold to England and Switzerland to secure an emergency loan of $2.2 billion from the International Monetary Fund—and kicked off an era of economic reforms.

In some ways the so-called liberalization of the Indian economy in 1991 paralleled Deng Xiaoping's decision to open China to

Western investment in 1978, and until recently India seemed to be following the same path as China, just thirteen years later.

Per capita incomes rose more than tenfold, from 583 Indian rupees a month in 1991 to 7,774 rupees a month in 2016, while the salary of India's highest-paid CEO rose by a multiple of thirty-five, to 22.5 million rupees from a paltry 6.5 million in 1991. Other indicators are equally dramatic. The market capitalization of the Bombay Stock Exchange has soared from just 32 billion rupees in 1991 to nearly 95 trillion in 2016. From a mere handful in 1991—when the government owned all of India's banks—the number of Indians with bank accounts has skyrocketed. A government initiative started in 2014 has brought 200 million more Indians into the formal banking system in just the last few years.[5]

Along the way, the era of sanctimonious deprivation has given way to one of unabashed consumption—complete with a new ideologue, the Art of Living guru Sri Sri Ravishankar. An Indian version of Deng Xiaoping, Ravishankar travels the country speaking to his followers and has effectively told a generation of Indians—once anxious about materialism—that "to get rich is glorious," and spiritual too.

But China's boom since the mid-2000s has widened the gap, exposing the vast differences between the two countries. The most obvious are in infrastructure and manufacturing—and that translates into dramatic contrasts in the way e-commerce operates in each country.

INDIAN RETAIL

Even as India opened its industries to competition—sometimes more rapidly than China did—it held fast to certain vestiges of Gandhian thought. As China began to grow, it took advantage of the size of its market to woo foreign investment and plowed money into factory infrastructure to reach massive economies of scale. But until recently, India preferred homespun cloth, retaining tax breaks and other incentives for small-scale producers and regulations that made it difficult for larger companies to grow. (For example, the government enforces strict labor laws for companies with more than a hundred workers, which helps to protect millions of tiny sweatshops around the country.)

Nowhere has this way of thinking prevailed more thoroughly than in the retail sector—where government policies have long curtailed foreign investment, ostensibly to protect the little guy.

Retail plays an incredibly important role in the Indian economy, accounting for $600 billion in trade, or about 22 percent of India's GDP, according to a recent Boston Consulting Group report. Yet "modern" or "organized retail"—large chains and supermarkets—accounts for only a tenth of those sales.[6] Most commerce still is transacted in the small mom-and-pop shops known as *kirana* stores.

In many ways, the kirana shop is the symbol of Indian retail, a small store stacked with hundreds of products crammed on shelves in an area sometimes no more spacious than a large closet. India has twelve to fourteen million kirana stores, or approximately one for every twenty households. Like the general store on the US frontier during the 1800s, the kirana store is more than just a retail shop. The owner often knows many of customers by name, understands the tastes of the neighborhood, delivers orders large and small, and will even sell to customers on credit.

Given the importance of the kirana store in India, it's easy to understand why many Indian immigrants to the United States get their start as convenience store owners. The Asian-American Convenience Store Association estimates that India American entrepreneurs own 80,000 of the 132,000 convenience stores in the United States. Most of these entrepreneurs hail from Prime Minister Modi's home state of Gujarat, which is known for the entrepreneurial spirit of its *baniya*s, or traders.

Along with the kirana stores, India's unorganized retail market includes a legion of boutiques, as well as handcarts and street sales from the back of a bicycle of everything from mops and brooms and fruits and vegetables to balloons and wicker furniture. Sit on the balcony of a middle-class house in any Indian city, and you can't help but hear a constant litany of singsong sales pitches floating up from the street. Vegetable vendors shout out their selection: "Carrots, spinach, tomatoes, onions!" Snack vendors bang on the side of a wok with a metal spoon. The balloon man blows a kazoo. Every so often a guy with a performing monkey shows up, whirling a little drum called a *dug-duggi*.

It's chaos. But don't underestimate its charm.

In recent years, as the Indian economy has liberalized, some Indian retailers have moved to consolidate and grow the organized retail sector. But some also have found Indian shoppers slow to adjust. Take Pantaloon Fashion & Retail, which operates eighty-six department stores across the country.

Pantaloon's CEO, Kishore Biyani, built out his retail chain, at first by emulating the large, uncluttered, Western-style supermarkets he'd visited when traveling abroad. But he soon realized that, despite their efficient layout, they don't generate the same sales volumes in India as they do in the West.

As the *Wall Street Journal* reported, he had to redesign his stores to make them more like the shopping environment that his lower-middle-class shoppers were used to—louder, messier, cluttered, and chaotic. As if to bring to the traditional bazaar to modern retail, he replaced his grid layout with narrow, crooked aisles. Changing the design of one store to make it more haphazard increased sales 30 percent, he said—suggesting parallels in India with the customer preference for chaos that Alibaba found in China.

In a traditional Indian boutique, three or four salespeople may assist in a sale, taking dozens of folded saris from the shelf, for instance, and repeatedly unfurling them before the customer with a flourish, until it seems rude to leave the shop empty-handed. Especially when the proprietor punches up the total and shaves off a few hundred rupees to seal the deal.

That's why Biyani staffed three times more employees per square foot than a typical Walmart. Although employees are not allowed to haggle on price, they do walk around with megaphones to make promotional announcements to shoppers, often using several local languages to make them feel more at home. And in his cluttered grocery section, instead of displaying only the shiny, unblemished produce, his employees leave dirty, wilted stragglers in the bin, because they give customers a sense of triumph—and boost sales—when they find the choice fruits and vegetables.[7]

The success of Pantaloon and similar chains suggests that organized retail will gradually supplant India's small boutiques and kirana stores, as it did in the West—at least to some degree. Boasting air-conditioned comfort and clean surroundings, Western-style shopping malls already have mostly eclipsed the bazaar, except for the sale of traditional items like jewelry and saris. Thus organized retail was expected to grow 20 percent a year between 2017 and 2020, compared with 10 percent growth for traditional trade, according to the Boston Consulting Group.[8]

But the continued growth of the traditional sector hints at its surprising resilience, and the woes foreign retailers face illustrate the deep commitment (at least on paper) of Indian policy makers to protecting the little guy. While China swiftly encouraged direct foreign investment in retail so as to improve the efficiency of its supply chain and get its massive manufacturing output to market, India has been slow to open up its retail segment. Many Indians argue that opening up the retail sector will spur growth and thus generate employment, but others contend that more efficient superstores will result in massive job losses for the forty million Indians engaged in retail and logistics. At the same time, homegrown tycoons like Sunil Mittal, founder of Bharti Enterprises, and Mukesh Ambani, chair of the Reliance Group, have capitalized on those fears and have begun to build their own chains while enjoying protection from the international giants.

Until 2011, foreign direct investment was prohibited in multibrand retail, making supermarkets, convenience stores, or other general retail establishments off-limits to the multinationals. In November 2011 the Indian central government announced that it would open India's retail sector to foreign direct investment but tabled the reforms after encountering intense opposition from retailers. The next year the central government decided to allow the states to determine whether to liberalize retail. But given shifting public opinion and the need to comply with twenty-nine different state tax regimes, foreign retail expansion has been limited.

Even those reforms engendered an instantly negative reaction, and politicians rushed to the defense of the small shop owner. It got so bad that a senior politician in Uttar Pradesh said he would set Walmart stores on fire and India's parliament ground to a halt.[9]

Nonetheless, retail reform has its proponents. Indian retail is highly inefficient. Supply chains and logistics are unreliable, meaning that as much as a third of a vegetable shipment may spoil before ever reaching the market. Farmers argue that they could sell more produce if retail was modernized. Consumers argue that modernizing retail would save everyone money, especially the poor. But the proponents of reform have so far made little progress.

One of the great challenges for India is that government officials often benefit from the inefficiencies. Whereas China for the most part acts as a national market, India's states set taxes and other policies; that is, products that move from one state to another incur taxes. The policies are not always clear, and officials along the way, eager to collect bribes, always are willing keep delivery trucks waiting at state lines if necessary.

Despite all these challenges, foreign retailers are beginning to make headway in states that allow them to. Some states are allowing retailers like Walmart, Tesco, and Carrefour to open stores. But modern retail still accounts for only 10 percent of the Indian market compared to 85 percent of the US market.[10]

That translates into an even bigger opportunity for e-commerce.

THE INDIAN CONSUMER

As the varying state taxes and regulations suggest, India's diversity also poses a different challenge than China's relatively homogeneous market. China is unified by the common use of Mandarin and the dominance of the Han Chinese—who make up nearly 92 percent of the population. But India is splintered by language, religion, culture, and geography. Its federal structure means that the twenty-nine states do not operate by the same rules, and their degree of development varies widely. Lifestyles also vary from state to state. Some Indians are living much as they did a thousand years ago, while others have purchased all the gadgets and conveniences familiar to the wealthiest consumers in the United States or Europe. On one hand, the country boasts 185,000 millionaires and nearly a dozen billionaires. On the other, nearly half of India's 1.2 billion people live on less than $2.50 a day.[11]

In some respects this means companies must approach the Indian market as though it were many different small countries rather than one big one.

Even so, many demographic factors in India favor of the growth of e-commerce. Half its 1.25 billion people are younger than twenty-five. And incomes have been growing at a steady 10 to 12 percent per year.[12] Most of all, Indian entrepreneurs are optimistic that recent policies are improving their lives.[13] As studies have shown, optimism is often a self-fulfilling prophecy. And nowhere is the optimism higher than in India's booming e-commerce sector.

THE RISE OF E-COMMERCE IN INDIA

I made my first trip to India in 2000, when I traveled to New Delhi with Jack Ma to attend an Internet conference. Interest in the dawn of the Internet had drawn thousands of locals of all ages to the expo grounds to hear experts talk about this exciting new technology. Indians' interest in the Internet was even greater than what I'd seen in China.

But although the Internet had been available in India since August 1995, the infrastructure didn't come close to matching the enthusiasm. Our five-star hotel didn't have Internet service, and dial-up was painfully slow and expensive. Probably as a direct result, only about five million Indians—fewer than 1 percent of the total population—were online, despite their widespread fascination with the new technology. (Indians nationwide had only 5.7 million PCs.)[14]

It seems crazy now, but that minuscule level of penetration didn't stop e-commerce entrepreneurs from taking a shot. And, just as in China, the first opportunities they identified were for B2B portals designed to help isolated companies find trading partners. One of the earliest firms was a company founded by Bikky Khosla, who'd begun publishing the *Exporters Yellow Pages* in 1991. As Jack Ma was introducing his China Pages to connect Chinese exporters to buyers overseas, Khosla saw he could use the Internet to give Indian exporters a better way to find buyers for their products. In 1996 he began TradeIndia, a B2B site designed to give Indian exporters a platform for promoting themselves globally. While countless other players have come and gone, TradeIndia survives to this day.

Meanwhile, entrepreneurs in India thought they could apply technology to help improve another kind of marketplace. But it wasn't C2C or B2C they found the most attractive in 1996. Rather, it was B2G—bride to groom. Aware that Indian newspapers were earning massive sums from classified ads placed by parents seeking suitable matches for their sons and daughters, several innovators launched matrimonial websites that made the search easier and more efficient. With 90 percent of marriages still arranged by parents, it was a massive opportunity—and still is.[15]

The sites provide details about individuals' job prospects, salary, education, caste, religion, and dietary restrictions, as well as height, weight, and complexion, making it possible for parents to instantly search for, say, a Tamil-speaking bride of the Brahmin caste with a degree in primary education—eliminating hours of combing the classifieds. Needless to say, matrimonial sites have proved to be hugely popular. Countless sites today specialize in specific regions, religions, and social classes, as well as visa holders permitted to work in the United States, widows, widowers, and divorced people, accounting for a $36 billion market, according to Frost & Sullivan, an international consulting firm.[16]

That may sound entirely unrelated to the buying and selling of goods and services online—the bread and butter of e-commerce. But it illustrated something important.

Finding a suitable mate requires a lot of trust. In traditional matchmaking trust usually is based on existing social relationships. But the Internet created a challenge by introducing greater anonymity to the process. The "prematrimonial detective" arrived alongside the matrimonial sites to fill the trust gap. These third parties follow and investigate potential mates to assure the parents that the people behind the profiles are who they say they are.

The emergence of matrimonial sites proved that the lack of trust in India's online environment could be overcome. If a marketplace for a bride or groom could successfully bridge the gap, surely a marketplace for products could do the same.

Only not right away, as Baazee, one of the earliest players, quickly learned.

THE EBAY OF INDIA

As the worldwide Internet investment boom hit a peak in 2000, investors and entrepreneurs began to look at India. As in China, India's Internet boom gave rise to thousands of e-commerce sites that replicated the models of the two US e-commerce success stories—eBay and Amazon. But when the Internet bubble burst, India suffered more than most countries, because Internet entrepreneurs were only starting to invest in India.

The first casualties were those that had used the Amazon retail model, companies that stocked their own inventory and sold it to customers themselves. As in China, they found that it's impossible to build an inventory-led model in a country with low Internet penetration, slow and expensive online connections, lack of trust, and insufficient infrastructure.

In contrast, one company followed the eBay marketplace model—facilitating sales rather than selling its own inventory—and managed to survive the bursting of the Internet bubble. Started in Mumbai by Harvard Business school grads Avnish Bajaj and

Suvir Sujan, Baazee set out to be the eBay of India and raised money from some big names, including News Corp.

"There were twenty-two eBay clones at the time," Niren Shah, the company's fifteenth employee and former CFO, told me. "We were trying to start our own eBay of India, but we realized very quickly that the auction model is not very popular in India. Used goods were not very prevalent in India, and at one point we had 90 to 95 percent new goods. So we did not waste too much time in pivoting to a fixed-price model rather than sticking with auctions."

That decision became even more significant when the Internet bubble burst and plunged India into an Internet winter. Baazee had to close regional offices, lay off staff, and bring operations back to Mumbai. "There were ten thousand websites started in 1999 and 2000, and, other than two or four, everything shut down," Shah said. "2001 to 2004 was real nuclear winter. A lot of guys working with us were under tremendous pressure. They quit because working at a dot-com meant they couldn't get married. A lot of bride-to-be parents would say, 'Hey, you've got to get a real job.'"

Baazee carried on, struggling to get vendors to sell online. "Basically, we were selling the Internet at that time. Not just e-commerce. We had to go out and convince sellers," Shah said.

Just as in China, plenty of skeptics said e-commerce could never work in India, he said. "There were tons of people that said you couldn't offer online marketplaces in India. People would say Indians are very different. Indians like assistance. They like touch and feel. There were big trust issues. 'E-commerce will never work.' My parents were very supportive, but a lot of my friends, even some of my cousins and distant family, were, like, 'What are you doing? This is all a dot-con. The bubble has burst. Head back to the US.'"

In fact, the skepticism was the least of Baazee's problems. Its registration list read like a who's who of India, with celebrities and industrialists buying and selling online. But those were just about the only Indians on the Internet at the time.

With only five million Indians online, reaching critical mass was impossible. "After a couple of quarters you realized that the market is just not there," Shah said. "The entire debate that we would have was whether the market size was a million or million and a half users."

Instead of giving up, though, Baazee pivoted and entered the B2B reverse-auction businesses, modeling its business on Free-Markets, a US reverse-auction pioneer. (In a reverse auction, sellers bid for the lowest price at which they are willing to sell their goods.) This accounted for 80 percent of Baazee's transaction values. "We understood that the value did not lie in the B2B business," but it was necessary for survival, Shah said. Baazee also began a payment service, essentially the PayPal of India.

By 2004 India had seventeen million Internet users, and the company was still losing money. "We had a great team of rowers, and everybody was pulling his oar like crazy," Shah recalled. "There simply wasn't any water in the river."

Baazee's one million registered customers represented a respectable percentage of India's small number of Internet users, but they weren't enough. So when eBay approached with an enticing offer, Baazee's founders decided to sell. "We thought the market was still a little farther away, and they gave us a good offer," Shah said.

Because they had modeled Baazee on eBay, it was a good fit, and many of Baazee's senior staff rose to important positions with the global firm. However, eBay squandered Baazee's leadership position by making the same kind of mistakes in India that it had in China. Within a few years Baazee went from Indian e-commerce leader to laggard. And when the e-commerce wave finally hit, the early entrant was left out.

"Candidly, I think eBay focused too much on profitability," Shah said. "It's a bit unfortunate that they weren't able to capitalize on the three- or four-year head start. But it is the way it is. I have no regrets."[17]

5

INDIA'S E-COMMERCE GOLDEN ERA FINALLY ARRIVES

INDIA'S EARLY ATTEMPTS AT E-COMMERCE DURING THE DOT-COM boom offered little hope that e-commerce would take off. While e-commerce in China was hitting its stride between 2004 and 2007, in India it was still languishing. Computer and Internet penetration rates remained among the lowest in the world. Data speeds were slow. And the infrastructure remained extremely fragmented and inefficient. Then, in 2007, the same year that Apple brought the first smartphone to the world, India's e-commerce caught a second wind when two former Amazon employees opened an Amazon clone. The name of that company was Flipkart.

FLIPKART

About seven years after Sachin Bansal and Binny Bansal—who are not related, although they share the same surname—founded the company that showed e-commerce could be a winning proposition in India, I received an email from Sachin inviting me to Bangalore to talk to his staff about my experience at Alibaba. I found an impressive collection of new employees drawn from McKinsey, Amazon, and the leading business schools. They'd given up the stability of jobs in the United States and leading companies in India's IT services sector to join the Indian start-up.

I asked Sachin what he'd like me to talk about. How e-commerce works in China? Strategies for building an online marketplace? I was surprised by his answer.

"The thing we most need right now is to hear about the organizational issues—how Alibaba grew and kept a strong company culture. We have a lot of new people on board with great experiences and are having some growing pains."

It was a good reminder that the difficulty of growing a huge business is often overlooked in the discussion of e-commerce strategy. After all, the business model Flipkart was replicating depended on selling on a massive scale to keep costs down. And during the previous seven years, Flipkart's workforce had quickly grown to fourteen thousand employees.

Both Sachin and Binny are graduates of the Indian Institute of Technology Delhi and former employees of Amazon. They had set out initially to build a price comparison website for India in 2007. But they quickly realized that wouldn't work because not enough items were for sale online to provide comparisons, and they converted Flipkart to an online bookstore, striving to build an Amazon for India. They chose books for many of the same reasons that Amazon had in the United States. Books were less expensive to ship than other items, and they had a long shelf life—so they were a good fit for an online model that allowed for virtual stocking of specialized items on the "long tail"—which refers to selling a large number of unique items with relatively small quantities sold of each.

They had an important additional reason for choosing books as the category to focus on in India—lack of trust for e-commerce. "Books are something that has a lower transaction size. A book [costs as little as] one hundred rupees. So it's very easy for a customer to trust you with that first transaction," instead of more expensive items such as mobile phones or cameras, Sachin told an interviewer for CNBC's *Young Turks* program.[1]

They started Flipkart in their apartment with an initial investment of $8,000. In the early days, instead of holding inventory, they would get an order and then run across the street to buy books from the local bookstore. To attract customers they used some clever guerrilla marketing tactics, such as handing out Flipkart bookmarks to people coming out of bookstores. "In order to make sure that our targeting was right, we would give bookmarks to only those who were coming out with books in hand—the people who have made purchases," they explained.[2]

The strategy worked. Flipkart raised $1 million from Accel Partners in 2009, $20 million from Tiger Global in 2010, and more than $500 million from a group of investors, including Naspers, in 2012. The money helped grow Flipkart's asset-heavy model as the company moved into buying its own inventory and operating its own warehouses. By 2010 Flipkart had 120 employees, was selling one book per minute, and was poised for rapid growth of its organization to keep up with the demand.

Flipkart's book buyers were all over India. Most were urban, English-speaking white-collar workers. Half the transactions came from large cities and half from small cities. Flipkart shipped all over India, to places where bookstores and books could be hard to find.

As the company grew, Flipkart strived to differentiate itself from its competitors with customer service. Much as Jingdong had done in China, Flipkart wanted to control the customer's experience from end to end to make the process seamless and reliable.

Sachin and Binny had good reasons. The Indian postal service was so notorious for losing packages that most people sent everything by registered mail, just to make sure somebody would be accountable. India had a host of courier companies but nothing like UPS, FedEx, or DHL.

Flipkart therefore built an extensive logistics and delivery infrastructure, complete with a motorcycle fleet that races around the country with yellow FLIPKART signs on its scooters. Owning the fleet has helped not only with deliveries but also with reverse logistics for product returns, something India's logistics companies were woefully unprepared to handle. Owning the fleet also helped the company to more easily accept payments through cash on delivery, which proved to be the breakthrough that e-commerce in India needed. In interviews with various news outlets, the two founders boasted that their logistics capabilities would protect them from Amazon's inevitable assault on the market in India—in 2011 India's market was still closed to the US behemoth because the rules governing foreign direct investment in multibrand retail also applied to online retailers.[3]

By 2013 Flipkart was receiving more than a million visitors per day and had about ten million registered users.[4] Its reach was growing as well, with the company claiming that five out of six online Indians visited their site. Having established Flipkart as the primary shopping destination for Indians, its founders then decided to open a marketplace that would allow third-party vendors to sell on the platform and plug into Flipkart's fulfillment infrastructure, as Amazon had done in November 2000. Designed as a virtual mall, Flipkart's marketplace was meant to give shoppers a wider selection of products while spreading some of the inventory risk from Flipkart's own operations to those of the third-party merchants selling on the site.[5]

In expanding to a marketplace, the challenge for Flipkart was to live up to its reputation for a high level of service to customers. The company soon ran into problems, as buyers reported receiving bricks, stones, cheap knockoffs, and even mangos instead of iPhones and other expensive products, while scammers reportedly demanded refunds, telling Flipkart they'd been cheated.

In 2014, just as Alibaba was preparing for its initial public offering, Flipkart astonished the Indian tech scene by raising $1 billion, valuing the company at a reported $7 billion. But Flipkart was no longer modeled on the founders' former employer, Amazon, but on Alibaba. "In 2008, Amazon was a dominant player and a role model for most of the people starting in e-commerce. But over time, I've realized that India is different and Alibaba Group's model is better suited for the Indian market," Sachin Bansal told the Indian start-up news site *YourStory* after Flipkart acquired the online retail clothier Myntra.com in May 2014. "The supply chain, the customers, their thought process . . . there is a lot of similarity between the Chinese and Indian online retail markets," he said at press conference related to the acquisition. "What's happening in China is inspiring, it is bigger than anything in the US."[6]

Indeed, Alibaba's IPO sent a signal to the world that e-commerce could work by using a different business model in emerging markets. Flipkart was becoming an Alibaba of India. But across the country in New Delhi's Gurgaon tech district, another company—Snapdeal—was hoping to lay claim to that title.

SNAPDEAL

In 2014, when Flipkart announced it was switching to an "Alibaba-like model," Sachin and Binny found themselves in a public spat. Kunal Bahl, founder of Snapdeal, felt his own business philosophy was closer to Alibaba's than Flipkart's was, and he said so to reporters.[7] The public dispute between the two star Indian companies only a few months before Alibaba's IPO made it clear that India's e-commerce would develop more like China's than like e-commerce in the United States.

Following in the footsteps of Alibaba also was a directional change for Snapdeal. When Kunal Bahl and his childhood friend, Rohit Bansal, started the company in 2007, it was a coupon business. They had met as classmates in 1999 and bonded over a shared interest in math. "We were very clear that at some point we were going to do something together, but it was only a matter of time," said Bahl.[8]

Their paths diverged when Kunal went to the United States to study at the University of Pennsylvania's Wharton School of Business and then work at Microsoft. Rohit stayed in India, where he studied at IIT Delhi. But they ran into each other at a wedding and rekindled their interest in working together. The day after the wedding they started brainstorming ideas for what would later evolve into Snapdeal.[9]

At first it wasn't even an Internet company. Bahl and Rohit Bansal started it in 2007 as an offline business that printed coupon books. As they made the transition from white-collar workers at multinationals to entrepreneurs, they knocked on the doors of small businesses. They made sales, but they didn't enjoy the rollicking success they'd expected, Bahl told NDTV, an Indian TV network.

"It had very, very average traction," he said of the original business. "We realized building a business is not easy. We ran out of money every month."[10]

Nevertheless, they kept plugging away and eventually started an online daily deals platform in February 2010, when Groupon was heating up in the United States.

In 2016 I visited Bahl in his offices in Delhi to hear the Snapdeal story firsthand. He explained that deals were a hot sector when he and Rohit Bansal turned Snapdeal into an online deals site. "There were seven players in the online deals business when we started," he said. "Within six months there were fifty players."

But despite the plethora of competitors, within a year and a half Snapdeal owned about 70 percent of the market. "We had an advantage because we've always been about the small businesses," Bahl told me. "[Our] fathers are small business owners. We've seen the life of pain and agony that the small business owner has in India. We wanted to see how we can change that."

They soon realized that the deals site wasn't going to be enough to bring about that change because it didn't create enough sales. Some venture capitalists encouraged the two friends to go to China, where e-commerce was booming, to take a look at the market there. During their trip in December 2011, they were shocked by the volume of goods that companies were selling.

"We saw companies shipping 500,000 or a million products per day," Bahl told me. "We thought, 'This is amazing. This is where India is heading too.'"[11]

They came back and announced to their board that they wanted to pivot to a marketplace model, even though they had already raised $57 million for their online deals business. Not everyone on the board was persuaded at first, but they eventually agreed. Within two months Kunal and Rohit had shut down their deals site and restarted their company as an online marketplace. That was December 2011.[12]

Because of the similarities of the two markets, they based their platform on what they'd seen in China. "It was very clear to us that this is where India was headed, for the same structural reasons," Bahl said. "Both markets have very long-tail, fragmented retail and lack of access to what people need, especially in small towns." Those conditions meant small business owners suffered "a life of acute pain, agony and stagnation" in both countries. They also shared what Bahl describes as "a deeply entrepreneurial culture." Pointing to the busy street below his office window, Bahl elaborated: "Even sitting here there are a hundred entrepreneurs in front of us. That guy running the food truck. The guy operating that rickshaw—they're all entrepreneurs. They are just waiting for an outlet, platform, or channel. Realizing that, we pretty much overnight shut down our deals business and said we were going to build a marketplace."

From the outset Snapdeal eschewed the inventory model; by creating a platform for businesses, the marketplace could offer a larger assortment of products. "We always wanted to be a platform company helping small businesses," Bahl said. "If they are motivated to be successful, we'll be successful as a result. We never even thought about the inventory model as an option.

"For us, marketplace is not so much a business model as a philosophy," he said, and pointed to a cup of coffee on a table. "Our philosophy is, if I have a thousand such cups in our warehouse that we own, and there are five sellers selling the same cup, which cup will I sell first? I'd sell the stuff that I've locked my working capital in. Automatically you're going to compete with your own sellers, which we never wanted to do. We never wanted to put ourselves in a conflict of interest with our ecosystem."[13]

Because Snapdeal didn't own any inventory, its digital marketplace was more like Alibaba than Amazon. For India it was a unique proposition. But even Alibaba's business model required a little tweaking. In China, Alibaba started purely as a facilitator of sales—letting other companies handle logistics. Over time Alibaba began to dip further into logistics. But Snapdeal figured early on that it needed to control more of the ecosystem to match the service provided by the companies such as Flipkart and Amazon following the inventory model.

"Traditionally it's been 'own everything or own nothing,'" Bahl said. "We feel the answer is somewhere in the middle. Whatever parts are really underdeveloped, you build, but for the rest we will use what is existing. I think that thoughtful approach to logistics has helped."

Of course, Snapdeal was not the first digital marketplace in India. EBay had also tried but was languishing. I asked Bahl why he thought eBay had not succeeded in India. "They were probably thinking, 'Let's get to the market early and establish a dominant position there,' but they were five or six years too early. In 1999 there were only twelve thousand Internet connections in India. They made a lot of mistakes, self-admitted."

Despite its inability to crack the India market on its own, eBay decided to back Snapdeal and in April 2013 invested an undisclosed sum in the company. The deal allowed Snapdeal product listings to show up in eBay India search results if the product was not available on eBay India.

Snapdeal's digital marketplace functioned at first much like Alibaba's Tmall—which was set up to differentiate brand owners and authorized distributors from C2C merchants. But Snapdeal didn't have to worry about differentiation, because it didn't have any C2C sellers, or any sellers at all, for that matter.

"We needed people who already had some products," Bahl explained. "They didn't answer our phones so we literally just showed up at their shops and asked them, 'Why don't you just put this online?'"

Their first customers agreed practically out of pity, he said, chuckling, and Snapdeal did all the work to get them online—from photographing the products and writing the descriptions to up-loading the content to the site. But once those customers started clocking sales, they bought in.

"The moment they saw some sales, they got excited, because their expectations were zero. Not low. Zero."

After that, nobody had to convince other sellers to sign up. Now tens of thousands of new sellers join the platform every month, purely as a result of word of mouth.

Because India lacked a sophisticated logistics infrastructure, Snapdeal's business had to include a more comprehensive set of shipping and logistics services than Alibaba originally did in China. To fill these gaps, Snapdeal provided warehouses in which sellers could store inventory. Snapdeal picks up vendors' products and holds them at its warehouses, accounting for 80 percent of the products sold on Snapdeal. Bahl explained Snapdeal's philosophy this way: "The lethal combination is marketplace with intermedi-ated supply chain. The e-commerce business of the future is a marketplace with no inventory and intermediated logistics. Even when I talk to John Donohoe at eBay, he says if he had started eBay again, this is how he would run the businesses."

As of May 2016, Snapdeal had spent eighteen months pump-ing $300 million into beefing up its logistics operations, according to the *Economic Times* of India. During that period, its volume of shipments nearly doubled and the number of sellers on the platform tripled, from about 100,000 at the beginning of 2015 to 300,000 in May 2016. To accommodate those volumes, the company ac-quired two million square feet of warehouse space in 63 locations in 45 cities.[14]

That's the same amount of warehouse space Amazon India uses for its inventory model and slightly more than the amount owned by Flipkart, according to the *Economic Times*.[15]

Snapdeal acquired FreeCharge in 2015 to add a payment ser-vice to its ecosystem and modeled it after Alipay, with an escrow-based TrustPay feature that holds money for seven days before forwarding it to the seller. By 2016 FreeCharge was handling one million transactions per day.

Bahl stressed the value of the thirty million registered addresses it holds; clearly he is thinking about expanding into banking. "Most banks don't even have thirty million registered addresses, but because of deliveries we have them," he said. "In extending loans, where you live is the most important" factor.

And what about keeping customers from straying to another platform? "People are not likely to go outside the platform," he said. "Our whole platform works on ratings and reviews. Without that we would just die. We provide so many protections—such as trackability, seamlessness, recommendations—that people are happy to stay in the system." To help maintain the system's integrity, Snapdeal also rates buyers. "Some customers order the same product from five places and just keep the one which comes first," Bahl said. "So we have a system to score buyers. If you return the offer [with no good reason], COD will go away as an option to pay."

In operating an online marketplace, language is a big issue in India that China didn't have to deal with. "India is like a bazillion countries in one country," Bahl said. "One hundred twenty million people is the number of people who can use English for e-commerce. One billion people can't. That means that, for one billion people, going to an English Snapdeal app or site is like reading Arabic." To address this problem, in December 2016 Snapdeal became the first marketplace to offer its platform in multiple languages.[16] "That's what's going to unlock the next one hundred to three hundred million users. You'll start hitting a ceiling otherwise," Bahl said.

I shared with Bahl my surprise at the negative reaction that e-commerce so often receives in the Indian media, where reporters seem to focus on the growing pains instead of the opportunities for entrepreneurs in the country. But Bahl explained that Indian businesses that lobby for government benefits are the source of most of the whining that media have been reporting. He said Snapdeal had not encountered much resistance from existing stakeholders, such as large retailers or middlemen, because Snapdeal hasn't really cut into their business. That, after all, is the key to the marketplace model: Snapdeal isn't selling products; it's helping its partners make sales.

"We are not doing replacement commerce," he said. "We are doing incremental commerce. That commerce was not happening earlier. If we own our own inventory like Flipkart does or an Amazon does, then I would understand that. But we tell retailers, 'Snapdeal won't compete with you, we actually want to work with you to provide you with nationwide reach.'"

The attitude of traditional retailers has been changing over time. Many have tried to open their own e-commerce platforms and failed, then made their way to Snapdeal. "We actually work very closely with the offline retailers to say, 'You have the product, you understand what people want, we will provide you with the reach,'" Bahl said.

The story for the middlemen is different. For centuries middlemen have exploited India's infrastructure problems and poor communications to reap huge fortunes—and Bahl said they do it by making products unaffordable for millions despite low manufacturing costs. By cutting those guys out of the loop, Snapdeal is increasing profits for manufacturers and savings for consumers—which translates into greater sales volumes, he said.

Take a sari made in Surat, Gujarat, for about 350 rupees. When it arrived at a shop in Delhi through the traditional network of middlemen, it would cost more than 2,000 rupees. But on Snapdeal it sells for 799, including free shipping anywhere in the country.

"Everyone who should make money makes money, which is the manufacturer, ourselves, the courier company, and the consumer," Bahl said.

Brands, too, have started to embrace e-commerce, after initial concerns that online sales were disrupting the traditional bricks-and-mortar sales channels. The locally owned mobile phone company, Micromax, for example, surpassed Samsung to become the market leader before Chinese-made smartphones started flooding the market in 2015–16.[17]

Although Micromax has its own branded outlets and sells phones through various other electronics and mobile phone retailers, it now makes a whopping 40 percent of its sales online, Bahl said.

One reason: deep discounts. Until April 2016, when the practice was outlawed, marketplace and payment solution companies alike were dipping into their reserves to offer deep discounts and essentially buy market share. As of now, brands like Micromax can offer discounts if they want, but they can no longer participate in the price war in which Amazon, Flipkart, Snapdeal, and the like are engaged, because nonmanufacturers are no longer allowed to offer discounts. According to the *Economic Times*, online sales of electronics products plunged 30 percent as a result.[18]

Because the online marketplace is a less expensive and more efficient way to reach customers, companies are finally beginning to look at e-commerce platforms as a way to build brands, Bahl said. "We offer landing pages with creative [services] for brands. We do exclusive deals with phones and brands. We do joint press conferences with media and have a 150-person team which only works with brands."

One of the most productive such exercises was a joint promotional campaign with Nestlé's Maggi noodles. Among the most popular brands in India, Maggi had suffered a huge setback in 2015, after a regulator in the state of Uttar Pradesh claimed to have discovered unacceptable levels of lead and monosodium glutamate in a batch sent to him for testing. With rumors swirling of a missed payoff or a guerrilla attack by a competing brand, India decreed a nationwide ban that pulled India's most popular instant noodles from the shelves and forced Nestlé to destroy hundreds of tons of the product. Although subsequent tests showed nothing was wrong with Maggi noodles, newspapers ran articles about the health hazards of instant noodles and other such foods for weeks on end. In February, after the flap was over, the Swiss food giant said it could take three years to recover the lost revenue.[19]

That's where Snapdeal came in.

"When it came time to relaunch, they had limited stock," Bahl explained. "It was a great opportunity [for Nestlé] to work exclusively with Snapdeal to amplify their relaunch. We ran a flash sale for Maggi and got one million registrations and sold out 720,000 packets of Maggi in less than a minute."

That partnership only hints at what Snapdeal has planned for India's e-commerce scene.

The company is looking to host twenty million transactions a day by 2020, by allowing people to pay their utility bills and book airline, bus, and movie tickets with the Snapdeal app. The idea is to be the one app that users keep on their phones for e-commerce and to handle everything else. To make it happen, Bahl believes Snapdeal will have to continually expand its offerings.

One way Snapdeal planned to do that was by entering the C2C market with a brand extension called Shopo, a zero-commissions C2C marketplace it opened in July 2015. China's Taobao led to the start of Tmall, but in India the same thing was happening in reverse, Bahl explained.

Between 2012 and 2016 Snapdeal rejected half a million sellers because they were too small. These were people making long-tail items like handmade baskets and jewelry—and they exist by the millions in India's towns and villages. With Shopo, Snapdeal had given them a way to connect with customers across the country—which is why the site had already attracted 100,000 sellers and five million listings in its first five months, Bahl said.

"Within the next year we want to get to one million shops," he said.

The idea made sense to me, but in February 2017 Snapdeal closed down Shopo, explaining that it had decided to focus on other, more profitable areas of its business. It was understandable, given an increasingly competitive environment with investors applying more pressure on Indian e-commerce companies to turn a profit than ever before. But with 100 million or so entrepreneurs and would-be entrepreneurs across India, I felt it a shame that the service had been closed down. There is clearly an untapped opportunity to build a marketplace that captures the vibrancy of India's "kirana economy" of small retailers. But perhaps it will come at a different time with a more patient set of investors.

AMAZON

Among US e-commerce companies, eBay was by far the most aggressive about expanding internationally in the early years of the Internet. Amazon was a relative latecomer to emerging markets. Instead of expanding in these riskier areas, it focused on building operations and expanding in the United States and other developed economies such as the United Kingdom, Germany, and the rest of Europe. But that strategy came with a cost: by leaving the assault on China to eBay, Amazon lost a massive opportunity, albeit to Alibaba and not its American competitor. It's hard to be the world's most valuable e-commerce company without being a key player in the world's largest e-commerce market. So it's clear that Amazon does not want to compound its mistake with an error in India.

Thanks to the legal restrictions on foreign direct investment in multibrand retail, Amazon was slow to enter the Indian market too. But when CEO Jeff Bezos did make the move in 2013, he entered the market at full tilt.

Bezos had groomed Amit Agarwal, a Stanford grad from Mumbai who had been working at Amazon since 1999, to build a localized site. When Amit first presented his business plan for India, Bezos said it was not enough. "He challenged us to think like cowboys, not like computer scientists," Agarwal said. "We need to move very fast."[20]

Moving fast is possible only if you have the power to make decisions locally. Back in 2006 Bezos described why US Internet companies struggled in China: "The Chinese management team in the China market is busy trying to keep their American bosses happy, instead of trying to keep their Chinese customers happy. And that's a mistake we will not make."[21]

His diagnosis may have been correct, but during the next few years Amazon seemed to be falling into exactly that trap. The company never managed to capture more than 1 percent of the total market in China. But Amazon insiders laid the blame on simple arithmetic: the company just didn't invest enough money to win the battle. In India Amazon's leaders have vowed not to make that mistake again.

Since Amazon entered the Indian market in 2013, the battle between Flipkart and Amazon has become intense and the subject of news stories. In July 2014 Flipkart announced it had raised $1 billion in fresh funding to invest in the market.[22] One day later Amazon counterpunched by announcing that it would commit $2 billion to the Indian market.[23] And in the next two years the numbers kept going up and up—with Amazon's commitment reaching a planned $5 billion at last count.[24]

But if there's one thing Western Internet companies have proved, it's that money can't buy markets. Winning the market also requires the right business model. And in the case of India, Amazon had to adjust its US model so it could comply with India's regulations, which were even more restrictive than China's.

For several years Amazon had operated in a kind of limbo, selling products through a joint venture called Cloudtail India, although it warned investors, in a filing with the US Securities and Exchange Commission as early as October 2014, that the joint venture might violate local laws. Then, in March 2016, India finally clarified the rules for foreign investment in e-commerce firms.[25]

Under those rules India allowed wholly owned foreign companies to sell to consumers as well as businesses online. But in an effort to protect local retailers, it restricted the foreign companies to using the marketplace model, rather than buying and selling inventory. At the same time it issued regulations that limited sales by a single seller (such as Cloudtail) to 25 percent of total goods sold on the platform.[26]

Even before the rules were finalized, Amazon had relied more on a marketplace model than the inventory model. That was not a huge challenge, because about half the sales on the company's US site are made through third-party merchants. And India's regulations may well be a blessing in disguise for Amazon, since they force the company to focus on what I believe is a much more exciting business model for the country.

In pursuit of the largest gross merchandise value, or GMV, the marketplace model's term for the total value of all goods sold through the website, Amazon has been engaged in a breakneck race with Snapdeal and Flipkart to sign up retailers. As of March 2016, Amazon had signed more than 400,000 sellers, 85,000 of whom were so-called active sellers, whereas Flipkart and Snapdeal boasted total sellers of about 300,000 and 100,000, respectively. That $5 billion Bezos promised to invest seems to be aimed at widening that gap even further. After Flipkart announced in early 2016 that it would hike its fees and pass on the cost of shipping and returns to its sellers, Amazon said it would slash its commissions on smartphones and software in June 2016.[27] Such products account for a third of all online sales in India.

Getting that many sellers wasn't all about spending money, however. As Snapdeal had learned, Amazon has had to do much of the legwork for retailers, helping them take photos, upload product descriptions, and get their businesses online. Amazon even fills out tax forms for some sellers. The company will also handle phone orders on behalf of sellers and pick up the products, as well as pack and deliver them in Amazon boxes. Amazon undoubtedly hopes that as retailers begin to make sales online, they will take on more of these responsibilities themselves.

Amazon's operations in India have had to take a different form than in the United States. As in the United States, Amazon has invested in huge warehouses to handle fulfillment. In India it has built twenty-one large warehouses, with more than two million square feet of storage space across ten states.[28] Its largest warehouse, in Hyderabad, is a 280,000-square-foot monstrosity with capacity for two million items. But while Amazon relies on the US Postal Service, UPS, FedEx, and regional shippers for its US delivery, in India the company has followed Flipkart's example and hired its own motorcycle couriers who weave in and out of traffic with packages on their backs. Amazon has also partnered with local kirana, small family-owned shops, where motorcycles drop off packages. The local kirana owner then calls customers when their packages arrive and collects the money on behalf of Amazon. For the kirana, it's a good way to bring foot traffic to the store.

As Amazon grows in India, it will have to do a delicate dance as a foreign operator in the market. In the United States retailers protested Amazon. But in India it will also have to deal with a healthy level of resentment of foreign investment. Amazon has passed the first hurdle, getting regulatory approval to operate an online marketplace in the country. But it will no doubt struggle against protectionist forces as it continues to grow.

Perhaps Amazon's best argument for gaining acceptance in India is that it is bringing online tools to small businesses. Amazon is commonly perceived as a retail Goliath that has driven small retailers out of business. Yet by 2016, nearly 50 percent of the products sold on Amazon were from third-party sellers, a fact that, in my opinion, Amazon does not do enough to promote. If Amazon can position itself as a company that is harnessing India's kirana spirit and empowering entrepreneurs with tools to sell both domestically and abroad, it can gain acceptance as a friend and partner to India's small retailers, rather than resistance as a fearsome challenger.[29]

PAYTM

Just when Flipkart, Snapdeal, or Amazon seemed likely to dominate India's e-commerce, a relative outsider—Paytm—leaped into the fray and surprised everyone. Until February 2014 Paytm was a mobile payment leader but had shown little interest in running a marketplace.[30]

Billed as a "mobile wallet" company, Paytm, or "payment through mobile," started off as a website to allow users of prepaid cell phones to top off their balances online. Then it expanded to facilitate the purchase of other goods and services, such as movie tickets and taxi rides.

But behind the scenes, Paytm's founder, Vijay Shekar Sharma, had been thinking about building a marketplace company as early as 2011, when he attended a conference in Hong Kong at which Alibaba's Jack Ma was one of the keynote speakers. Eventually, the attraction proved to be mutual, and Alibaba took a 25 percent stake in Paytm with an initial investment of about $500 million in early 2015.[31]

Paytm was then India's fastest-growing mobile payments company, and Sharma had gone to Hong Kong with the goal of figuring out what a world reliant on the smartphone is like. "In that year, I learnt that if you want to learn what is happening in mobile Internet in the world, you don't go west, you go east," he said. As he listened to Jack's speech, Sharma was impressed by the numbers and enormous growth of e-commerce in China. What he learned, he said, is that "payments and commerce go hand in hand."[32]

When I interviewed Sharma in 2016, he told me that Jack's vision completely transformed his own ideas about where Paytm should be headed. Blown away by Jack's offhand reference to the company's growth from $64 billion to $126 billion in revenue in one year, "I came back and told my board members, 'We will build a Taobao for India,'" he told me.

Nearly everyone was telling Sharma to stick with payments—a big business opportunity in itself. But he found Jack's enthusiasm to be infectious. Sharma read virtually every word that had been written about Alibaba, Taobao, Tmall, and Jack Ma—and even bought old business magazines from a secondhand dealer to find articles. Finally, in October 2014 Sharma finagled a meeting with the Alibaba founder in Hangzhou.

"[They told me that] Jack was only going to come for twenty

minutes, but in the end the meeting lasted two and a half hours," Sharma recalled.[33]

The Paytm founder spoke as much about his life as he did about his company—which, a few months before, had officially become India's largest e-commerce company by transaction volume; it was processing about 300,000 transactions per day.[34] Sharma shared how he'd grown up in a modest family with no special advantages—this impressed Jack: "I was surprised that Jack thought it was an advantage that I had gone through tough times."

Sharma went from pitching to Jack to being pitched by Jack. Essentially, both men had the same idea in mind. If everyone from Alibaba to Flipkart was building or acquiring a payments company to ramp up sales on their marketplaces, why couldn't Paytm leverage its payments app to drive customers to a marketplace of its own?

A few weeks later Paytm raised more than $500 million, surprising the Indian tech world. But Snapdeal's founder, Kunal Bahl, remains a skeptic.

"It's unclear to me what business they are in," Bahl told me. "We are an e-commerce company backing into payments. We've never seen anywhere in the world a payments company backing into e-commerce. The skill sets are very different. Technology requirements are different. Capabilities you need to build around a supply chain are very different. Our strategy seems a little more logical and well put together. I feel like a commerce business without payments is like a car without wheels. But the wheels by themselves are not particularly useful, either."[35]

E-COMMERCE IN INDIA TODAY

Booming Numbers

It's safe to say that e-commerce in India has now reached a turning point; sixteen years after Baazee was founded, the river finally has water. Smartphones now account for one quarter of India's 900 million mobile phones, and Internet data prices have come down. This is helping to push Internet penetration from 32 percent in 2015 to 59 percent in 2020. It's predicted that India will have one billion people online by 2030, adding more people online than any other country.

Indian e-commerce is leaping to mobile even more quickly than e-commerce did in China. Snapdeal's mobile business grew from 5 percent of all transactions in 2013 to 75 percent in 2015. Because mobile commerce was growing so quickly, Flipkart even tried to do a mobile-only platform but was forced to reverse its decision when sales dropped off. It might have made the move too soon. But it is safe to assume that India is gradually shifting from mobile first to mobile only for many platforms.

Fortunately for the e-commerce players, these shifts are all coming at a time when the Indian economy is strong. If the Indian economy keeps bucking the emerging market trend, by 2025 per capita income could be double the 2014 figure of $1,570. But assuming that its growth pattern holds steady, there will be ever more traffic jams and bad offline shopping experiences, because of India's notoriously poor infrastructure development. That is why I can imagine that the emerging middle class in India will spend more of its money online than its counterparts elsewhere.

In 2015 e-commerce sales in India had already reached $16 billion, and the top three e-commerce companies had exceeded sales of the top ten offline retailers for the first time. Morgan Stanley predicts that e-commerce sales in India will grow by 700 percent by 2020, slightly faster than the rate that China grew from 2010 to 2014.[36]

Drawn by the opportunity to participate in "the next China," all the major global players are scrambling for a berth in India. Alibaba, Softbank, and former rival eBay have invested in Snapdeal. Alibaba has hedged its bets with its investment in Paytm. Naspers, the South African media company that is a major investor in China's Tencent, has invested in Flipkart. In 2017 Tencent, eBay, and Microsoft also joined Flipkart's roster of investors. Amazon, of course, has focused on Amazon India. Facebook has launched a payment platform for India via its WhatsApp messenger system.

As of early 2016, the market was still led by Flipkart, which held 45 percent of the market. Snapdeal followed at 26 percent, and Amazon was at 12 percent. But these numbers were very much in flux, with Amazon beginning to bridge the gap. As of June 2016, for instance, the Seattle-based giant had inched up to a 15 percent share in terms of GMV, but it had passed both rivals in terms of overall web traffic, including desktop and mobile users, *Forbes* reported.[37]

The scramble for the India market has created an investment frenzy. The frenzy is most evident during massive sales, which are modeled on Alibaba's Singles' Day. In a mad rush to enhance the all-important GMV figures, retailers have subsidized prices, in many cases losing money on every sale. A boon to customers to be sure, but this has led to a backlash from local retailers, who argue that they cannot not compete. And the government stepped in to say that retailers cannot set prices themselves. It will be interesting to see how the market share recalibrates when prices are no longer subsidized and return to market levels.

Cooling the market may be good for e-commerce in India, as the sector had the feel of a valuation bubble. In the long run, this could be healthy in a market where intense investor pressure for market share may be encouraging wasteful marketing spending. As Niren Shah told me, "People are destroying value."

Uncertainty about regulations has also slowed growth. As I noted earlier, in March 2016 the Indian government helped clarify some of the rules for foreign investments in e-commerce retailers. Whereas China generally erred on the side of allowing more foreign invest-ment, India went the other direction, prohibiting foreign companies from investing in direct retailers and requiring that no retailer on any marketplace could account for more than 25 percent of overall sales for that marketplace. This forced Flipkart and Amazon to scramble to find a way to comply; they explored such ideas as breaking down their operations into individual businesses based on categories.

Yet despite these setbacks, the investment frenzy and resulting media coverage has been good for India, accelerating the growth of e-commerce in the country. In China the battle between eBay and Alibaba ignited people's interest in e-commerce, persuaded sellers to go online, and convinced shoppers they could find deals and trust e-commerce. The rivalry created a public debate. And it has given rise to a sector that is capturing the imagination of future entrepreneurs—and lifting them out of poverty.

Already Flipkart, Snapdeal, Amazon, and Paytm offer Indian craftspeople access to a much wider market for their products than they ever could have imagined. Snapdeal, for instance, offers a wide range of goods manufactured by two hundred or so entrepreneurs from the Dharavi neighborhood of Mumbai. A sprawling warren of shacks built from cast-off sheet metal and plastic tarps, Dharavi is Asia's largest slum. But it's also one of India's most productive commercial centers, home to leather manufacturing and a host of other industries. Before the advent of e-commerce, Dharavi craftsmen, like twenty-eight-year-old Nadeem Sayed, who makes leather jackets, struggled to find markets for their products and were at the mercy of larger traders when it came to pricing. But with direct access to millions of buyers, some of these grassroots entrepreneurs have dramatically increased their incomes. Sayed once made and sold leather jackets that brought him about 15,000 rupees per month. But through Snapdeal he's increased his sales to 1.5 million rupees a month by selling to customers in the United States, United Kingdom, and Canada instead of to Indian wholesalers.[38]

TRENDS AND PREDICTIONS

E-commerce will take longer to take root in India than in China . . .

At first glance, India looks like it could be "the next China" for e-commerce. But although e-commerce growth in India will be dramatic, taking root in India will take longer than in China because of the many additional frictions in the Indian market. These include the large number of languages spoken, infrastructure inefficiencies, and competing state tax regimes. That India is a democracy with a history of protectionism also introduces more regulatory uncertainty, which will present hurdles to the adoption of e-commerce in the short and medium terms. This is why, even with rapid growth, total retail e-commerce sales in China are still expected to be thirty times greater than in India by 2020.[39]

But when it does take root, it will be more important
to India than even to China . . .
In the long run, these inefficiencies represent the greatest opportunities for entrepreneurs in India. Once they are resolved, it's easy to imagine that e-commerce will play an even more important role in India than in China, because India's infrastructure woes will make the gap between physical commerce and e-commerce even greater. E-commerce grew dramatically in China once the digital infrastructure was in place, and in India it will rocket forward once infrastructure problems are solved. And in doing so India's e-commerce will become a seven-course meal when retail, from branding to delivery, moves online.

Resistance to Chinese products bought directly online
will emerge in India
As I noted in the previous chapter, the Indian government is supporting a "Make in India," campaign and celebrating innovation while encouraging foreign investment. But even as it does this, an increasing number of inexpensive products will be sold directly from China into India from cross-border e-commerce websites such as AliExpress. Two leading marketplaces, Snapdeal and Paytm, have Alibaba as a partner, which will accelerate the flood of Chinese products. This will lead to tensions and perhaps even restrictions on Chinese goods coming into the country at the same time that "Make in India" is getting a huge push.

*India will emerge as an e-commerce incubator
for other emerging markets*
The early e-commerce entrepreneurs in China looked to the United States for inspiration. The current e-commerce players in India look to China for inspiration. And it's likely that entrepreneurs in emerging markets will look to India for inspiration in the future. India's economy is a better model for them than China's.

Ideas from India will spread more quickly to other countries
Indian e-commerce companies are correct in focusing on the Indian market now. But once the market has stabilized a bit more, and companies become profitable and leaders emerge, we can expect the Indian companies will begin to look for opportunities overseas. India has an advantage over China in that India is not hampered by an authoritarian regime, so its technology and services can grow without censorship. This will make India's services more palatable to markets outside the country. India also benefits from its use of English as the language of business as well as from internationally savvy Indian tech industry managers who could help India's companies expand globally.

*E-commerce in India will grow from a battle
of marketplaces into a battle of ecosystems*
Just as in China, e-commerce business models in India have converged on the marketplace model. And they will likely follow the Chinese example and expand into ecosystems that include payments, logistics, and other services as e-commerce companies scramble to increase the number of ways they can reach consumers and sellers. This is already clear from the battle between Paytm and FreeCharge for the taxi payment business. As e-commerce companies scramble to grow their ecosystems, we are likely to see an aggressive phase of mergers, acquisitions, and consolidation.

E-commerce will give rise to a new generation
of homegrown brands

"India is a very long-tail market" with a highly fragmented set of suppliers and manufacturers, Sandeep Aggarwal, founder of e-commerce marketplace ShopClues, explained to me. He cited the fact that in the United States, the top twenty brands of shirts constitute a majority of the overall market share, but in India there are many more manufacturers, with no clear brands taking outsized shares of the market.[40] In fact, Indians are not as obsessed with foreign brands as the Chinese are. And Indians want specialized products because of their deep and diverse cultural and religious differences. So as e-commerce allows creators to gain instant access to a nation of buyers, homegrown brands will appear, often making their debut on the Internet. It's easy to imagine that we will soon be hearing about "Snapdeal originals" or "Paytm originals" that can only be bought online.

Offline retailers will try but fail to do e-commerce well

Throughout the world offline retailers have proved themselves to be bad at transitioning to the online world. In the United States, even long-standing titans with broad national reach, such as Barnes & Noble and Toys "R" Us, haven't made the transition. So it is hard to imagine that in India, where organized retail accounts for such a small portion of retail in the country, traditional offline retailers will be any more successful at creating their own online stores. Instead, offline retailers like Pantaloon should follow the old adage "If you can't beat them, join them." When approaching the online market, major players should look to maximize their sales on Amazon, Snapdeal, and Flipkart as vendors rather than try to compete with them. As Sandeep Aggarwal told me, "The Walmart of India will not be Walmart Corporation—it will be an online company. And that online company will not be an inventory-led model; it will be a marketplace."[41]

The ultimate winners will be consumers and small merchants

Most of the attention for e-commerce in India has focused on the top players, who use their billions to subsidize the growth of e-commerce. It is not yet clear which of these titans will survive, which will be gobbled up, and which will become the most successful. But there are clear winners: consumers and small merchants. Consumers will benefit from the lower prices and greater availability. Merchants will benefit from having national and even international reach for their products. So it's in their best interests to stay friendly toward all the top players and make their stores available across a diversified range of e-commerce marketplaces.

Foreign brands will discover huge opportunities

From the perspective of foreign brands, e-commerce in India is now at about the stage China was in 2008, the year Taobao spun off Tmall to become an independent entity. Judging from the China experience, now is the time for foreign brands to get into India. All the major players have services that allow brands to sell their products and tell their stories in ways that are more sophisticated than a simple photograph and text description. Yet few brands are taking advantage of the opportunity. Tmall remains crowded with global brands competing for attention, but e-commerce in India is at a critical point, and getting in now is well worth considering.

E-commerce in India will prove to be more creative than disruptive

The China market has proved that e-commerce creates sales where none would otherwise have occurred. In India e-commerce should be an even more creative force, since it is creating a platform from which the entrepreneurial spirit of the kirana store can be harnessed online, giving eager retailers national reach for the first time. Unfortunately, the proponents of the status quo—existing retailers and other intermediaries—are convincing bureaucrats to see things their way by arguing that e-commerce is a largely disruptive force. E-commerce leaders in India need to do a much better job of touting the benefits that e-commerce is bringing to grassroots entrepreneurs there. E-commerce in India is not a case of large retailers sucking up all retail opportunities. Rather, it is about giving small retailers the tools they need to become large retailers.

E-commerce leaders should do more to highlight the successes of merchants selling on their sites. They should point to small retailers in rural and impoverished regions who have improved prospects for their families by selling online. They should highlight the growing numbers of jobs e-commerce is creating for workers who have found jobs as delivery people. Until e-commerce leaders make this compelling case, they will be met with resistance from those in the media and the government who have a stake in protecting the incumbents and the status quo.

E-commerce will give rise to a banking revolution

Banks in India have largely remained bureaucratic, inefficient, and woefully unable to serve the needs of small merchants and micro-entrepreneurs. Part of the problem is a thicket of regulations that make a sheaf of forms necessary for something as simple as opening an account. But it's also the legacy of the era of state-owned banks. Privately owned banks became legal only in 1993 and have not yet fully modernized. In the Internet era, as mobile commerce moves India toward a cashless society, will the State Bank of India really need its nearly 200,000 employees in almost 10,000 branches? Without the need to physically process deposits and withdrawals, probably not.

Just as it did in China, e-commerce will drive a banking revolution in India. As e-commerce companies in India collect the transaction histories of buyers and sellers, they will be gaining important credit information. Over time this credit information will allow them to extend loans, an area that some payment companies are already exploring, although it's not clear that banking laws will permit them to do so.

The biggest hurdle e-commerce companies face in becoming e-banks is resistance from the heavily protected banks, which will undoubtedly protest the emergence of online financial institutions. The banks will argue that e-banks are unreliable, can't be trusted, destroy jobs, and introduce financial instability to India's economy. But government policy has so far had the effect of accelerating the demand for the mobile payments, helping the leading service providers such as Paytm. When the Modi government banned the use of large banknotes in late 2016 in an effort to stamp out black market activities and generate more tax revenue, the daily number of digital payments jumped 271 percent.[42]

C2C will take off . . . eventually

It's surprising that e-commerce in India has gotten as far as it has without the emergence of a massive C2C player, such as Alibaba's Taobao, which allows small businesses and individuals to sell online. But despite many attempts, C2C simply hasn't taken root.

However, in a nation of entrepreneurs, this should change quickly. With its strength in purely mobile marketplaces, Paytm may be able to move into the market that was left wide open when Snapdeal shut down its Shopo service. We should expect that, in the next few years, C2C mobile-based marketplaces will become an important frontier for e-commerce players in India.

Logistics: A problem that creates opportunity

Logistics will remain one of the fastest-growing industry sectors in India as new solutions are found that take the country into the e-commerce era. Because India is starting from scratch, we can expect interesting spin-offs in the logistics arena. Flipkart's initiative to spin-off its own logistics company is one such example, but there are many others—logistics has become one of the hottest sectors for investment over the past year or two, according to *Tech in Asia*.[43] E-commerce companies themselves are expected to invest about $6 to $8 billion in logistics, infrastructure, and warehousing in the next few years, according to one recent study, while stand-alone logistics firms like Delhivery, Ecomm Express, and GoJavas have attracted venture capital and private equity investment.[44]

Multiple players will coexist in the market

Alibaba still manages to hold about 80 percent of the China e-commerce market. Some have argued that this is because of protectionism. But Alibaba has such an outsized position in the China market because people simply were unaware of the opportunity there; for several years eBay was Alibaba's only real competition. Once Alibaba vanquished eBay, the Chinese start-up had the playing field to itself for several years, which enabled it to grow and consolidate its share of the market. India is different. The success of Alibaba made people aware of the opportunity in India and attracted more competition. Thus share of the market in India will be more evenly distributed among the major players for the foreseeable future.

Private label will become an important segment for e-commerce players

Because cobbling together a fulfillment infrastructure is so expensive, players like Flipkart and Amazon are finding themselves pressured on their profit margins. So it is not surprising that they have begun experimenting with private-label products as a way to capture more of the value chain. By tracking purchase data through their systems, companies will be able to identify high-volume, commoditized items, such as iPhone chargers or men's dress shirts, for which they should start their own private labels. It will be important not to lose focus on their core e-commerce business, but private-label items represent an opportunity to capture more profit when fierce competition is squeezing retail margins.

SOUTHEAST ASIA

Alibaba is a crocodile in the Yangtze River, but we are the komodo in the seventeen-thousand-island archipelago.
—*William Tanuwijaya, founder of Tokopedia*

IN 1985 MY MOTHER TOOK ME AND MY SISTER ON OUR FIRST TRIP to Asia, when I was fifteen years old. The most memorable part of the trip was a visit to one of Bangkok's floating markets. To reach the market we rose at dawn and took a long-tail boat through a web of canals lined with homes on wooden stilts, temples, and shanties with corrugated metal roofs. The poverty of the city was evident as we floated past the poorest of the canal dwellers, who lived in makeshift homes beneath the bridges, bathing in, and cooking and drinking from, the river.

When we arrived at the floating market, we found a colorful collage of women in straw hats plying the narrow passages in wooden boats to sell fresh fruits and vegetables. Not yet overrun by tourists, the market remained largely as it had been for hundreds of years, a way to buy and sell fresh produce before the widespread use of refrigeration. The floating hawkers would congregate in the central floating market before rowing up and down the river to serve passing boats and the homes they encountered along the way. As a fifteen-year-old accustomed to shopping for groceries at the local Safeway, I was enthralled.

Today Bangkok's floating markets exist almost entirely for the sake of tourists, and shoppers are more likely to find trinkets and knickknacks than papaya salad. But the markets do offer a window on how trade was carried out along the rivers and canals of Southeast Asia for hundreds of years. And life along these waterways and small islands helps explain the way e-commerce has evolved in the region, which can be summed up in two words—it's fragmented.

The rivers and canals of mainland Southeast Asia, which includes Thailand, Vietnam, Cambodia, Myanmar, Laos, and Peninsular Malaysia, have served as important trading routes, moving crops from fertile plains to other parts. The Mekong, Chao Phraya, and Red rivers spread commerce, culture, and religion throughout the region while providing geographic barriers that allowed pockets of unique cultures to emerge and evolve.

The great rivers end in deltas that led to lowland settlements, which became commercial centers that later grew into today's large cities. These cities became centers of trade for the region. The seas and oceans of maritime Southeast Asia, which includes Indonesia, East Malaysia, Singapore, and the Philippines, have served as important maritime trading routes connecting India and China. Trading and migration not only moved spices between regions but also brought Islam and Buddhism to Southeast Asia from India and the Arab world.

The sixteenth century ushered in an era of influence from European powers that viewed Southeast Asia as another region to divvy up in their global land grab. The Portuguese were first to arrive, taking up a base in the Moluccas, also called the Maluku Islands, an archipelago (part of Indonesia today). The Spanish came next, settling in the Philippines. During the next several hundred years, the Dutch would claim what is now Indonesia, and the French would plant their flag in Vietnam, Laos, and Cambodia. The British claimed Singapore, Malaysia, and Burma.[1] But despite foreign influences, the unique identities within the region still exist with their cultural roots going back thousands of years.[2]

E-COMMERCE'S EVOLUTION IN THE REGION

Fast-forward to the twenty-first century, and this complicated history helps explain why e-commerce got off to such a slow start. With a population of 620 million, Southeast Asia certainly represents a huge opportunity. But Internet penetration was low, and the e-commerce infrastructure too inefficient to attract significant investment.

EBay, which opened its Singapore marketplace in 2001, was one of the first US e-commerce companies to establish a presence in the region. Given the country's English-speaking population, large expat community, and mature retail infrastructure, it was a natural choice. Not surprisingly, eBay established a leadership position in the Singapore e-commerce market, as the city-state's conditions were more of a mirror of the United States or Germany than of its neighbors in the region. Ebay's next appearance in the region was eBay Malaysia and eBay Philippines in 2004, followed by debuts in Vietnam and Thailand in 2007. In many ways eBay has fared better in Southeast Asia than in other emerging markets, and many of its properties in the region survive today. The company has no doubt benefited from the size of the individual markets, which at first were too small to sustain large independent players, so having one platform that served all the markets proved to be an advantage. But as the markets have grown and matured, eBay's decision not to localize its websites has become more of an issue, and over time it has moved toward serving as a platform that plugs local sellers into its global marketplace for cross-border trade rather than as a strong domestic player itself.

Some homegrown players tried to introduce e-commerce in the region outside Singapore, but what they offered was little more than classified ads that allowed sellers to list products while conducting transactions entirely offline. One example in Indonesia, Tokobagus, which was started in 2005, allowed sellers to post product photos and simple text descriptions that could include the seller's phone number and email addresses. Interested buyers would simply contact the seller and negotiate payment and logistics off-line. OLX, which is led by Naspers, the major investor in China's Tencent, later bought Tokobagus.

Another company that took a crack at the Southeast Asian market is Rakuten, Japan's leading marketplace operator, which provides a digital platform similar to Tmall. Starting in 2009, the company moved into the region aggressively, setting up shop in Thailand, Indonesia, Malaysia, and Singapore. But Rakuten struggled to adapt its Japanese business model and management style to the Southeast Asian markets. In 2016 Rakuten had announced it was shutting down its marketplaces in the region.

Significantly, one company that did not make aggressive moves to target Southeast Asia's 600 million consumers is Amazon. The only good explanation for Amazon's staying out of the market is the region's fragmentation. The Amazon model relies on large scale and an efficient infrastructure, and perhaps Jeff Bezos was deterred by such a fragmented market for a business model that relies so heavily on scale and efficiency. But this is likely to change in the future as the market matures and Amazon sees more opportunity there.

ROCKET INTERNET: ATTACK OF THE CLONES

The first twenty years of e-commerce in Southeast Asia were small attempts and baby steps, but one company did finally enter the market in a big way in 2012—the ever-controversial Rocket Internet, the Berlin-based "clone factory" known for churning out e-commerce companies for emerging markets. Rocket, which has also been active in India, has come under a fair amount of controversy and criticism, but its efforts in Southeast Asia have been one of the company's relative bright spots. Rocket started its operations in Indonesia, Malaysia, the Philippines, Thailand, and Vietnam in 2012, rolling out "mini-Amazons" throughout the region. The company raised more than $647 million, which it used to build large warehouses and develop logistics and last-mile delivery infrastructure. Alibaba Group acquired Rocket's local company, Lazada, in 2016, providing some validation to Rocket, whose business model had been criticized as not sustainable. Rocket's influence extends far beyond its efforts in Southeast Asia, and I discuss Rocket companies elsewhere in this book, specifically in the sections on Latin America and Africa. That was why I decided to hop a plane for Berlin and visit Rocket's headquarters; I needed to better understand its vision and what it was learning from its efforts in emerging markets.

At the crossroads of East and West, Berlin is a fitting place for the headquarters of Rocket. While Rocket is not a household name in the West, no e-commerce company has expanded more aggressively into emerging markets in recent years. Part incubator, part venture capitalist, part e-commerce empire, the controversial company became either a beacon of hope for Europe's innovators or a lightning rod of criticism. One thing is for sure—its experience in operating more than a hundred companies in a far-flung empire stretching from Nigeria to Colombia to Argentina to Pakistan offers lessons for e-commerce operators in emerging markets.

The roots of Rocket go all the way back to the US Internet boom. It's no surprise that, in that heady time, Europeans quickly adopted US e-commerce models. Oliver Samwer, Rocket's founder, created the first example, an eBay clone called Alando, with his brothers, Marc and Alexander, and three college friends. The six founders sold it to eBay for $43 million just three months after it opened for business in 1999.[3] That became a template for Rocket Internet, which Samwer and his brothers started eight years later.

Oliver Samwer was born the middle child in Cologne, Germany, in 1972. His parents were prominent lawyers; his father once represented Karl Carstens, who was later elected president of Germany. As teenagers, the brothers decided that one day they would start a company. Their mother reportedly did not like this risk-taking plan and encouraged them to pursue more stable careers, such as something in insurance.[4]

The brothers brushed aside her advice and pursued their interest in entrepreneurship. In 1998 all three were living in the San Francisco Bay Area and studying US start-ups. The result of Oliver's efforts was a 167-page book called *America's Most Successful Startups: Lessons for Entrepreneurs*, which he wrote with Max Finger. The highly detailed, analytical book offers a window on the approach he and his brothers would later take. The philosophy of Rocket, and the reason the company is so reviled in innovative circles, is captured by a line in the book: "To be a successful entrepreneur, you do not have to come up with your own ideas. You have to recognize great ideas when you see them."[5]

To write the book Finger and Samwer interviewed seventy-five entrepreneurs and attempted to crack the code of entrepreneurship. Their final product covers everything from how to identify business opportunities to how to unveil a start-up, grow a business, and build a company culture. The book attempts to lay out a sort of science of building a company and is a surprisingly useful read for entrepreneurs. Its lessons include "Find a large market that is not well-understood" with opportunities that "have not been exploited by the dominant players because of institutional resistance." The authors note that Bezos could start Amazon from scratch and beat Barnes & Noble because the latter was weighed down by its physical stores. "Even though you might be smaller than the incumbent, you have the advantage of starting over," they advise. "Therefore you should look for an opportunity where the incumbent cannot move quickly enough."[6]

The Samwer brothers recognized one such idea when, while they were interning at various tech companies in Silicon Valley, they saw how quickly people were taking to eBay in the United States. Thinking that its business model could work in Germany, the brothers tried to contact eBay to see if it would allow them to establish a German operation. When they received no response, they moved back to Germany and decided to set up their own German clone of eBay, which they called Alando.

They weren't the only ones to focus on setting up an eBay-like business in Germany, but they moved quickly. And they had Oliver's salesmanship on their side. The acquisition of Alando three months later proved to be a tremendous success for eBay. As Meg Whitman would write in her autobiography, eBay Germany "took off like an absolute rocket," becoming eBay's most important market outside the United States.[7]

The sale made the Samwer brothers Germany's first Internet millionaires, but Oliver would later cite the early sale of Alando as one of his biggest mistakes, saying that they took a deal too early and could have held out for more money. However, the idea of cutting and pasting a US Internet model onto the German market clearly had legs. The brothers' next venture was a ringtone company, Jamba! They sold the company, best known for creating the "crazy frog" ringtone, to Verisign for $273 million in 2004.

The Samwers' next successful clone came during the Groupon craze. They cut and pasted the Groupon model onto Europe and called their clone MyCityDeal. In just a few months it led the daily-deal e-commerce sites in thirteen European countries. Groupon acquired MyCityDeal in 2010 for $170 million worth of Groupon shares.

After several successes the Samwer brothers believed they had developed expertise in identifying US companies whose business models they could transplant to other markets before the US companies began to look beyond their borders. If they could do this with three companies, the brothers concluded, why couldn't they do it with hundreds? In 2007 they set up Rocket Internet, with the explicit goal of replicating the cut-and-paste model on a global scale.

Critics claim that Rocket is nothing more than a clone factory. But as Europe's most successful Internet entrepreneurs, the Samwers have also been hailed as an inspiration for the European start-up community. Oliver Samwer even appeared on the cover of *Wired* magazine as the most influential person in European tech.

For the most part, Oliver Samwer has been media shy. But in the few public comments he has made, he has defended the company's approach, telling *Wired*, "We are builders of companies, we are not innovators. Someone else is the architect, and we are the builders."[8]

So what, then, is Rocket Internet?

Rocket is best described as a "venture builder." The company scans the global market to identify proven business models, selects those it wants to focus on, and then quickly builds a virtual team within its corporate headquarters to ramp up and start the business. Each wall of the company's offices sports a poster for a "100 day launch plan"; these set out a clear timeline and flowchart for each step from idea to market, covering everything from setting up the legal structure, hiring local staff, and deciding on the company's graphic design to coding, buying keyword ads, and the initial publicity campaign. A business starts on the top floor of Rocket and works its way down; if successful, it "graduates" and moves into another office nearby as an independent company.

Rocket has grown to into a sprawling empire of companies with operations around the developing world, from Nigeria to Buenos Aires to Colombia to Pakistan. It went public just two weeks after Alibaba, a move timed to ride the surge of investor interest, as a public relations executive at the company acknowledged. Rocket's companies range from taxi-hailing apps to fashion to general merchandise to food delivery services. In many cases Rocket serves countries that are big enough to be attractive but small enough to lack the start-up ecosystem of financiers, entrepreneurs, engineers, and managers that gives birth to a homegrown company. While an entrepreneur in Pakistan might take years to develop an idea, build a team, and attract venture capitalists, Rocket can quickly assemble a team and, with its relentless focus on being early, gain an early-mover advantage in a new market. Then, the theory goes, the company can be spun off or sold back to one of the giants it was modeled on.

Rocket's most successful company to date is Zalando, a clone of Zappos. The company moved out of the Rocket corporate structure and had its own IPO in 2014. Notably, Zalando has succeeded largely in western Europe. By moving into emerging markets, Rocket has taken on entirely new frontiers.

Given Rocket's acknowledged goal of succeeding through mimicry, perhaps some of the criticism it receives is deserved. But when I looked closely at its business model, it was clear to me that the company itself is actually quite ingenious, and—dare I say it?—innovative. In theory Rocket's approach combines the most important aspects of the start-up phase. By providing a ready source of funding, it fulfills the function of angel investor and venture capitalist. By providing a place for companies to grow from concept to debut, it serves as an incubator and accelerator. And by connecting all its companies within a single family of businesses, it offers many of the benefits of a multinational company. In that sense, it was the first of its kind. And on paper it looks quite attractive to the investors who have already put in billions of dollars.

The question, then, is, how well does this model work in practice, especially in emerging markets? I visited Rocket's headquarters in Berlin's hip Mitte district. Housed in a former hotel, the company offices are surrounded by art galleries, falafel shops, fetish shops, and—when the city thaws out from a long, cold winter—beer gardens sandwiched between graffiti-covered buildings.

My first meeting was in 2015, with Andreas Winiarski, the head of public relations at the time. Andreas had essentially become the public face of the company, a surrogate for the senior management team, which was not particularly interested in speaking to writers. "Oliver doesn't like to talk to the media, and it creates some challenges for us, especially as a public company," Andreas told me.[9]

Andreas came to Rocket in 2012, after a private email Oliver had sent to staff was leaked to the media. In the email, the subject of which was "When is it time for blitzkrieg?," he wrote, "I do not accept surprises. I want this planned confirmed [sic] by all three of you: you must sign it with your blood. . . . I will only do a plan that you 100 percent believe in and that is signed with blood."

He continued: "There are only 3 areas in e-commerce to build billion dollar businesses: amazon, zappos and furniture. The only thing is that the time for the blitzkrieg must be chosen wisely, so each country tells me with blood when it is time. I am ready—any time!

"I am the most aggressive guy on Internet on the planet. I will die to win and I expect the same from you!"[10]

Blitzkrieg, if you're not up on your World War II history, was Hitler's description of his aggressive military strategy of taking a country by storm—literally, a lightning war. Borrowing a management philosophy from the Nazis didn't sit well with the European press, and Oliver was roundly criticized for the email.

But it also provided a crucial insight to the approach of Oliver and his brothers: execute, execute, execute, with both speed and fastidious attention to detail. The focus on fast execution was no doubt a result of seeing how just a few months made all the difference for their businesses—after all, in three months' time, they built $43 million in value for Alando.

I found Andreas to be surprisingly open, and the company agreed that as my research progressed, I would be able to interview someone in senior management. Six months later, on a follow-up visit to Berlin, I sat down with Rocket's chief technology officer, Christian Hardenberg.

Christian, too, had joined Rocket in 2012. He trained in college as a programmer, had previously been a consultant, and spent some time at a start-up. So I asked what had attracted him to Rocket.

"The chaos, clearly the chaos. At that time we had this big e-commerce launch. We started e-commerce companies in a weekly rhythm, sometimes three countries in one week. We didn't have PR. We didn't have legal. We didn't have anything you would expect from such a global company. As a programmer, I really like to structure," he said, and working at Rocket was an opportunity to bring structure to chaos.

Being based in Berlin has been a big advantage in attracting talent. "Every interview people always say, 'I heard good things about Berlin,'" Christian said. Within Europe, Berlin has become the place for creative types who want space and a low cost of living to be able to take risks—unlike rival tech centers in Europe, such as London, Stockholm, and Dublin, which are known for their expensive real estate and high costs of living. The fall of the Berlin Wall also meant the end of government-subsidized businesses, which drove industrial production out of the city and left large empty spaces that young people could convert into clubs, lofts, studios for artists, and offices for start-up companies.

Berlin's proximity to eastern Europe has also been a great way to attract programmers. "We get a lot of people from eastern Europe. That's our main source of [engineering] talent right now," Christian said. "Moscow has great universities, but people don't want to work there."

In many ways Rocket is irresistible to anyone with an international mind-set, especially those in Berlin, which has few global companies. Christian said he has enjoyed this aspect of Rocket: "We are in more than a hundred countries now. Just before talking to you, I had a phone call with a guy in Singapore, and after this I'm talking to someone in Africa. I'm constantly jumping around the globe in my mind, and it's really something you wouldn't find in other places in Berlin."[11]

The company is also attractive to employees who want a taste of the start-up life with fewer of the start-up risks. "You have the combination of corporate security . . . [and] the thrill of a start-up, and this combination is unique," Christian said.

Many Berlin-based Rocket employees jump from location to location, doing a stint in Nigeria, followed by a job in Mexico City, and then rotating back to Berlin. Christian himself spent some time in Vietnam helping to build the tech team for the Southeast Asian operations of Lazada. He lived in Ho Chi Minh City and first brought in European engineers before developing a local team to do the work. Since then, Lazada's operations in Vietnam have grown to hundreds of developers.

On its website at the time of my first visit, Rocket's stated mission was "to be the largest Internet company outside the United States and China." The main markets that Rocket first entered were those where the big players had no presence. "For Oli [Oliver], he has had this clear idea—e-commerce will change everybody's life. This is a fact. And now is the time," Christian said. "There is still so much wide space on the map, and he basically saw this as the biggest opportunity in his life to conquer this, get into these places where Amazon didn't find time for yet."

Rocket's approach is all about execution, not innovation. "It's speed. That's what Rocket stands for. I once made this example with exit velocity. From astrophysics you have this certain velocity a rocket needs to get out of a gravity field. And this is somehow a minimum velocity you need to get off the floor. And I think for start-ups it's a bit like that," Christian said. "If you are too slow, others will just eat you and you'll never get off the ground. So we use that as a principle to endow a bias for action. You get so used to it that you don't even realize it anymore. The common denominator is speed. If someone is slow, it slows everyone down."

His employees are used to this tilt toward execution. "They are comfortable with the process," he said. "Once you kick off a company everyone knows what to do, more or less, and after three months we pretty predictably get a quite good quality start-up out there. And then we learn and then we use that data."

It helps that Rocket has grown so many businesses. "We have all of these companies already waiting. In all countries we have shell companies we can just start tomorrow," Christian said. "Sometimes, in some countries, it takes a long time just to get something registered, so we have the contracts and legal entities ready and know how to do business in Indonesia [for example] and what licenses you need."

And if the data show that the business is not working, Rocket also doesn't waste any time shutting it down. "We ask what does the data show us? . . . If the facts are negative, we close things down quickly."

Rocket's core businesses started with the goal of creating mini-Amazons throughout the emerging world, except for China. Rocket's general merchandise businesses target Africa through Jumia, Latin

America through Linio, and (before its sale to Alibaba) through Lazada it targeted Southeast Asia. To build these the company set up a proprietary online shop system, based on Amazon, and licensed it to all the Rocket e-commerce companies doing business in those regions. This is one of the main arguments in favor of Rocket's model: it has the scale necessary to apply universal platforms in a variety of markets.

But over time Rocket has learned that some aspects need to be customized and that the one-size-fits-all approach simply doesn't work. "They [Rocket's businesses] all used the same system," Christian said. "But it was soon clear these companies could not be successful with a tech team in Berlin with an eight hours' time zone shift and completely disconnected from their local markets."

Rocket decided to decentralize its engineering. It flew engineers from the local companies into Berlin, trained them on Rocket's software, and then "handed everything over to them and, step by step, pushed them into independence," he said. "At that point we allowed them to take what we built as a starting point and take it from there. If you would have tried to keep everything on one platform, we would have slowed down everyone." This helped the local businesses to accommodate the unique needs of each market, such as digital goods or providing pickup stations in local villages. In some areas the local platforms could initiate "try on delivery" for clothes, so that customers could simply try a shirt on at home before paying the courier. "I think that is key to success, that you can innovate on your own," Christian said. "Of course, it's inefficient— every company needs their own tech team—but I think it's good to accept this inefficiency [in exchange] for speed."

As the companies began to localize, Rocket realized that it was important to move from a retail-led model to a marketplace. "It was a [matter of] learning along the way that retail-only is not going to work," he said. "The margins were not good enough, and there is a lot of gray-market competition, so [a marketplace] was smarter." Christian conceded that Rocket was "a bit late, but then [made] a quite radical move to move from retail to marketplace, but I'm proud that it worked out." But he believes it may have been a necessary step in Rocket's evolution: "I think we were right because you need first a certain size to be attractive to vendors as a marketplace."[12]

Over time the company went from modeling its retail operations after Amazon to modeling them after Alibaba. "We were all focused on building Amazons, and then one day we shifted, and everything was, 'We are building Alibabas,' " one of Rocket's senior managers told me.

The companies are allowed to separate from the mother ship over time, find their own investors, and stand on their own. They even develop their own corporate cultures. Christian explained: "I would say the relationship to our companies changes over time. It's a bit like childhood. In the beginning, [the companies] are like a little baby, and you need to do everything and nurture them because they are helpless. And then they grow up and have their own ideas like a teenager and basically push back on Rocket, typically a bit, and say, 'We can do things better on our own.' And later, beyond that, they see the advantages of the parents and ask for help when it makes sense."

From a strategic perspective, Rocket's approach to localization was a pleasant surprise. The story of US e-commerce companies' failure in China was very much about trying to use a one-size-fits-all global approach for their platforms. But the one place Rocket's philosophy did not seem to apply was top management. Almost universally, Rocket's local companies are headed by nonlocals.

I asked Christian whether this is a weakness. He acknowledged that he wonders whether these companies should be headed by local managers who know the country and have a network. "We are coming a bit from outside into these countries, into Nigeria from Paris," he said. "Typically it's [a] European at the top [of the company]. But also we are very selective [with] these people, and they typically have [had] a career at McKinsey and have some execution skills or experience that are not so available locally. I think it's also a cultural thing. In the end, these top management people are quite similar in their [makeup], and that also helps. All [are] young, ambitious, coming more from a consulting background . . . Maybe if you would have some very different cultures, some Indians and Chinese and everyone speaking their own language, it would be more difficult to make this very transparent cohesive group."

So what is working for Rocket Internet like? In talking with managers other than those provided by the company's PR team, I was surprised to find a fair amount of cynicism about the company. Stock options are not extended as incentives to most employees, and this creates resentment.

Being a Rocket employee in Berlin requires a fairly thick skin in an industry that prizes innovation over execution. Outside Rocket, many Berliners also are cynical about the company; one senior manager told me: "I was looking for an apartment in Berlin, and it came down to me and one other person. When the landlord found out I worked at Rocket, they . . . gave it to the other person." Within Berlin's gritty culture, some regard the company's business model as having much flash but little substance, and this employee's would-be landlord didn't want a tenant who might soon be out of a job.

It was not difficult to find former employees who had bad experiences at Rocket. To be sure, some simply could not keep up with the hard-driving, results-driven approach that Rocket maintains. But the negative reports seem to go beyond that.

A former head of one of Rocket's Latin American ventures told me that a common complaint is that the company lacks any coherent company culture. Often, co-CEOs run the companies, and this can lead to confusion and lack of organization. People didn't seem to understand what the goals were and what their place in the organization was. While this can be true of any start-up, the lack of discussion about values sometimes means that there is no unifying purpose for some employees.

Employees and former employees are not the only ones voicing grievances about Rocket. By the summer of 2016 investors also were beginning to lose patience. Rocket's life as a public company

has been fraught with ups and downs, starting with its stock drop-
ping 13 percent below its offering price on the first day of trading
in Frankfurt. After briefly rising to a peak of EUR56.6 per share,
the company fell to nearly EUR15 per share by the spring of 2017.
Along the way, it began to generate headlines such as "Rocket Falls
Back to Earth."[13]

Yet Rocket's model got a major validation when the Alibaba
Group acquired Lazada for $1 billion in 2016, hoping it would
give Alibaba an early start in the Southeast Asian markets served
by Lazada. From Rocket's perspective, it was a page straight out of
the Alando and MyCityDeal playbook, only this time the buyer
didn't come from the United States but from China.

The Lazada deal was a bright spot, but other parts of the company have struggled to reach profitability, and the Rocket mother
ship has shown signs of a deteriorating balance sheet. I think one
reason that Rocket is struggling is that it has not found its soul. In
its quest to execute, Rocket has not given its employees a unifying
purpose beyond execution itself. I asked Christian about this, wondering aloud whether Rocket has an idealistic "change the world"
motivation. He immediately shook his head and dismissed this
idea. He said he thinks Rocket and Silicon Valley "have different
roles in the world. Silicon Valley is the place for innovators, for
world changers. We need those people. . . . They are our heroes. . . .
But I think here we are a bit more the engineers who sweat all the
details and say, 'Vision aside, what's the problem at hand?' And
maybe that's also why Rocket fits a bit better [in] Germany, because
in the end adapting Amazon to India or Indonesia is not so much a
vision problem but more like many little things, like how do I do
payment, logistics, sourcing, and so on?"

I also asked him about the criticism that Rocket lacks an innovative spirit.

"I personally find it a bit ridiculous, as I think if you would
open a pizza place on the corner, no one would ever come to the
idea and say, 'You just cloned the pizza business next door!' It's just
that's how competition works all over the world. . . . I think com-

petition should allow for more [than one person] doing e-commerce in the world," he responded. "Of course, if we jump on very early ideas, I can understand that it feels wrong that . . . we just wait until the risk goes down . . . [and] there's some proof of success and then get in, but I think it's prudent. It's not our money we are spending. It's the investors'. It's basically our story to investors that we look for the proven business models, not the completely unproven ones. That's a different business. If you take a higher risk, you have a different return."

So what will happen to Rocket?

"I hope it works out. . . . At least from the outside it looks like such a smart combination of taking proven business models—put the smart people on it—but also have this repeatable approach to things." And Oliver is "an amazing salesperson. I've seen him with investors." But "I don't want to sound like we know" what the recipe for success is, Christian said. "Not all of these companies are profitable yet, but I think so far almost every one we started is growing nicely."

Will Rocket Internet achieve exit velocity? Or will it fall to Earth? It's a bit early to say, but whatever the outcome, it will be especially instructive for others looking to enter the market.

As the interview ended, Christian told me, "My main fear is for our German car industry. That's really what Germany relies on still. There are so many jobs in cars—it's like half of the Germany economy." He cited Tesla's electric cars as a threat to the German car industry.[14]

As I walked away, I couldn't help but feel that his final comments summed up the very argument against Rocket's approach. Perhaps he missed the irony, but the future of Germany—like its car industry—relies on its ability to innovate rather than copy. It made me think that Rocket may be an interesting company. It may even prove to be a very successful company for its investors and employees. But Berlin—and European tech—needs a better role model.

THE KOMODO IN THE JUNGLE

I first met William Tanuwijaya, founder of Tokopedia, in 2013 and was immediately impressed. I was in Jakarta to show my film, *Crocodile in the Yangtze*, and received an invitation to give a private screening for him and his team. William is bright and passionate about his company, and while he didn't have international polish or a Harvard degree, I recognized in him a spirit I saw from the most successful Internet entrepreneurs. A couple of years later, when his company raised $100 million from Softbank and was hailed as a local champion, I wasn't surprised.

I caught up with William again in the spring of 2016 at a tech conference in Tokyo. A lot had changed since our first meeting. There were reports his company had raised an additional $147 million. Through its investments and growth, Tokopedia could reasonably claim to be the highest-valued marketplace operator in Indonesia.

Despite all his success to date, Tokopedia's founder remains humble. "I'm an entrepreneur by accident. An entrepreneur by necessity," he explained to the audience at the Tokyo conference. His father had encouraged him to leave their home island in Indonesia to pursue an education. So William traveled four days and three nights to get to Jakarta, where he studied computer science at a local university. After his father fell ill, William needed to find a job to support himself, so he became an Internet café operator, working there for three years while pursuing his degree. Although the work was taxing, he describes it as a "blessing in disguise," because the Internet in Indonesia was expensive at the time. He had free access and "fell in love with the Internet," he told me.

He graduated from university in 2003 and dreamed of working at a big company like Google, but he worked in other industries because the US Internet giants did not have much of a presence in Indonesia. In 2007 he decided to seize the opportunity to start his own e-commerce company. Inspired by eBay in the United States, Rakuten in Japan, and Alibaba in China, he "realized that if I can build the first online marketplace in Indonesia, I can solve this trust issue, connecting strangers from seventeen thousand islands to meet online and facilitate transactions online."[15]

He went to the CEO of his company at the time and pitched the idea of the marketplace, but the CEO was skeptical, asking, "William, can you tell me one person in Indonesia who has become wealthy and successful from doing an Internet business?"

"We didn't have a role model in Indonesia," William explained. "There was no Steve Jobs or Mark Zuckerberg of Indonesia. No Jack Ma of Indonesia. So, lacking of role models, the potential investors cannot see how they will get their money back."

Potential investors were also concerned about competition from international players. "They told me that Indonesia is a large potential market, the fourth-most-populous country in the world, with [a] 250 million population. 'If you prove to the world that you need a Tokopedia or a marketplace, then all of the global giants will enter the market. You are not reinventing the wheel. EBay, Alibaba, Rakuten may enter the market, and how would you compete with them?' I didn't know how to answer these questions at the time.

"People also asked about my background—which family do you come from?" In a country where family status and reputation are important for business, this proved to be a challenge. "I come from a very humble family," William said. "Investors would ask, 'Which university did you graduate from?' If I [had] graduated from an Ivy League university, I would have [had] a better chance against the Internet giants. But, no, I graduated from an Internet café. And they will ask me if I ever studied business before, and I had to tell them no."

But it was one investor's comments that spurred him to action: "William, you are still young—don't dream too high, don't waste your youth. You are thinking all of this story about the American dream, the Silicon Valley dream. But Indonesia is not Silicon Valley. And all of these successful founders were born special and you were not." The discouraging words made him doubly determined. "That became a moment that changed my life," William said.

"For me, Tokopedia is an underdog story," he said. "And as an underdog, you need good colleagues. We were lucky because we had colleagues to believe in ourselves when no one believed in us. We had colleagues who helped us realize that the past is something you cannot change. . . . But you can still save your own future. We realized we should not give up. If we can create this platform, Tokopedia, then we will help millions of people, the next generation, [and] they will be able to start their online businesses.

"Another quality an underdog needs to have is perseverance. A lot of people ask why I have so many investors from Japan. I don't speak English well. Global investors could not understand my English. But I didn't give up. Thankfully, Japanese investors understand the pain of trying to speak English and have more patience, so they took the time to listen to and understand my vision.

"I spent two days [at] my university trying to get people to join my company but could not attract people. I realized I needed to work harder and change my style. I am a very quiet, introverted, and shy person. But I realized that if I never speak in public to tell my story about my dream and my vision, then no one will understand it. [Even] today, it's still a struggle for me to speak in a public space. But I understand that I need to do that. So through that perseverance, we grew our team. We started with the launch with two people. Today we already employ five hundred people from around the world. And now we receive twenty-four thousand applications from around the world and can only hire twenty people. I remember [that] the founding father of our nation, President Sukarno, once said that you need to dream as high as the sky, because if you fall, you fall amongst the stars. And for me it is a simple and beautiful saying."

E-commerce in Indonesia seems to have finally hit a turning point. The Internet came to Indonesia in 1995 but was considered a luxury product, and it did not become affordable for a long time. Because Indonesia is spread out over thousands of islands, connecting Indonesians to the Internet meant bringing cable across seas before third- and fourth-generation smartphones became available.

So, in its early years, the Internet was available only in the big cities and had low adoption.

William describes the early wave of e-commerce as classified ad platforms such as Tokobagus, "basically like Craigslist in the US." Classifieds took off because logistics and payment for goods were an issue, not to mention lack of trust between buyers and sellers. Some wealthy Indonesian families tried to start Internet divisions of their conglomerates, using an Amazon model, but it was too early and the market proved too small. Aside from the electronics retailer Bhinneka, which persisted in its efforts for years, few companies were able to make a go of e-commerce.

But by 2016 William's efforts had produced results. The company counted half a million small merchants who were using Tokopedia and shipping fifteen million products per month. "That's fifteen million 'trusts' already created per month," William said.

E-commerce is beginning to revolutionize Indonesia's retail sector. The small plantation town where William grew up had no mall, and consumers would drive three hours to the island's capital to shop. Small mom-and-pop stores back home provided daily necessities, but the city offered greater variety in categories such as electronics and at prices as much as 50 percent lower than in the smaller towns.

So what is the potential of e-commerce in Indonesia? William points to figures that say small and medium-sized enterprises contribute as much as 58 percent of Indonesia's GDP. They are not online yet and e-commerce in Indonesia is still less than 1 percent of total retail. But Indonesia is a nation of entrepreneurs, and William expects e-commerce there to develop much as it did in China.[16]

He also sees similar characteristics in the behavior of buyers and sellers in Indonesia and China. Before Tokopedia went online, e-commerce platforms made too little provision for social interaction. "That's why people were doing e-commerce on social media like Facebook and Instagram," William explained.

Does that mean Facebook has an opportunity to participate in

e-commerce in the region? And could Facebook challenge the leading marketplaces?

"Small businesses owners have very limited time," he said. "So
when they don't have business, they are very happy to start selling
on social media. But when they start to get ten orders per day, a
hundred orders per day [the merchants] have to go back and forth
with a lot of comments and answering questions. There is a lot of
wasted time on social media. Our merchants used to sell on social
media, but now they understand that commerce is not only about
social, it's about efficiency as well. It's about building a business.
Reputations on social media can be faked [more easily] when
people [encourage] fake friends to 'like' their products or companies. The social networks are already a challenge to the classified
platforms. But you need time to create a network effect by building
out the details, like how to track a package through the logistics."

Given the geographic challenges in Indonesia, logistics tend to
be localized, so Tokopedia's approach is to work with all the logistics
providers. Buyers and sellers choose the providers who are strong
in their local area. Tokopedia's website is integrated with the providers' so customers can look online to see where their purchase is
in the system.

In William's view e-commerce in Indonesia will benefit from
strong tailwinds from the government, which has created a relatively favorable regulatory environment. "The president and ministry in Indonesia is progressive," William explained. "The first time
I visited the US was together with the Indonesian delegation. They
have a vision of becoming a leading digital economy in Southeast
Asia."

In fact, the president is so progressive that he invited William's
rival, Jack Ma, to serve as an adviser to Indonesia on e-commerce.
So how does William plan to fend off Alibaba and its Lazada of-
fensive? "We were very inspired by Alibaba, and now it is so lucky
for us that we can compete with the best in the world in our play-
ground. This will push us to provide the best quality and services
to our customer," he said. "You start small, you have this bench-

mark and idol that inspires you, and today we are head to head with them. Alibaba is the crocodile in the Yangtze. We are the komodo in the seventeen-thousand-island archipelago. We are lucky . . . that 'work until your idols become your rivals' happened to us."[17]

SOUTHEAST ASIAN E-COMMERCE TODAY

The numbers that have long hinted at the potential of the region are finally beginning to add up. Indonesia alone has more than 250 million inhabitants. The Philippines has 102 million; Vietnam, 95 million; Thailand, 68 million; and Malaysia, 30 million.[18]

With the rapid adoption of the mobile phone, Southeast Asia's large population is increasingly online. As data speeds increase and prices come down, an increasing number of Southeast Asians have an e-commerce shopping infrastructure at their fingertips.

But Southeast Asia has more than a large total population. The region has a growing middle class with solid spending power. China was able to build a healthy online retail ecosystem with a per capita GDP of $8,028 by 2015. Singapore is the outlier, with a per capita GDP of $52,889. Malaysia is next at $9,768 per capita, followed by Thailand at $5,815 and Indonesia at $3,347.[19] Yet the actual consumer purchasing power of the middle class across the region is higher than these numbers suggest because GDP per capita is weighed down by low rural incomes.

Another important factor for e-commerce is that Southeast Asia's populations are young and optimistic. More than 67 percent of residents in Southeast Asia are under the age of 35, with the region leading the world in optimism globally in 2015, according to Nielsen.[20] This optimism translates into greater consumer confidence to purchase the latest products.

All these factors create fertile ground for e-commerce. To gain a better understanding of the market on a macro level, I spoke with Sheji Ho, chief marketing officer at aCommerce, the largest e-commerce solution provider in Southeast Asia. The company works with brands, retailers, and marketplace providers to help companies set up online shops, market to consumers, and fulfill deliveries across the region. With nine fulfillment centers, 1,300 staffers, and $40 million in venture capital, aCommerce provides a sort of one-stop shop that helps offline sellers go online in Southeast Asia. Like the publicly traded Baozun in China, aCommerce has tied its fate to selling cyber picks and shovels to others participating in the gold rush.

An outspoken commentator in the region, Ho has both an in-the-trenches view from working with many of the major players as well as a bird's-eye view of trends in all markets. He has worked in China, and he helped me to link several key trends. Let me share several observations based on our discussions.

COMPARISONS WITH CHINA

Given the geographic and cultural proximity of Southeast Asia and China, you might expect that Southeast Asia's e-commerce would resemble China's more than perhaps any other region's. Sheji estimates that based on Internet penetration alone, e-commerce in Southeast Asia is eight years behind China. However, because e-commerce is coming of age later in Southeast Asia than it did in China, it will come of age faster. The result, Ho argued, is that e-commerce in Southeast Asia is really only about five years behind China. This is largely because of the structural similarities in the markets, including

- weak offline retail infrastructure, especially outside first-tier cities
- surging domestic consumption spurred by growth in GDP per capita
- major capital investments in Southeast Asian e-commerce businesses
- young and digitally savvy consumers
- high import duties and taxes that keep cross-border e-commerce to a minimum

- hypercompetitive e-commerce players that will drive media interest and growth in the sector

Ho is quick to point out some of the differences between Southeast Asia and China:

- Southeast Asia is more of a mobile-first/mobile-only market than China.
- China had a head start in logistics infrastructure because of the government's predilection for a top-down, planned economy.
- The massive distribution power of Alibaba encouraged China's rapid transition from COD to Alipay as the preferred payment method.
- Southeast Asia is more competitive because it is an open market, one much easier for foreign companies to enter than China's.[21]

All these observations but one ring true to me. While I do think that e-commerce in Southeast Asia will benefit from maturing more quickly than it did in China, the fragmented nature of its markets also holds it back. And the lack of a solid logistics infrastructure means that it will take longer for e-commerce to take off in Southeast Asian than it did in China.

So I think it's optimistic to say that Southeast Asia lags China by only five years. But whether it takes five, eight, or ten years, e-commerce will be a big market in Southeast Asia.

SOCIAL MEDIA

One of the first things I noticed in Southeast Asia was that entrepreneurs were using Instagram and Facebook to set up online shops. Ho explained that e-commerce users in China had basically jerry-rigged their own version of Taobao. "One third of Thailand e-commerce is estimated to originate on social platforms," he explained. "This is unique to Southeast Asia and is happening throughout the region, with the only exceptions being Singapore and Malaysia." The data back it up—ecommerceIQ surveyed online shoppers in Thailand and found that 48 percent had purchased something through Facebook, Instagram, or the chat app Line in the previous three months. In fact, the number of people shopping on Instagram, Line, and Facebook exceeded the number of people shopping on the largest e-commerce platform, Lazada.[22]

Ho walked me through the process of buying through social media. Small sellers post products, such as fashion and clothing items, on Instagram and Facebook pages and build a following. Shoppers browse the product images until they find something they like. They then connect with the seller by using their preferred messaging app, Japanese messenger app Line, to ask questions, discuss the items for sale and haggle on price. Once they agree to a sale and the terms, the seller provides bank account information so the buyer can wire payment. The buyer sends the seller a photo of the receipt to confirm it was wired. Once the buyer receives the product, the seller typically sends a note of thanks.[23]

Although this process seemed new, it was also familiar. The online users were using the features of different apps to achieve the same result achieved on Taobao. Taobao sellers were allowed to set up highly personal profiles and blogs, express their own personalities, write blog posts, and build followers. Buyers could judge the credibility of sellers based on their number of followers, connections, reviews, and communication style. Although Facebook and Instagram were not designed for e-commerce, they did roughly the same thing, allowing users to build their online reputations through their social networks. By seeing how many friends and followers a potential seller had on Facebook, buyers in Thailand could decide whether this person was trustworthy. Buyers could further evaluate the seller according to the quality of product images and selection of products.

Taobao had allowed buyers to send real-time messages to sellers to initiate live exchanges on their mobile phones, and buyers and sellers in Southeast Asia similarly wanted to connect in real time, to get to know each other better before doing business. This allowed buyers to ask questions and get answers, and also helped buyers and sellers build trust in the process.

So what explains this similarity? Why, in the absence of a Taobao in Southeast Asia, have users basically cobbled together their own? I would argue that the cultural similarities in how Chinese and their Southeast Asian counterparts do business in the offline world carry over to the online world. This suggests that e-commerce players have a huge opportunity to step in and fill the gaping hole in the Southeast Asian market. Alibaba or Tencent could open a more Taobao-like marketplace in the region to serve domestic markets. And Facebook, Instagram, and Line should be looking at moving into e-commerce in Southeast Asia. Whereas regulatory restrictions in China have prevented these foreign companies from putting down roots there, Southeast Asia represents as unique opportunity for them. It's not surprising that Facebook has first offered a payments mechanism and its "Facebook shop" feature in Southeast Asia. Line has started its own Line stores and Line shop. But these companies will have to do more than take baby steps—they will have to go all in or face the prospect of losing out to more focused marketplaces as the market matures.

NO DOMINANT PLAYER

Southeast Asia's cultural and geographic fragmentation is reflected in the market today. Lazada is the only company with strong market shares across the region, and even its penetration is only about 20 percent. The rest of the market is divided into tiny slivers. Even in relatively mature Singapore, twelve different platforms have fairly evenly divided 90 percent of the market.[24]

This tells us a few things about the Southeast Asian market. First, the market reflects the region's fragmentation. Second, the market demonstrates that it is still in its early stages, with the ultimate winners yet to be determined. Finally, because investors are stuffing cash in the pockets of all players at the same time and at about the same rate, no one competitor can take the lion's share of the market, as Alibaba did in Southeast Asia.

A MOBILE-FIRST MARKET

To understand just how much the mobile phone is reshaping e-commerce, consider Thailand, where the average user has 1.4 cell phones. As Sheji Ho pointed out, the mobile phone penetration rate in Thailand already exceeds that of developed countries like the United States and China, making Southeast Asia the only true "mobile-first" region. Key factors in the growth of mobile have been increasing data speeds and lower prices. Less than one year after third-generation phones entered the market, mobile penetration in Thailand passed that in the United States and in China. This is helping extend the Internet beyond the cities, as 85 percent of mobile commerce penetration in Thailand is outside the cities, and 79 percent in Indonesia is outside the cities.[25]

Another important factor is that Southeast Asians are using mobile phones as a gateway to shopping.

Southeast Asians initially used mobile phones to research and learn about products. Lazada reported that by April 2014, more than 50 percent of its traffic was already coming from mobile only as mobile users were increasingly beginning to move from research to purchases. Southeast Asians also prefer cell phones with larger screen sizes, which is giving brands an important opportunity to take their branding beyond a simple list of products.[26]

E-COMMERCE INVESTMENT IN SOUTHEAST ASIA

Just before the Alibaba IPO in 2014, global investors began to up the ante in Southeast Asia. A landmark investment was the $100 million that Softbank, the early Alibaba investor, put into Tokopedia. Not long afterward, traditional retail operator Mahatari Mall announced that it was investing $500 million in creating a digital marketplace (although it later declared that it still had to raise some of this money from investors). Indeed, after years of remaining relatively low, the amount of venture capital coming into Southeast Asian e-commerce reached $603 million in 2015, making it the industry sector that received the most venture capital in the region that year.[27] The competition, media attention, and advertising e-commerce is receiving will undoubtedly drive the adoption of e-commerce in the region.

PAYMENT: A CHALLENGE

Southeast Asia lacks both physical retail infrastructure and payment options. Large sections of Southeast Asia's population have no bank and/or lack credit cards. Only about 36 percent of Indonesia's population older than eighteen has a bank account, and the same is true for 31 percent of both Filipinos and Vietnamese. This contrasts with China, where about 79 percent of the population older than eighteen has a bank account (a huge help in fueling the growth of Alipay, which relied on bank accounts for customers to fund their accounts). In addition, credit card penetration is low in Southeast Asia, from about 8 percent to 18 percent in the largest markets. One of the latter is Vietnam, where a mere 3.5 percent of the population has a credit card.[28]

While some would see the lack of credit cards and bank accounts as a major barrier, I see a major opportunity. COD has become the key method for paying for online purchases. But as I explained earlier, COD is likely to fall out of favor when online payment systems grow and establish a critical mass. So online payment systems in Southeast Asia are likely to morph into Internet-based financial institutions, which will disrupt the banks in the region, forcing them to either fully embrace e-commerce or struggle. But this will be more than just a disruptive force—it will be a creative one, too, providing a way for entrepreneurs and small businesses to receive credit.

LOGISTICS: ANOTHER CHALLENGE

As Sheji Ho contends, the growth of e-commerce in Southeast Asia is highly dependent on logistics and payments. Right now, only Singapore ranks highly on the World Bank Logistics Performance Index (LPI), between Germany and the United States. But serving a tiny city-state of one island and serving countries made up of thousands of islands is an entirely different matter. No wonder Indonesia and the Philippines rank below even India on the LPI.[29] This helps explain why companies such as Lazada and aCommerce have built their own fleets to complete deliveries.

TRENDS AND PREDICTIONS

So how will e-commerce in Southeast Asia evolve?

Brand stores will have a better chance of growing
China almost skipped the development of online brand stores, such as Nike.com and Apple.com in the United States. Alibaba's head start was simply too big: it had established itself as a de facto storefront for shoppers, which led brands to simply open stores on Tmall and, later, Jingdong Mall.

But the fragmented nature of the market in Southeast Asia means that no one player has become the dominant player, creating an opening for brands to build stand-alone online storefronts. Brands might integrate with Line to allow staff to chat with shoppers. They also could build up a following, establish trust on Facebook, and accept payments through Facebook's payment system or LINE Pay. Building their own online stores would mean brands would have to run their online stores, including logistics and operations, but they would not have to pay commissions to a marketplace operator. The brands would have more control but also more responsibility.

The option for brands to build their own online stores also has important implications for search engines. In China search engines did not, and still do not, play a significant role in e-commerce. Government policy essentially forced Google out of the country. Tao-bao and Tmall blocked Baidu from crawling them. So customers started their shopping on Taobao and Tmall, rather than on search engines, which had been so important in the West. But Google could benefit in Southeast Asia from brand sites that buy keyword ads on Google's search engine rather than on Tmall.

Alibaba will seek to create China-like ecoystems in the region

Alibaba's acquisition of Lazada initially surprised me. Alibaba had long believed in local entrepreneurs' serving local markets, instead of having McKinsey and Harvard Business School grads parachute in from Europe to run local markets. An Alibaba-Lazada alliance seemed like a cultural mismatch.

But Alibaba may have calculated that gaining a foothold across the region was worth suffering through a cultural mismatch while it nudged Lazada from an Amazon-like marketplace to an Alibaba-like marketplace. According to Sheji Ho, no other e-commerce player is in Alibaba's position to build out the ecosystem, and it is already doing that through investments in several regional companies.

Alibaba will certainly not go unchallenged. And as e-commerce becomes more established, players in the region will expand into other related industries to try to create as many ways to interest customers as possible, particularly as online payment becomes important. The companies will grow, form more partnerships, and e-commerce players and cab-hailing apps, online entertainment, and specialized online retailers are likely to merge and acquire each other. The consolidation of the market will play out differently in each market and will depend on the strength of Alibaba-Lazada's local competitors.

E-commerce growth will spill over to online finance and fintech, disrupting the banks

With so many customers in Southeast Asia who don't use banks, one of the major opportunities will be e-commerce's growth into financial technology. The reliance on COD and the paucity of bank accounts and credit cards mean that the fight to establish a leadership position in online payment will be fierce, because the leader in e-commerce payments will be in a great position to move into financial technology. Online banking and financial technology are likely to become incredibly important to e-commerce companies.

Cross-border trade into Southeast Asia will increase, spurring conflicts

Protectionist regulations and restrictions have largely kept cross-border e-commerce from taking root in Southeast Asia, with the exception of Singapore. But with more Southeast Asian shoppers going online, a large amount of cross-border activity into and out of the region is all but inevitable, as Southeast Asia's growing middle class searches for branded products not available in the region as well as inexpensive imports from China. Southeast Asian countries will have to balance their interest in protecting local retailers and in accelerating e-commerce. Brands will be lining up to get into the Southeast Asian market. Alibaba has already begun to connect its Chinese sellers with Southeast Asian buyers as well as to try to convert Tmall Global sellers into Lazada Global sellers, opening the doors to 600 million additional customers.

However, cross-border trade within the Association of Southeast Asian Nations (ASEAN) will represent another set of challenges and opportunities. The online ecosystems of Thailand will compete with those of Indonesia and the Philippines. If countries are too protectionist, they may hamper the growth of their own ecosystem, putting themselves at a disadvantage relative to other countries in the region.

O2O and Omnichannel commerce will take root much earlier in Southeast Asia

Southeast Asian retailers have had the benefit of watching the China experience, so they know that e-commerce soon will challenge them. That means they are much more likely to embrace online to offline (O2O) early as a way to drive foot traffic to their bricks-and-mortar malls. This is already happening: the Siam Paragon shopping mall in Bangkok is Instagram users' most popular place from which to post pictures. Savvy retailers will make O2O an important part of their operations, embracing e-commerce rather than viewing it as a threat.

Indonesia will become the major battlefield
for e-commerce in the region
Indonesia will perhaps be the best laboratory for new ideas in e-commerce in the region. Its large population is attracting the lion's share of investment in e-commerce, and its battle for e-commerce primacy is the most intense. The battle to watch: Softbank-backed Tokopedia versus Alibaba's Lazada. A future merger of these two rivals would not be surprising because their business models are complementary.

7

LATIN AMERICA

It's better to be the head of a rat than the tail of a lion.
—*Spanish proverb*

THE COUPLE TANGOING ON MY HOTEL TELEVISION CONFIRMED that I had arrived in Buenos Aires. It was my first trip to Argentina and second trip to South America. I wanted to get this trip off to a better start than my last one, which had ended in my getting mugged in a Bogotá slum, so I headed to the hotel restaurant for a peaceful cup of coffee.

But it wouldn't quite work out that way.

When I opened the heavy metal lid of an improperly assembled buffet warmer, it unexpectedly flipped back, kicking a Sterno tin full of flaming gel onto my chest. When I looked down to find that my shirt was on fire, I dropped the plate I was holding; it shattered, piercing the silence. I immediately whipped off my shirt and tried to stomp out the flames. When the room full of diners in suits and business attire turned to see what the commotion was about, they saw a crazy shirtless man dancing in the middle of their breakfast.

Luckily I escaped my breakfast unscathed. But it was a good reminder that life in emerging markets always comes with hidden risks.

I'd come to Buenos Aires to meet the pioneers of e-commerce

in Latin America, founders of the firm Mercado Libre. The company first appeared on my radar in 2004, when Google flew me and several other international clients to the Googleplex for meetings and I met some of their marketing team members. Now I would get to see the Mercado Libre team on their home turf.

I stepped out of the hotel into a gorgeous day. Buenos Aires was living up to its name. I strolled across town through the leafy neighborhoods and admired the ornate colonial buildings that gave the city a European feel.

But these once-immaculate buildings were showing signs of wear. The last hundred years had not been entirely good for Argentina. During the prosperous belle époque period (1871–1914) that preceded World War I, Argentina was a magnet for European immigrants. In those forty-three years Argentina's gross domestic product grew at an annual rate of 6 percent.[1] Argentina was more prosperous than France, Italy, and Germany, enjoying one of the ten-highest incomes per capita in the world. Its per capita GDP was more than four times greater than that of its neighbor and rival, Brazil.[2]

Buenos Aires was the heart of Argentina's prosperity, serving as a major international port from which Argentinian beef and other agricultural products were exported to the rest of the world. The country adopted technologies from other parts of the world, applied them to its industries, made the country rich, and saw its arts and culture scene boom.[3]

But after World War I external shocks rocked the Argentinian economy, and then the Great Depression and World War II exacerbated the country's problems. To explain the struggles Argentina faced, economists today seem to agree that while the country was focused on exporting commodities, it failed to invest in education and, as a result, had no innovations of its own that might have led to more diversified industries. This made Argentina vulnerable to swings in global demand for its commodities, as well as those of its internal political pendulum.[4]

During my 2015 visit to the country, it was clear that isolationism was taking a huge toll. Currency controls had created a huge gap between the official and black market exchange rates. High tariffs limited the products that were entering the country. The government had defaulted on its debt in 2014, and the economy was shaking under the pressure of being an outcast in global financial circles. For young white-collar workers in the more prosperous sections of Buenos Aires, the upcoming election presented an opportunity to change the leadership and return to freer markets. E-commerce, which had been languishing in Argentina for several years, looked forward to a change.

Although Argentina was poised to grow again, its neighbor to the east, Brazil, was in the throes of a deep recession. For years the country and its population of 200 million—the world's fifth largest—had enjoyed Brazil's status as a member of the BRICS association of five major emerging economies (the others: Russia, India, China, and South Africa). As one large market, Brazil had also attracted the lion's share of e-commerce investment in South America, giving rise to a healthy start-up community.

But despite Latin America's 620 million people and large middle classes, its e-commerce development still lagged behind that in China. Argentina in particular had not seen e-commerce take off as quickly as in China, even though Argentina had a head start. In early 2000 it was estimated that 50 percent of Latin America's start-ups were based in Argentina, which also had the fifth-largest number of registered Internet domain names in the world. So what happened?[5]

I'd come to Buenos Aires to talk with leaders of the one company that had pioneered e-commerce across the region and had a broad sense of the history of the industry as well as the form of its evolution in the region—Mercado Libre. It's the only Latin American Internet company that's gone public on the Nasdaq. I was in Buenos Aires to find out why the company was a shining exception rather than the rule.

MERCADO LIBRE

The headquarters of Mercado Libre (Free Markets) is a modern skyscraper with colorful art in the lobby. Located in the Vincente Lopez section of Buenos Aires, it offers sweeping views of Uruguay, from where many of the senior managers commute, because it has become more stable than Argentina in recent years. The team had organized a full afternoon of meetings with senior management, including Stelleo Tolda, the COO, who had joined the company in its first months, and Sean Summers, the Pepsi marketing executive Mercado Libre had lured to Buenos Aires to run its marketplace division.

Mercado Libre was founded by Marcos Galperin, an Argentinian born into a family that had made a fortune from Sadesa, one of the largest leather sellers in the world. After he graduated from high school in Buenos Aires, Galperin had headed to the Wharton School for undergraduate studies. He worked at an Argentinian oil company before returning to the United States for a master's in business administration at Stanford from 1997 to 1999, during the dot-com boom.

Like so many of the early international pioneers of e-commerce, Galperin saw the rapid growth of eBay and became interested in bringing the eBay model to Argentina. Tolda, a classmate at Stanford, recalls running into Galperin at the library on a day off from class. "Marcos was not one to be found in the library. I asked, 'What are you doing here?' He told me, 'I'm doing research for this company I want to start, researching US models that might work in Latin America.' "

As they studied for their MBAs in the heart of Silicon Valley, they watched the investment boom from a front-row seat. "We saw what was going on in the US. We were there for eBay's IPO. Other companies were being launched and gaining traction," Tolda said. "EBay was our early inspiration."[6] Three months after Galperin started Mercado Libre, Tolda joined him to help set up the company's operation in Brazil.

Galperin had begun laying the groundwork for Mercado Libre as a student and had asked his finance professor, Jack McDonald, to introduce him to investors. His break came when McDonald arranged for Galperin to drive the venture capitalist John Muse to his private plane after a speaking engagement. In the time it took to get to the airplane, Galperin had convinced Muse to invest in his business. After graduation Galperin returned to Buenos Aires and set up shop in a small space connected to the basement parking garage of an office building. He also enlisted his cousin Marcelo Galperin to be the company's chief technology officer and convinced Stanford classmate Hernan Kazah to come aboard. The latter would later become the company's CFO.

Galperin and his team started their Argentina website in August 1999 and the next month expanded to Brazil and Mexico. To keep up with the many other eBay clones that were popping up throughout the region—they estimate there were more than fifty in Argentina alone—Galperin, Tolda, Marcelo, and Kazah soon had a website that was serving most South American countries, fueled by two rounds of investment totaling more than $50 million.

I asked Tolda why Mercado Libre had never faced any tough competition, and he quickly corrected me, showing me that I'd made a mistake a lot of others have made. "Because a lot of our competitors didn't survive, everyone thinks that we didn't have competitors," he said, "but actually we had a lot of competition in the early days." He described Mercado Libre's major rivalry with DeRemate, another Argentina-based auction site. A team of Harvard Business School graduates led by Alec Oxenford had founded DeRemate. Oxenford and his team, mostly former colleagues at Boston Consulting Group, took the lead in gaining consumer recognition in the region.[7]

The rivalry between Team Stanford and Team Harvard became intense. As Oxenford explained in a Harvard Business School case: "We were both excellent management teams—very different, yet alike at the same time. We were from HBS; they were from Stanford. The story of our competition was plagued with face-to-face encounters at industry conferences, at potential investor's offices—even on airplanes. Perhaps the most astounding and portentous co-incidence in all of this was when we held our launch parties on the very same day."[8]

DeRemate licensed technology from a European technology provider—this gave it a head start over Mercado Libre, which developed its own technology. But over time DeRemate found that being beholden to an inflexible technology was a disadvantage, while Mercado Libre was able to make localized modifications to serve its local market.[9]

When the Internet bubble burst in 2000, investment in the Internet slowed, but the battle to become the eBay of Latin America was still in full force. But another company was also interested in becoming the eBay of Latin America— eBay. In February 2001 eBay gained control of a leading auction site in Brazil, iBazar, when it acquired iBazar's Paris-based parent company, which also operated several European auction sites. During the dot-com boom, iBazar was valued at nearly $500 million. But it sold to eBay for just over $100 million in stock, with iBazar's CEO, François Grimaldi, telling the press, "We didn't find bidders to propose better conditions . . . with what has happened to Internet stocks, we now have to be reasonable."

After dipping its toe in South American waters, eBay was ready to search for a local partner by the fall of 2001. It came down to Mercado Libre and DeRemate. Given the pressure to find investors at the time, gaining a partnership with eBay was essentially a make-or-break proposition. For the winner it would mean vital funds and a partnership with the dominant e-commerce company. The loser would find attracting new investment difficult while facing an eBay-backed competitor in a down market.

The decision came down to a beauty pageant between Team Stanford and Team Harvard, which had a home field advantage because Meg Whitman, like Oxenford, is a Harvard Business School graduate. In the end Galperin was able to convince Whitman to switch sides in Latin America, even though Mercado Libre had fairly low transaction volumes. "With the volume we had at that time [2001], [eBay] told us that the decision was not about buying market share, that we were way too small for that. The decision was about which firm would be better positioned to capture the growing market in the future, and it was about fit with the management group—who eBay thought it could work with to be successful in Latin America."[10] As one executive told me, "Marcos is a great salesman."

EBay acquired a 19.5 percent ownership interest in Mercado Libre for an undisclosed amount. The deal gave Mercado Libre, which was still in the red, important funding, control of iBazar in Brazil, and a partnership with eBay, which was to share its best practices. EBay gained a foothold in the region while agreeing to not compete with Mercado Libre there for the next five years.

The eBay deal was a knockout blow for many of Mercado Libre's competitors. Mercado Libre began to swallow them, beginning with its 2002 acquisition of Lokau, a Brazilian auction site and strong competitor. Beginning in 2005 Mercado Libre acquired DeRemate in two stages at fire-sale prices.

In addressing the Latin American market, Mercado Libre found what other players in emerging markets also have found—the auction model did not fit developing countries at an early stage of e-commerce. Mercado Libre had set out to build an auction site modeled after eBay. But despite its best efforts to make auctions take off, Mercado Libre found that the majority of its clients were small entrepreneurs selling new products. Nobody wanted to wait around for the results of an auction. So Mercado Libre broke with the pure auction model and introduced a "Buy it now" feature. "We launched 'Buy it now' before eBay did because we thought it offered a better experience," Tolda explained. "What we learned from our sellers, and they were smarter than us, was if you start your auction at your buy-it-now price, you essentially had a fixed-price sale. For quite some time we lived with three types of listings, with 'auction,' 'buy it now,' and 'fixed price.' At some point we did away with 'buy it now' and just did auctions and fixed price." By 2004 auctions accounted for 67 percent of items sold on eBay, but only 14 percent of the items sold on Mercado Libre's sites were auctioned; the rest were fixed price.[11]

Mercado Libre also faced a quandary about which revenue model to use. In the early days the company relied heavily on banner ads for revenues, but eBay's model had been wildly successful in the United States because the company had found a way to charge both listing fees and transaction fees, achieving a "take rate" of about 7 percent on each eBay transaction. But eBay had a virtual monopoly. In Latin America the intense competition of the early days forced Mercado Libre and its biggest rivals to forgo listing fees. This meant they relied on transaction fees, most of which have low values, making the generation of money from these fees much more difficult. But when Mercado Libre began to acquire its competitors and see others die off, the company began to charge listing fees.

Mercado Libre differentiated itself from some of its counterparts in other emerging markets by concluding early that its revenue model would have to rely on innovations. In addition to the "Buy it now" feature, it introduced such features as allowing sellers to pay extra to highlight their listings or to use a boldface font for the item heading. It also allowed sellers to pay extra to have their product listings appear at the top of category lists and search results. These value-added feature fees accounted for 30 percent of Mercado Libre's revenue and have an interesting parallel in the pay-for-performance keyword ads that Taobao created half a world away. The message appeared to be similar—e-commerce merchants in emerging markets like to display their wares at a minimal cost and then have the option of paying extra for value-added listings. You could argue that this approach fits the sale of new products as it more resembles traditional retail and gives cost-conscious small sellers the opportunity to calibrate their costs and promotions to find the right revenue formula. Still, Mercado Libre's revenues were slow to take off. In 2002 the company generated only $1.7 million in revenue.[12]

By 2004, 57 percent of Mercado Libre's gross merchandise value (GMV) was coming from Brazil, 19 percent from Argentina, and 12 percent from Mexico. Colombia, Venezuela, Chile, Ecuador, Uruguay, and Peru contributed the remaining 12 percent. Its website closely resembled eBay's, down to the format, font, and colors. But Mercado Libre also made sure to introduce some homegrown features, such as buyer protection plans.[13]

It had initially seemed that the bulk of Mercado Libre's market might be in Argentina, where the company was founded. Argentina originally was the regional center for start-ups, but Brazilian e-commerce managed to take off sooner, aided by a larger population, greater banking penetration, and more Internet penetration. In Brazil "people didn't really see a start-up as something attractive ten years ago," Tolda explained. "Many young people looked for stability more than anything else, and they were more after [jobs in] typical investment banking, consulting and multinational companies. Others were looking for perhaps something even safer, with a career in the public service. There were not so many risk takers. I think that has changed. There are alternatives for people who want to take risks. In the past, if you were a businessperson in Brazil and were unsuccessful, there was a stigma and it was hard to do away with that. [The] Internet became cool, and failure became more acceptable, changing the culture."

Tolda added that the investment climate changed as well. "For many years it was safer for you to just buy Brazilian treasury bills and earn a nice return instead of investing capital in more risky ventures," he said. "That also changed over time, and today you do have a VC [venture capital] community here that supports those businesses." Despite its heavily regulated business climate, and interstate and intercity taxes levied on products moving from place to place, e-commerce did take off in Brazil, attracting investment and drawing in competitors such as online retailers Cnova and B2W and offline competitors such as Walmart. But Mercado Libre held its own and emerged as Brazil's Internet marketplace leader.[14]

"One thing that I found not only in Brazil but in all countries is that competition has helped us more than it has harmed us," Tolda said. "We are still at a fairly early stage of development, there is still enormous potential for e-commerce. As others, particularly those who have bricks-and-mortar businesses, identify the potential of selling online, they also drive new users to e-commerce. More than us competing with them for clients, what they have done is help in building this client base for e-commerce as a whole. I firmly believe that. If you look at e-commerce penetration for retail in Latin America, it ranges from 4 percent in Brazil to 2 percent in other countries. What Brazil has benefited from the most is that the retail sector as a whole caught on to e-commerce early on, and that has helped drive the business."

Argentina and Chile have followed paths similar to Brazil's. Other countries, particularly Mexico, have lagged. "The big question mark for us has been Mexico," Tolda said. "If you look at the potential on paper versus realized potential, there is a much bigger gap in Mexico than any other country. Brazil is bound to be our biggest market because it is the largest country with the largest population, with more economic potential for e-commerce. Mexico would naturally come second, but it doesn't—it's not the case. Argentina is bigger than Mexico. I think retail has been more conservative in Mexico, telecom access has been more expensive, and banking services are less penetrated."[15]

The remarkable thing about Mercado Libre is that it actually grew while its cousins Baazee (in India) and EachNet (in China)—other recipients of eBay funding—foundered. You could argue that because eBay only held a minority stake in Mercado Libre and never gained majority control, being independent of eBay's operational control was a blessing in disguise for Mercado Libre. From 2002 to 2008 Mercado Libre's annual revenues grew from $1.7 million to $135 million. This was when eBay was exerting operational control over its India and China subsidiaries only to see them sink. Meanwhile, Mercado Libre was able to customize its marketplace for the specific conditions of the emerging markets it served, innovating localized solutions to logistical and payment challenges. In 2003 it started Mercado Pago, a payment platform. It customized the service so that people could buy on credit and installments, a common consumer expectation in Latin American retail. It also grew its platform in a way that favored small B2C sellers using fixed-price sales rather than auctions, which simply didn't work in developing countries.

Mercado Libre's independence from eBay was not always a given. When making its initial investment in Mercado Libre, eBay was no doubt pursuing the model it had used in many markets—make a small investment in a market leader, watch its development, and then buy the whole company. And in fact eBay and Mercado Libre circled around this several times, but they could never agree on price. "We thoroughly enjoy what we are doing, and if we were part of a bigger company, that might not be the case," Tolda said. "EBay used to be a golden standard, and it's certainly not the case for us now. We even feel a twinge of sadness to think of what eBay is now, compared to what it was in the past. In hindsight we are happy with the decisions that we have made along the way. There's a saying in Spanish: 'It's better to be the head of a rat than the tail of a lion.' "

When negotiations with eBay fell through, Galperin decided to flex Mercado Libre's muscle and go another route—take the company public on Nasdaq. In August 2007 Mercado held its IPO, which doubled in price on the first day and reached a valuation of $1.6 billion. It was a major milestone for Mercado Libre and the Internet in Latin America, and it made the company something of a role model for entrepreneurs in the region. The company had shown that an Internet start-up in Argentina could go public and that a company from outside Brazil could become a market leader in Brazil's notoriously insular market, one that marketing plans often skip because of Brazil's language (Portuguese, not Spanish), culture, and protectionist barriers.

Since its IPO, Mercado Libre has weathered the global financial crisis, which saw its stock drop to a fraction of its post-IPO peak, then rebound and steadily rise during the past few years. The company has continued to expand through several acquisitions and started its AdSales platform as well as a logistics platform, Mercado Envios, further extending the company's ecosystem.

The company sets as its mission "democratizing capitalism" and has taken the approach of building an "enhanced marketplace" that encompasses marketplaces, payment, and logistics. Mercado Libre rolls these different elements out in new markets when they are ready. For example, in Brazil the company has C2C for individuals, B2C for small retailers, and B2C for large retailers and brands. Its Mercado Pago and Mercado Envios logistics services complete the loop.

Sean Summers, who runs the marketplace, explains: "For everything we do, we have a platform that works across markets. The only thing that changes is the level of sophistication or development."[16] The one area Mercado Libre won't go into—but its competitors do—is buying and selling its own inventory alongside the merchants in its marketplace.

One major new initiative for Mercado Libre is brand stores. Much like Tmall, Mercado Libre's major goal is to attract new vendor segments such as brands, manufacturers, and large retail to create a premium, curated marketplace. The company didn't feel the need to establish a separate environment like Tmall because South America does not have quite the problem of fake goods that China does. Rather, Mercado Libre wants to expand from a simple flea market to a shiny shopping mall within the same website.

As of 2015, Mercado Libre's major priorities were to drive payment growth both on and off its marketplace, expand its services on mobile platforms, and drive adoption of the shipping services offered through Mercado Envios on the way to building a complete logistics environment. In addition, Mercado Libre building out a developer's ecosystem on top of its open platform, with the goal of unleashing external innovation by third-party service providers who can innovate and sell additional services on its platform. Over time Mercado Libre plans to expand into markets that now are too difficult to serve because they are so small.

Because it operates a pure marketplace, Mercado Libre has a head start on payments in the region. Mercado Pago at first simply facilitated transactions on the Mercado Libre marketplace and then introduced services allowing third-party merchants to accept Mercado Pago payments outside of the Mercado Libre marketplace. They have been pushing more into mobile payments and offer mobile point-of-sale (POS) payment options. And as I noted earlier, Mercado Libre offers financing, an important feature in Latin America that includes installment sales. The company estimates about 65 percent of total Brazilian retail purchases are made using credit financing, whereas on Mercado Pago about 75 percent are made this way. These types of financed payments are particularly important in high-inflation environments. If it takes cues from PayPal and Ant Financial, Mercado Pago could grow into much more than a payment platform; it could become a large financial service business. "The vision for Mercado Pago is huge and it can be enormous," an executive said.

Mercado Libre's vision of its core business has been evolving from that of a marketplace to that of e-commerce facilitator. And the goods it carries have evolved from mostly electronics to a broad general selection of merchandise. At the same time it is bringing in more small and medium-sized businesses and large retailers, rather than just hobby sellers.

Mercado Libre estimates that about half of Latin America's 600 million people are Internet users. Of those, two-thirds are online shoppers, showing a high penetration. About 50 percent of Mercado Libre's revenue still comes from Brazil, but other Latin American markets are accounting for bigger percentages of its revenue, with Argentina accounting for 30 percent; Mexico, 8 percent; Venezuela, 7 percent; and the rest of Latin America, 6 percent. With 121 million registered users, Mercado Libre estimates that 28 percent of Latin American Internet users access Mercado Libre every month and that 155,000 people make a living by selling on Mercado Libre. Its key metrics of GMV are growing at the healthy rate of 25 percent a year.[17]

After my day of meetings, my impression was that Mercado Libre is run by a strong team. It reminded me of my days at Alibaba. Everyone seemed to be on the same page, had admirable goals, and the company had a friendly, down-to-earth culture. It was no surprise to me that Mercado Libre has won awards in the region for being a great place to work.

"I think I would have a hard time finding a group of people where I would enjoy the culture as much as I do here," Tolda said. "We have a passion for what we do. We like changing the world. That sounds kind of trite and too big of a goal, but when we started sixteen years ago, the stuff we had to do seems very basic. It's a new world and we've been a part of making this new world. . . . As a marketplace we have changed the lives of sellers tremendously. There are a number of entrepreneurs who got their first entrepreneurial experiences with the shops they started on Mercado Libre."[18]

Mercado Libre's assessment of why e-commerce hasn't taken off in Latin America as much as it should made sense to me. But I couldn't help wondering whether the company perhaps needed to inject e-commerce with a more urgent sense of innovation and revolutionary spirit. Compared with the websites of its Asian counterparts, Mercado Libre's website seemed a bit stale, not really a reflection of the vibrant spirit of the small and medium-sized entrepreneurs it serves. It also wasn't interactive, so people could not chat in real time, despite a culture mad for connectivity and a tradition of haggling. Whereas Asian e-commerce companies were allowing a rich graphic and multimedia branding experience for brands with storefronts on their sites, Mercado Libre offered little beyond the chance to post products with text. Although I had just parachuted into Latin America, it seemed to me their team was missing an opportunity.

Could it be that Mercado Libre's growth was sandbagged by its closeness to the US market, that it clung too heavily to its US role models for inspiration, rather than designing more robust marketplaces that meet local conditions? Could being a public company and having the concomitant investor pressure have somehow diminished the company's taste for taking bold risks? Members of its team alluded to a time when that was the case, and I couldn't help but think they could be doing more.

The good news for Mercado Libre was that e-commerce was reaching a turning point. As in Asia, the mobile phone was providing the breakthrough that e-commerce needed in the region. By 2014 mobile purchases were accounting for 16 percent of the company's GMV. Mobile was a powerful enough force to overcome the economic downturn in many markets by putting a new tool in the hands of shoppers and entrepreneurs alike. This was accelerating the growth of e-commerce and attracting new investors and competitors. Mercado Libre's one-time partner, eBay, was growing in the market—expanding into the region without the limitations of a noncompete agreement with Mercado Libre, because it had expired several years before. Amazon also was beginning to grow in the region. Alibaba's AliExpress was making inroads. And Galperin's former rival, Alec Oxenford of DeRemate, had started the classifieds site OLX, which was expanding in the region.

Most important, up in Mexico City, another company was aggressively moving into the region and lighting a fire under Mercado Libre—Rocket Internet, with its Latin American e-commerce operation, Linio. Not since Mercado Libre's early days had another company made such an aggressive attempt to build a region-wide e-commerce marketplace. Could Rocket take on such an established player? I headed to Mexico City to meet with the Linio team and see what I could find out.

MEXICO

I've visited quite a few markets in my time, but none quite like La Merced Market in the heart of Mexico City. One of several hundred in the city, the market has been in existence since the colonial period (1521–1810), catering to merchants who congregated on the edges of the city's historic center to trade goods from around

Mexico and the rest of New Spain. In the 1860s the government established a permanent market in the area, and in the last century and a half it has become the largest traditional retail food market in Mexico City.

I walked through La Merced Market to get a sense of how Mexicans have traded for centuries. Filling buildings that span the space of several football fields, the market is like a fireworks show of bright colors, sights, sounds, and smells. Vendors themselves are almost hidden, sitting behind their neatly stacked pyramids of limes and corn, with large Mexican flags hanging from the ceiling over their heads. Other sections of the market are home to piles and piles of green, orange, and red peppers. Anchos. Jalapenos. Habaneros. My mouth would have been watering if a peppery mist hadn't been stinging my eyes—the revenge of peppers that had fallen into the aisles and gotten crushed by the feet of shoppers and the carts pushed by laborers.

Walk a full city block and you leave the produce section, then enter the meat and dairy section, where plucked chickens hang from hooks and men push wheelbarrows piled high with butchered cows' heads. (This market is not for the faint of heart—or stomach.)

Next is the toy section, where vendors sell toy tarantulas, Christmas ornaments, and colorful Disney piñatas, some with smiles and others with scared expressions, seemingly aware of their fate. On the perimeter of the market, where the official market ends, small vendors hoping to sell to passersby tend makeshift stalls covered in brightly colored plastic tarps. Although officially not allowed, they are tolerated for the price of a small bribe to the officials overseeing the market.

The offline marketplaces in Mexico City all have the main characteristic of the floating markets in the Bangkok canals or the souks of Mumbai—a raw entrepreneurial energy. The vendors are driven more by the need to survive than a passion for building a business, but I have found this usually translates into a healthy and vibrant online marketplace.

So why have online marketplaces thus far been unable to tap the potential of Mexico's 122 million consumers? With the US e-commerce boom just across its northern border, wouldn't Latin America's second-most-populous country be a natural place for e-commerce to grow? Although Mexico has one of the fastest-growing economies in Latin America, e-commerce accounts for only about $4 billion of the nation's $200 billion in annual retail sales.[19] That's less than Alibaba sold in the first ninety minutes of its 2015 Singles' Day sale. Might that be about to change?

Early signs are good. Internet penetration is on the rise, a consequence of smartphone penetration. More than half of Mexicans older than six use the Internet, and 85 percent of those Internet users use social networks. However, only about a quarter of Internet users shop online.[20]

After strolling the markets, I headed to the regional headquarters of Linio, Rocket Internet's answer to Amazon.com in the region. Rocket Internet started Linio in 2012 and has since spun it off into an independently run company. While Rocket remains the largest shareholder, Linio has attracted additional investors, including Kinnevik, J. P. Morgan, and Holtzbrinck. The company is focused on Spanish-speaking Latin America, and when I visited Linio in the fall of 2015, it had already expanded to eight Latin American countries with plans to enter four more markets in the region. Linio estimated that its combined addressable market constituted the fifth-largest economy in the world, and claimed to have become the "most-visited multi-category e-commerce company addressing major Spanish-speaking Latin American countries, namely Colombia, Mexico, Peru, Venezuela, Chile, Panama, Argentina and Ecuador." Linio saw a revenue opportunity of $13 billion in the next five years, assuming it could capture 25 percent of the market.[21]

Linio claims to have 30 percent of all traffic to e-commerce sites in Spanish Latin America, just behind AliExpress. Not surprisingly, Mercado Libre disputes this ranking, saying that Linio is using a definition that excludes Mercado Libre. Sean Summers of Mercado Libre said, "It's a lot of bullshit marketing. . . . I think it's a lot of PR, which comes with the fact that they are raising a round of financing." Summers described Linio's approach as "Let's just ignore that Mercado Libre exists and then say, 'I am the biggest.' [Linio] is the tallest midget."[22]

It's a growing rivalry that didn't start off that way. Mercado Libre modeled itself after eBay; Linio started off, like its cousins Lazada in Southeast Asia and Jumia in Africa, as a small Amazon. Linio started as a pure online direct retailer, operating its own warehouses. Over time it has become what it calls a "controlled marketplace" with control of all aspects of the experience, including logistics and fulfillment. In a sense it is trying to mash together all the characteristics of various marketplaces in other countries. Like Amazon and Jingdong, it controls the supply chain. Like Tmall and Amazon, it allows others to sell on its platform. Like Amazon, it offers fulfillment. Like Alipay and PayPal, it offers financing. It controls every facet of the purchase and fulfillment process, and it sees this as differentiating itself from an eBay or Mercado Libre. And to extend its reach to new categories, it is even adding a grocery arm.

Linio's headquarters is located in the leafy commercial district of Mexico City. Outside the company's offices, steam rises from taco stands while guitar players serenade sidewalk diners. It's a reminder that, despite the reputation for drug violence and kidnappings that Mexico has gained in recent years, life—and business—goes on.

Linio's offices felt much more like those of a start-up than do those of its primary competitor, Mercado Libre. Aside from bright orange plastic "Linio" letters that fill up the office lobby, interior decorating seems to have taken backseat to moving and executing quickly in typically Rocket Internet style. In some ways it was a good sign—the team hadn't gotten too comfortable.

I met with Andreas Mjelde, CEO of the company. Dressed in a white T-shirt, dark pants, and white tennis shoes, he looked more like the dot-com entrepreneur he had become than the McKinsey consultant he used to be. He fit the profile and pedigree of a typical

Rocket CEO. I asked him how he liked the change from consulting to a start-up, and he told me, "It was amazing. Getting my hands dirty and doing real work and solving problems on a day-to-day basis. One exciting thing about e-commerce is that you see almost instantaneous results. That's 180 degrees from a McKinsey project." Mjelde joined the company in 2012 as a cofounder. He had originally intended to start an e-commerce company in the Nordic countries and got in touch with Oliver Samwer to discuss working together. Samwer convinced him to go into emerging markets, which offered more opportunities than the more mature Nordic markets. Oliver had asked Mjelde if he'd be interested in moving to Africa, Asia, or Latin America. Using consultant-speak, Mjelde explained how he arrived at his decision:

"For me, it was very simple logic. E-commerce is driven by retail. Retail is driven by the size of the economy and GDP, more specifically, disposable income. What was interesting about Mexico as a starting point for looking at Spanish LATAM [Latin America] is that it's actually a really big economy. If you look at Spanish LATAM, it would be the fifth-biggest economy in the world and growing faster than the number three and four, which is Japan and Germany."

Mjelde argued that the lack of physical retail in Latin America suggested that the potential for e-commerce in the region might ultimately be greater than in today's leading e-commerce markets. "In the US you've got forty-six square feet built out per capita. China is about eleven and a half. In LATAM it's two square feet per capita. So [the United States has] twenty times more retail . . . than what it is in LATAM. In terms of long-term potential, you should see that e-commerce should have a higher share of total retail."

Perhaps, I said, but why has it taken so long to take off?

"People have tried e-commerce several times in Mexico. There was a first round of people trying in the late nineties. A second round seven or eight years ago. And now the third round started around 2011 to 2013." With the first round, Mjelde said, the dot-com boom ended before Latin America had attracted much investment, so it never really got the support it needed. The second round was stifled by underdeveloped infrastructure, with one telecom company, Telmex, that was comfortable making margins of 60 percent to 80 percent as a national monopoly. Cell phones were not popular because cell phone service was a monopoly. But in 2012 the government broke the monopoly on fixed lines and cell phones. This led to greater penetration of the Internet as access increased and prices came down. As a result, "It's quite affordable now to have Internet both on the phone and fixed lines," Mjelde said.[23]

Another important front was logistics. Mexico had poor logistics coverage. But in recent years major players such as DHL and FedEx have gotten more aggressive there. The resulting competition has made logistics better.

Another factor, according to Mjelde, was a simple twist of the business model. "We went into the market and learned from what has worked in India and China and offered cash on delivery. I don't know why, but others didn't try to offer that before," Mjelde said, adding that he surmises that perhaps the local companies were too focused on doing what had worked in the United States. Offering COD was a key breakthrough that not only overcame the lack of trust but also addressed the problem that few people in Mexico have bank accounts.

In addition to offering COD, Linio and its peers have helped bridge the payment gap by allowing payments at the convenience store chain OXXO's thirteen thousand stores across the country. Customers print out a bar code, scan, and pay for the product at an OXXO market. While this is not a perfect solution, it's helped bridge a gap and solved a critical problem in the ecosystem. "It's important that the ecosystem around you is growing," Mjelde said. "Now we can see that it is really happening."[24]

One complaint I'd heard about Linio from a former country manager was that hardly anyone within the company ever spoke about values or a higher goal of some kind. Mercado Libre speaks in terms more familiar to Silicon Valley types, about a vision of helping change society. "Our mission is to democratize e-commerce" and "change the lives of millions of buyers and sellers in Latin America," Galperin has said.[25] I asked Mjelde what Linio's vision is, and he offered something somewhat less poetic: "Our long-term vision is to be the biggest provider of products for retail in the region, both online and offline."

To be fair, successful companies don't always start with an altruistic, world-changing ideal as their original goal, so I kept an open mind as he went on. "Latin America is characterized by high prices, because of high taxes. Also, if you talk to any brand out there, the price they set [for] LATAM is . . . higher . . . than the one they set for Europe, the US, and Asia. This has been a bit of a milking ground for many manufacturers. Prices are traditionally quite high, and then the second thing is that there is very little availability of products. You have decent availability in Mexico City, [but] the moment you go out to a tier-two city the options for shopping are very poor. And that's where we see the excitement of Linio. There is absolutely no reason why a person living in Vera Cruz should pay more than a person living in Miami, and you should be able to get the same products."

Linio's business model has shifted over time. "We held on to [a retail model] a bit too long," Mjelde said. "We always knew that marketplace would be important. But we thought it might be a fifty-fifty business. . . . I would expect that the business could one day be 80 percent marketplace or even 100 percent."

The company's expansion in the region proceeded in typical Rocket fashion—throw what you can at the wall and see what sticks. Mjelde said he thinks Rocket may have moved into too many new markets too quickly with its all-out strategy, without enough prioritizing. "We went quite aggressive in all of them. I think you also sometimes have to accept that some markets have a much higher growth potential than others. It's a huge region," he said. "To fly from here to Argentina is an eleven-hour flight. While people all speak the same languages and have roughly the same culture, there are a lot of nuances. In Mexico they have a brand culture. In Colombia they are not brand oriented, but they are deal oriented. In Peru there is no logistics industry, so there are fewer opportunities to push and scale the business up from scratch. In Argentina the market is more mature, so rather than focusing on every vertical out there, we needed to focus on certain product categories," such as books, which, surprisingly, have been a market underserved online. Buenos Aires has more physical bookstores per capita than anywhere in the world, which highlights the demand for books in the city and might suggest that there is an opportunity for online booksellers to undercut their physical counterparts by selling books online at a discount.

So why did Linio stick to Spanish-speaking Latin America and not enter Brazil?

Mjelde cited several reasons. The Brazilian market is much more mature, with more competition from strong local players, such as B2W. Taxes and regulations are complex with many different tax regions. And logistics are tough.

When I asked Mjelde about the differences between Latin America and other parts of the world, one thing that stood out was the importance of financing. "One thing that is very important in LATAM, maybe more so than in both Asia and Africa, is to have a financing arm. When you see the traditional retailers, you'll see that their financing arm is extremely strong. That might be as important a competitive edge as the stores themselves or product assortment or pricing. And that's something most e-commerce companies don't have as a core part of their value proposition. That's something we didn't initially plan to do, but it's becoming a core part of the business." To help serve this need, Linio introduced cobranded credit cards, and Mjelde expects the financing arm of the business to keep growing.

Does Linio see a big opportunity in moving into online financial services? "You have to take baby steps. . . . I don't know if that's where we're going to go," he said. "But I think we have to keep those options open." In fact, retail operations in the region often own a bank, so I expect online retailers in Latin America will make big moves into online banking.

So how about competition in the region?

"I'm not losing my sleep for the local retailers moving online. But the international players are tough competition. Not so much for the fact that they are going to move into the markets here. . . . We are seeing that Amazon and eBay already have operations on the ground in Mexico. It's not that easy for them," Mjelde said. "They are a big monster, and this little team they have in Mexico does not get that much attention or IT resources. . . . Since both of them entered the market, if anything, we have been innovating faster than they are." But the real issue is competition from cross-border trade, that is, Mexicans who buy products from overseas online retailers. "The [tax] legislation is not in favor of local companies [such as Linio]. The legislation is in favor of Amazon," Mjelde argued.

But Mjelde conceded cross-border trades also offer Linio an opportunity. Cross-border trade has become an important niche for the company, perhaps showing signs of being a new trend. Cross-border trade is one reason that AliExpress has become an important player in Latin America, one of the most used marketplaces in the region. "Now almost 20 percent of the business is international marketplace," Mjelde said. "We are finally in the position that we can offer you the Chinese price of the product, and we can soon offer you the same assortment. And that's a big game changer for people."

Mjelde didn't say much about Mercado Libre. Either he doesn't view it as a direct competitor or prefers not to point out the publicly listed elephant in the room. But the Mercado Libre folks had no reservations about taking a jab. An executive at Mercado Libre told me that, at Linio, "I see a very smart bunch of guys. They are incredibly aggressive and I respect that. I respect their determination. But they haven't proven they can build a sustainable business in the region."[26]

The trash talking could be a sign of things to come, as the two companies' business models merge. Mercado Libre has the benefit of being a publicly listed company with a long track record. But it also has the disadvantage of being a publicly listed company with a long track record. Linio can benefit from being able to build a platform from scratch without the encumbrances that come with a legacy business.

There can be no doubt that Linio and Mercado Libre will butt heads, and other competitors will join the battle soon as e-commerce accelerates. And as it does, large markets that have been off the radar, such as Mexico, will increasingly be in the spotlight.

Another market to watch is Colombia. Although Brazil has struggled in recent years and Venezuela is coming apart at the seams, Colombia is proving to be a bright spot in the region. Two years after I was mugged in Bogotá, I returned to the country, again as a guest of the government, this time the Ministry of Commerce. It was exciting to see the change there. On my first visit I was told that "we don't have e-commerce here, people don't really trust each other." Now the story was entirely different.

One of my hosts in the country was effusive in discussing how e-commerce has changed her whole life. "I buy everything online now," she said. "Clothes, groceries, tickets. It's so fun. And saves me so much time." She walked me through her favorite app, Rappi, developed by local entrepreneurs who also happened to be her friends. It was one of the most innovative and fun shopping apps I'd seen. You shop for groceries and other items on the app by lifting products to add to your virtual shopping basket, the best replication of the actual shopping experience that I'd ever seen. Choosing from colorful mangos, soursops, and coconuts piled in nice virtual stacks and dragging them to the scale felt more like shopping at the Merced Market than on a somewhat boring and dry Amazon platform. The homegrown app had done so well that Rappi has been exported to other countries, even for use in Spain.

Even more interesting is that it was solving the security problem in the city, finding opportunity in the face of problems. "When

I'm in a rush or don't want to go out to use an ATM at night, I even order cash on the app," which is hand-delivered by a courier, my host told me. Yes, you could pay digitally for a stack of pesos to be delivered to your door (by someone dressed discreetly, of course, so as not to attract attention from muggers).

Can it be that Colombia is ready to unleash its e-commerce potential? After a long wait, it seems the revolution is finally beginning to happen.

TRENDS AND PREDICTIONS

Latin America is (finally) on the verge of an e-commerce boom
It's hard to believe how slow Latin America's e-commerce development has been, considering that the region sits at the doorstep of the United States. You would think that Latin America's proximity to Silicon Valley would have sparked a greater degree of e-commerce growth, if only from the cross-fertilization of ideas. But e-commerce's golden era in emerging markets started across the oceans in Asia.

With the exception of Brazil, where e-commerce has enjoyed its own miniboom, Latin America's e-commerce has been held back by several factors. Government regulations and industry protectionism mean the Internet has not become as widely available and affordable as in, say, China and Southeast Asia. Latin America has also suffered from a more conservative investment culture in regard to start-ups, because many of the large investors are conglomerates or traditional businesses that apply "old economy" metrics to "new economy" businesses.

An additional factor is the lack of diversity at Silicon Valley companies. Although Asians make up 30 to 40 percent of the employee base of the tech giants in the United States, Hispanics account for only 4 to 5 percent of the employee base at such companies as Google, Microsoft, Yahoo, and LinkedIn.[27] The sharing of US know-how and tech experience by the Indian, Chinese, and Southeast Asian diasporas is largely responsible for the e-commerce boom in Asia. Without strong Hispanic representation in Silicon Valley's tech management ranks, ideas have taken longer to spread from the US tech giants to the local start-ups throughout Latin America.

These problems will be overcome in the next few years as e-commerce finally reaches its potential in Latin America. As in Asia, smartphone penetration will be the key driver, putting a shopping mall in the hands of Latin Americans for the first time. Entrepreneurs will continue to study new business models from Asia and adapt them to Latin America, creating a better fit for developing countries than models taken from the shelves of the United States. Seeing the potential, the tech-oriented venture capitalists and private equity funds will at last give Latin America's entrepreneurs the resources they need, fueling investment that will drive the ecosystem.

E-commerce will power through Brazil's recession
If we learned one lesson in China, it is that e-commerce is resilient in the face of macroeconomic headwinds and generally outperforms the broader economy. Yes, strong economic growth provides a nice tailwind for e-commerce. But it also breeds complacency, as traditional retailers fail to innovate while consumers are spending. But when tough times come, consumers start looking for deals as a way to stretch their budget, and the best deals are always online.

Even major crises, such as the spread of the Zika virus, create needs and opportunities for entrepreneurs to fulfill. When SARS hit China, people were afraid to do business face-to-face, and e-commerce accelerated as buyers and sellers moved their shopping activities online. So, while Brazil has seen its fortunes rise and fall with the volatility characteristic of emerging markets, e-commerce should continue to grow steadily over the long term.

Mexico has emerged as the most exciting e-commerce opportunity in Latin America
Whether you are building an e-commerce platform, looking to extend a brand beyond traditional retail channels, or are an entrepreneur looking for a new market, Mexico is the country to watch for

the next few years. With 122.3 million largely untapped shoppers gaining access to the Internet through their smartphones for the first time, the country is a bright spot, despite the question marks about the impact on its economy of a Trump presidency in the United States. Mexican shoppers will be easier to reach than ever before, through cross-border platforms such as Amazon.com or local platforms such as Linio and Mercado Libre.

Argentina is a close second for e-commerce opportunity

With a new government in place that advocates business-friendly reforms, Argentina's fortunes look like they are about to improve, and e-commerce should be one of the greatest beneficiaries. For years currency controls and tight regulation of imports have hampered e-commerce there. But with the pendulum now swinging toward the pro-business side of the spectrum, Argentina's e-commerce industry has a chance to bounce back and catch up with its neighbor and rival across the border, Brazil.

Colombia is an early-stage e-commerce powerhouse on the verge of liftoff

Latin America's third-most-populous country is at last poised for an e-commerce boom following the peace deal between the Colombian government and FARC (the Revolutionary Armed Forces of Colombia). If the peace holds, a more stable Colombia could bring economic stability and attract more venture capital. With a highly entrepreneurial culture and consumers hungry for a better life after years of stagnation, new ideas may take hold in Colombia faster than in other Latin American countries. And, yes, the security issues in Colombia can be overcome, so long as entrepreneurs embrace the opportunity to come up with localized solutions rather than wait for someone else to address security problems.

8

AFRICA—THE FINAL FRONTIER

IT WAS NOT THE FIRST UNSOLICITED EMAIL I'D RECEIVED FROM
Nigeria but the first I considered answering.

"I'm running an e-commerce company here in Nigeria. How
can we see your film about Alibaba here in Lagos?" wrote the
stranger.

"It's not available there now, but if you cover my travel ex-
penses, I'll fly over and do a screening with a Q&A," I responded.

"Really? We can do that. I'll put you in touch with my team to
work out the details."

When the initial excitement of traveling to a new country wore
off, I felt slightly uneasy, not sure what I'd signed up for. Like many
people, my only digital contact with Nigeria up to this point had
been requests to hand over my life savings to the family member of
a deceased Nigerian prince in exchange for the deed to a gold mine.
Was this email from Lagos for real? Or was it a complicated scam?

After some quick Googling, I was pleased to learn that, no, this
was not a scammer in a Lagos Internet cafe. It was Sim Shagaya,
founder and CEO of Konga.com. I'd never heard of Konga, so I
reached out to a friend who was connected with Sim on LinkedIn.

"Yes. Sim is a superstar," my friend said. "Really good guy—humble, super smart, driven, great reputation. We were classmates at Harvard Business School. His vision is to build his company Konga into Amazon for Africa."

A few months later I was boarding a plane from Houston to Lagos. The flight was packed with US oil executives visiting their Nigerian operations and Nigerian expats headed home to their families, with bags of American swag crammed in the overhead bins.

As we flew into Murtala Muhammed International Airport, we passed over the urban sprawl of Lagos, mostly one-story structures with patched tin roofs and intersecting dusty dirt roads, their red sand kicked up by yellow minibuses and motorcycles. As I disembarked the plane, a man with a Konga sign greeted me at the gate. He walked me to the immigration desks, where Nigeria's infamous corruption was immediately in evidence. While others waited in a long line, my escort walked me up to one desk, talked to the man there, and got me through. My companion turned out to be an agent whose main job is to whisk people through the line. Within the immigration area there were a number of such agents who helped people through the line, undoubtedly providing kickbacks to the immigration officers (other visitors I spoke to during the trip reported frequent shakedowns for bribes from the immigration officers when they entered without such escorts).

Outside immigration, my escort handed me off to the driver who had come to pick me up. As the sun was beginning to set, we drove down the highway past flaming piles of trash. Nigeria appeared to be a classic developing country, where everyone is an entrepreneur—I saw row after row of small, makeshift mom-and-pop shops, and men selling bottles of water, snacks, and trinkets to cars at stoplights. At major intersections stood police with AK-47s.

In its explicit poverty, Nigeria was much like India. Nowhere was this poverty more apparent than the Third Mainland Bridge, which hovers above the Makoko slum, an informal settlement of thousands of stilted shacks in the Lagos Lagoon. Residents paddle through canals and waterways to sell items from their dugout canoes in one of the world's largest floating cities, not unlike what I knew from the canals of Bangkok. On the edge of the lagoon, children pick through a giant, smoking trash heap.

This is the legacy of colonialism: a country with ineffective institutions. With an export economy 95 percent dependent on oil, Nigeria has suffered the so-called curse of resources, widespread corruption.

This corruption infiltrates all areas of life, making one of the key building blocks of e-commerce—trust—harder to achieve than in perhaps any other region of the world. I first encountered this while managing the website operations of Alibaba.com. The scams coming from Nigeria were so constant and voluminous that we briefly considered banning Nigerians from membership altogether before dismissing the idea as unfair.

But Nigeria's corruption goes beyond phishing. In his 2007 book *A Culture of Corruption: Everyday Deception and Popular Discontent in Nigeria*, Daniel Jordan Smith describes students bribing teachers, police extorting bribes at checkpoints, charlatans scamming patients with fake drugs, wives conning husbands, and gangs of youth shaking down minibus drivers. It's not uncommon to see THIS PROPERTY NOT FOR SALE painted on the outside of buildings, because Nigeria has a long tradition of people selling real estate that is not actually on the market.

Yet despite the struggles of day-to-day life, Nigerians consistently top worldwide polls for happiness and optimism. In just a few hours on the ground there, you can feel the abundant laughter and smiles, and the outside perceptions of Nigeria give way to a much warmer and happier reality. And in early 2014 this optimism took firm root in e-commerce, which had attracted hundreds of millions of dollars of investment after years of being ignored. Was Africa, and Nigeria in particular, on the verge of an e-commerce golden era?

If there was going to be a boom, Nigeria was the logical place. With 173 million people, Nigeria is Africa's most populous country and by some definitions has the largest economy in Africa, surpassing South Africa's. As the headquarters of the Economic Community of West African States, it is also the gateway to a trading bloc of fifteen countries, from Benin to Togo, with a population of 340 million people.

The popularity of mobile Internet increased the percentage of Nigerians online from 20 percent in 2009 to 41 percent in 2014. The middle class was growing fast, and it had a taste for international brands. With all the foreign investment, e-commerce in Nigeria was on the verge of surpassing $500 million in 2014—a low figure, but a sign of life.

Perhaps more important was the striking lack of organized physical retail: 98 percent of retail sales in Nigeria and Cameroon occur in small, local, and informal outlets and mom-and-pop shops. The figures are 96 percent in Ghana and 70 percent in Kenya. (As with many things, South Africa is an anomaly, with 60 percent of total retail sales occurring in formal retail shops.) Throughout the continent, 90 percent of the $823 billion in annual transactions in Africa are made through informal channels.[1]

And the organized retail that does exist leaves much to be desired. One of the malls most popular with the elites of Lagos, the Palms Shopping Center, is falling apart and takes an hour to reach by waiting in traffic on a small two-lane road. Although South African grocery chains are beginning to make some inroads in Nigeria, poor roads and infrastructure have hampered their growth.

My first conversation with Stanley, the driver I'd been assigned, made it clear that Nigeria was ready for e-commerce. When he found out I'd previously worked at Alibaba, he pointed at his jeans and said, "Really? I bought these jeans on AliExpress."

He'd had them sent from China to Nigeria? Why? I asked. Aren't lots of jeans available here in Lagos?

"Yes, but these are much cheaper," he told me. "I had to wait a few weeks but they arrived and are fine. I even bought a computer on AliExpress. Unfortunately, the guys cheated me. But AliExpress gave me my money back." He seemed unfazed. Stanley was even beginning to think about starting his own business, exporting kola nuts online. He asked for my advice, and although I'd never been in the market for kola nuts, I encouraged him.

When I arrived at the Southern Sun hotel, it was clear that the economy was booming. Located on the island of Ikoyi, on the more foreign and elite side of Lagos, Southern Sun was an average hotel by international standards. The hallways were dilapidated and rooms small. Yet the rate was more than $500 per night, driven up by a recent surge of investors visiting the city. And with Boko Haram raging in the countryside, it was comforting to know that two guards toting AK-47s stood outside the main gate.

As I was plugging in my computer, the power went out. Not just in the hotel but in the whole city. The lights flicked on and off all night long, which begged the question: Is it possible to run an e-commerce company without the *e*?

But that hadn't stopped African entrepreneurs from trying. One of the earliest e-commerce companies, which survives to this day, is the South African auction marketplace Bidorbuy. The company was founded in 1999 and, like so many e-commerce companies of the time, was modeled on eBay. Andy Higgins, the founder, was living in London and helping to roll out several auction sites in Europe when he was contacted by investors eager to start an eBay for Africa in his native South Africa. He did and soon expanded his marketplace internationally, creating a series of marketplaces from Australia to India. The dot-com crash brought Bidorbuy back to Earth, forcing Higgins to shut down most of his marketplaces and cut his staff to him and one other person.

Higgins did manage to sell off his India operations to a local competitor, Baazee. And he decided to do the bare minimum to keep Bidorbuy afloat, running the business while pursuing an MBA. The company managed to survive and by 2010 had grown to more than 1.1 million unique visitors a month, with a GMV of $2 million per month.[2] Still, even with his surviving foothold and perhaps the best e-commerce opportunity (on paper), e-commerce represented only about 0.59 percent of total retail sales in South Africa in 2014.[3]

Far up the coast from South Africa was one of the continent's most celebrated success stories, Kenya. With the fourth-largest economy in sub-Saharan Africa and a population of 44 million people, Kenya is often touted as the third-most-attractive e-commerce market in sub-Saharan Africa, behind Nigeria and South Africa. Its most remarkable contribution to e-commerce on the continent is the payment system pioneered by M-Pesa.

Safaricom, Kenya's largest mobile network operator, started M-Pesa in 2007 as a way to allow small entrepreneurs to repay their microfinance loans by phone. By 2013 two thirds of the country's adult population was using it, with transaction volumes equaling 25 percent of Kenya's GNP.[4] The service was so successful that it quickly expanded beyond loan repayments to become a mobile payment platform. Users fund their accounts and make withdrawals by visiting Safaricom's more than forty thousand agents. Its growth accelerated when elections turned violent in 2008 and Kenyans became skeptical of banks; they saw M-Pesa as a secure way to send money to friends and relatives trapped in Nairobi's slums.

Over time, M-Pesa expanded far beyond mobile money transfers and is evolving into banking services. In cooperation with its banking partners, it now extends loans to individuals and small businesses, using the threat of discontinuing phone service to discourage loan defaults. By 2013 it had accumulated about $50 million in savings and had extended about 300,000 small loans, averaging $12. That was nowhere near the $92 billion that Alibaba raised from people investing in Alipay's money market savings accounts but a start nonetheless. Based on its success in Africa, Safaricom was taking its model to other emerging markets, including those in India, Tanzania, and Afghanistan. While it faced the challenges all e-payment systems confront—people trying to use them for money laundering and fraud—Safaricom's success shows that e-commerce in Africa will be mobile. And it is a rare example of an e-payment system that preceded e-retail.

But in terms of financial payout, perhaps the greatest e-commerce success story in Africa belongs to the South African media conglomerate Naspers, known more for its investment in China than in Africa. Founded in 1915 as a publisher and printer of newspapers and magazines, the company grew into a media and pay-TV conglomerate. Naspers has been widely criticized for not opposing—and even occasionally supporting—apartheid in South Africa, a controversy it tried to move beyond in 2015 with an apology.

Naspers's most famous investment, and the one that has catapulted the company to titan status, was its early investment in Tencent. In a deal rivaled only by Softbank's investment in Alibaba, in 2001 Naspers purchased a 46.5 percent stake in Tencent from the Hong Kong tycoon Richard Li for $34 million. After reducing its stake to 34 percent over the years, the value of its investment in 2016 still was about $81 billion, helping make Naspers the largest company in Africa. Naspers has used the proceeds from reducing its stock in Tencent, and its rising status, to do its part to spread e-commerce to other emerging markets. Among its notable investments are India's Flipkart and the Middle East's Souq.

Naspers's own investments in Africa have achieved mixed results. It shut down its first major Nigerian e-commerce company, Kalihari.com.ng, in February 2014 after it failed to take off. Naspers hoped to redeem itself in the region with its investment in Konga.com, and its money helped Konga bring me to Nigeria.

On my second day in Lagos, I visited the Konga offices, based in the Yaba district. The distance from the hotel to Konga should be a ten-minute drive across the bridge from Ikoyi. But with Lagos's insane traffic, it can take as much as one hour.

Once at the office I met Sim Shagaya for the first time. Sim is tall and charismatic, with a deep voice and a big smile, and he immediately struck me as a born leader. I wasn't surprised when some influential bloggers in the region began calling him one of the "10 Most Powerful Men in Africa."

The son of a Nigerian army general, Sim was born in Nigeria and went on to serve in the Nigerian Army after graduating from the Nigerian Military School. He then studied at George Washington University and Dartmouth College before taking an MBA at Harvard Business School.

Sim started his career at the Rand Merchant Bank in South Africa but returned home to head Google in Africa in 2006. He also founded a successful billboard advertising business that he later turned into his first successful e-commerce company, DealDey, which he started in 2011. DealDey was an African Groupon funded by investors in the billboard company. In July 2012 he started Konga.com, for which he followed Amazon's retail model.

By the time I met Sim, Konga had moved into several stories of offices in a simple, nondescript building in the Yaba district. Inside, the company felt like any start-up in a developing company at this stage—employees crammed behind small desks in a space with plain white walls, because they were growing so quickly that no one had time to decorate or even hire a decorator. A web of tangled extension cords and wires ran across the floor. Outside, neighbors lived in makeshift shanties, cooking and eating outside, and bathing behind enclosures cobbled together from odds and ends of tin and plastic they had found in the neighborhood.

Sim brought me up to speed on Konga. The company had invested in a large warehouse that was full of inventory and was working on modernizing its inventory system. Konga ran its own delivery fleet, vans and motorcycles that could easily weave through traffic jams to make deliveries. While the sales figures were growing, so were the company's losses, as managing an entire operation from end to end is costly. The company was still trying to figure out which products to purchase and the categories it should carry. And while some fashion items carried high margins, they were also more likely to sit on the shelves.

The costs of running such a model were especially high in Nigeria. For instance, Konga needed generators to keep the website running in the event of a power outage. Although Sim didn't say so directly, I sensed that Konga was feeling pressure from its investors,

Naspers and Kinnevik, the Swedish investment firm, which wanted to see a path to profitability.

The main question at the time was the same one being asked at Lazada in Southeast Asia, Flipkart in India, and Jingdong in China—to what extent should the company try to expand into a marketplace model? And if it did, should it follow Amazon's example and build a hybrid marketplace/retail model? Or should it be more like Alibaba, a pure digital marketplace?

It is important to note that Konga was not operating in a vacuum. It had significant competition from Jumia, another Rocket Internet e-commerce venture, which started in May 2012, two months before Konga. A mirror image of Linio in Latin America and Lazada in Southeast Asia, Jumia was using Nigeria as its African base to roll out retail operations in more than ten African countries. Jumia was funded with multimillion-dollar investments from Rocket, Konga's investor Kinnevik, and other investors, making it a formidable foe.

These challenges were on Sim's mind as we walked to the Ozone Cinema, just a few blocks away, to screen my film for an audience of Konga staff and the start-up community in Lagos. A bit old and rundown, the theater had undoubtedly shown its fair share of the nearly two thousand Nollywood films produced each year on budgets that sometimes are less than $20,000 per movie.

"Pretty much all of the Nigerian tech start-up community is here in this room tonight," Sim told me as we surveyed the packed theater. "This is the first time we've all gotten together." There was Jason Iroko, who had started his iROKOtv, his own version of Netflix in Nigeria that specialized in home-grown Nollywood films. Heads of travel websites, real estate websites, and Google were there too. It was an honor to address the crowd and exciting to see that the tech start-up revolution was universal and even making inroads in Nigeria, after almost two decades.

When Sim addressed the crowd, the significance of what e-commerce could bring to Africa became clear to me from what he

said. "We have a duty to our country, especially from the point of
view of commerce," he said. "Africa has had a very long romance
with commerce. Sometimes that commerce has been unholy—
slavery. And sometimes it has been great. And for us that mission is
to use commerce to redeem this land and get all of us, irrespective
of tribe or religion or ethnicity or age, talking to each other and
making life a bit better for each other. And I suspect strongly that
if I keep thinking about it like this, and my colleagues at Konga
keep thinking about it like this in the context of the very long term,
then we will be fine."[5]

I have to admit that his hopeful message had me rooting for
Konga over its German adversary. Call me an idealist, but my travels had convinced me that to build a company with lasting value, it
has to have a soul. And Rocket's cut-and-paste approach, so geared
toward pleasing investors, didn't.

After the screening Sim invited me to spend a few weeks consulting with his team on various projects and providing insights
from China as Konga expanded to a marketplace. It meant the
company was facing some tough decisions, such as deemphasizing
the retail operation it had built and potentially eliminating jobs. But
it also meant unleashing the entrepreneurial energy of Nigeria.

Those few weeks at Konga reminded me of the early days of
Alibaba back in 2000, when not just a company but an entire new
industry was being born in China. On one evening during my
stay in Lagos, I spent some time with Sim at his house, where we
talked shop while chewing on *suya*, a spicy meat bought from a
nearby street vendor. "I don't want to just build a company that is
simply competing against all other retailers in Nigeria," he told me.
"I want to build something that fundamentally changes this country. We have to build a marketplace." He took me on a stroll around
Banana Island, an expensive enclave for Nigeria's elites. Sealed off
from the rest of Nigeria by several layers of security gates, Banana
Island is a large, master-planned neighborhood that guarantees
twenty-four-hour security and electricity to the expats, elites, and
(often corrupt) government officials residing within its high walls.

On our walk we passed the massive estate of Mike Adenuga, a Nigerian oil and telecom executive, who had adorned his compound with statues and fountains. The second-richest person in Africa, Adenuga would later go to war with the residents' association of Banana Island for the right to name his street Mike Adenuga Street. The stroll through Banana Island showed me just how much had to be done to spread the wealth on the continent.

I left Nigeria optimistic that e-commerce would take root. The quick adoption of mobile phones, combined with a booming economy, was good reason to hope that the country's e-commerce would follow a path similar to China's. Investment was beginning to flow in and even tragedies, such as terrorism and Ebola, were accelerating e-commerce adoption, providing an important means of doing business that would otherwise be difficult to pursue.

But this optimism was dampened in subsequent years, when Nigeria once again fell victim to the curse of resources. When oil prices crashed, Nigeria saw its economy fall into recession, and investors began to put even more pressure on the companies they had funded. The government imposed strict currency controls, making it difficult—sometimes nearly impossible—to get money in and out of the country. For e-commerce companies this meant that attempts to import foreign goods to sell online in Nigeria usually foundered. And on top of all of that, Internet penetration in the country actually began to decline, a rarity for any country.

With all the negative headlines about Nigeria's downhill turn, I was disappointed to read in January 2016 that after meeting with his investors, Sim Shagaya was stepping down as CEO of Konga and taking the more symbolic role of chairman of the company. Sim had become a visible symbol of Africa's homegrown e-commerce and was an inspiration not only to me but, more important, to the budding Internet entrepreneurs throughout Africa.

I emailed Sim in the hope of learning more about his decision to step down, but he didn't respond. Friends of his have speculated that the pressures of Nigeria's economic problems had put Sim and his long-term vision for the company at loggerheads with his investors, who wanted to see a faster path to profitability. Others speculated he had stepped down for more purely personal reasons. Whatever the true reason, I felt Africa had lost a Jack Ma of its own when Sim Shagaya stepped down.

But, of course, e-commerce in the ever-volatile Nigeria had found a way to live on, as it had in other emerging markets that had gone through similar downturns. And e-commerce heads in Nigeria were finding opportunity in crisis. Konga was rolling out its KongaPay, an escrow-based online payment system, as a step toward getting Nigerians to trust each other in an online payment environment. Jumia was setting up "customer adoption centers," where illiterate shoppers or shoppers without Internet access could have a company representative help them shop. And its JForce sales agents were beginning to go door to door with tablet computers to help others go online. Slowly but surely, they were building an e-commerce infrastructure and overcoming the lack of trust in the country.

Whether it is the heads of Konga or Jumia, or others who follow in their footsteps, entrepreneurs in Africa will eventually build an entirely new commercial infrastructure from scratch. And because it is starting from scratch on such an underdeveloped infrastructure, when it is built, e-commerce may prove even more valuable to Africa than to China and India. As Sim Shagaya has said, "Africa does not lack an abundance of people to buy things, sell things, or move them around. What Africa lacks is a twenty-first-century operating system to make it all work." It will take entrepreneurs with vision and daring, combined with investors who have patience and a long-term vision, to build this system. But as in China, India, Southeast Asia, and Latin America, this change is coming to Africa sooner than most people think. And it will transform the fortunes of entrepreneurs in e-commerce's final frontier, as it has already begun to do for e-commerce entrepreneurs around the world.

9

SIX BILLION SHOPPERS

I HOPE YOU'VE ENJOYED THIS JOURNEY THROUGH THE WORLD OF e-commerce. My goal has been to share my perspective on where e-commerce may be going. Along the way I've tried to provide the local context in which it is developing, in the hope that the next generation of e-commerce pioneers can avoid some of the mistakes, and learn some of the lessons, of the early e-commerce players.

It's an exciting time for entrepreneurs and e-commerce pioneers to be alive. Until about ten years ago, the benefits of e-commerce were largely limited to those in the developed world. But the future of e-commerce belongs to emerging markets. And e-commerce is now at the tipping point: the center of e-commerce is about to shift from the one billion shoppers of the developed world to the developing world's six billion shoppers.

With this in mind, I leave you with seven key takeaways.

We are now in the golden era of e-commerce in emerging markets
If you've read this far, I assume you agree that this is the golden age of e-commerce in emerging markets. Yet many business leaders

still think that e-commerce in emerging markets offers only marginal opportunity. In fact, the e-commerce opportunities in countries like China and India and in regions like Southeast Asia and Latin America are far greater than most people realize.

To understand the full scale of the opportunity, look at China, a country where, fifteen years ago, people thought e-commerce might never take off. In 2016 Alibaba's Singles' Day Global Shopping Festival

- generated $17.8 billion in transactions in a twenty-four-hour period (a 32 percent increase from the previous year) on Alibaba's websites alone
- attracted the participation of nearly 100,000 merchants
- saw at its peak the processing of 120,000 Alipay payment transactions *per second*
- saw 37 percent of buyers purchase from international brands
- processed 657 million delivery orders placed through Alibaba's marketplaces

And that's just *one* company in *one* emerging market on *one* day.

THE KEY POINT is this: The same revolution that occurred in China's retail market is gaining momentum in other emerging markets. Forward-looking companies and entrepreneurs can get into these other markets early, knowing that history is likely to repeat itself, albeit in a manner unique to each market. The market with the greatest growth potential in the near term is India's, followed by Southeast Asia's, Latin America's, and, long term, Africa's.

The key driver for global e-commerce growth
is smartphone adoption
The popularity of the smartphone, combined with the drop in Internet data prices, is powering Internet penetration in emerging markets. The result is that each week millions of new potential

e-commerce consumers are coming online in those markets. These smartphone users literally have a virtual shopping mall (or storefront) in their pockets.

Because e-commerce shoppers in developed markets started shopping online with desktop computers, they were slower to switch to mobile phones for their purchases than consumers in emerging markets. But for consumers in countries like China and India, a smartphone is often the first (and only) device they own for accessing the Internet, and they are therefore more likely to adopt the habit of using their phone to shop. Because consumers in emerging markets prefer phones with larger screens, companies can tailor all their branding activities to a smartphone screen, educating new consumers and building a brand for their products solely on the smartphone. Indeed, Alibaba's Singles' Day mobile sales figures overcame the concerns of the greatest skeptics: 82 percent of its sales came through mobile devices.

The preeminence of mobile use in emerging markets has important implications for e-commerce. It means that location-based marketing and services will become more fully developed. It means that mobile payment will become easier and that social commerce will play a more important role, because communication and shopping are more easily integrated on a mobile phone.

The failure to adapt US business models to emerging markets dominates the early history of e-commerce
In my travels to research this book, one common thread came through, no matter the market—the story of the first e-commerce attempts in emerging markets is the story of a failed attempt to apply the business model of eBay or Amazon to the local markets. Whether the company was 8848 in China, Baazee in India, or De-Remate in Latin America, those that stuck rigidly to the US business model either went out of business or limped along without achieving true success.

The reason for their failure is that US business models simply don't fit the conditions of emerging markets. EBay's auction model for secondhand goods didn't work in China, India, or Latin America because the big opportunity in these markets was to empower entrepreneurs to sell *new* goods—there was no big market for secondhand goods. Amazon's first retail-led model didn't work because the emerging markets were too inefficient for a comprehensive retail model that relies on large scale and low costs.

The companies that succeeded in the long run, such as China's Taobao and Latin America's Mercado Libre, may have started out as clones of their US counterparts. But they quickly pivoted and created something that fit the local market, starting with the local customer and working backward.

The Chinese model for e-commerce was the breakthrough that emerging markets needed for e-commerce to take off

The business model that Alibaba pioneered in China proved e-commerce could work in emerging markets, and its influence continues in other emerging markets today. The model is defined by a platform that empowers entrepreneurs and retailers by giving them the tools to create highly customizable storefronts and leaving responsibility for the success or failure of their business almost entirely in their hands. This platform is accompanied by an ecosystem that provides the services, such as payment and delivery, that buyers and sellers need to complete their transactions but that otherwise are nearly nonexistent locally.

In other emerging markets, e-commerce players have moved from favoring the Amazon and eBay models to favoring Alibaba's marketplace model. This does not mean that the Alibaba business model will work just as well in India as in China. And in fact the lesson from the China experience is that each market is unique and no one business model fits all. But entrepreneurs in emerging markets are now able to borrow from and adapt both the US and Chinese models while adding innovative services to meet local needs.

*E-commerce in emerging markets will prove more creative
than disruptive and will help lift millions out of poverty*
Creative disruption is a popular goal for entrepreneurs in the tech
world. But too often the creative aspects are celebrated while the
disruptive effects, such as job displacement, are overlooked. Amazon is a great example. Yes, it has brought less-expensive products
to consumers around the world. But it has also wreaked havoc
with the traditional retail it has replaced, driving bookstores and
retailers out of business as shoppers check out goods offline and
make their purchases online. "Amazon is not happening to bookselling, the future is happening to bookselling," Jeff Bezos famously
told the US television magazine *60 Minutes*. As much as I agree
with Bezos and admire Amazon for its innovation, I can't help but
also feel sympathy for the many traditional retail workers in the
United States who have been displaced.

Fortunately, the moral argument against e-commerce is harder
to make in emerging markets. Rather than replacing an already efficient retail infrastructure and displacing millions of workers,
e-commerce in emerging markets is likely to be creating opportunities
that did not exist offline. As studies cited earlier in this book have
shown, e-commerce has an additive effect in emerging market economies. And the inventory-free "China model" that companies in
emerging markets now favor tends to empower small retailers rather
than compete with them. As Jack Ma put it in Davos in 2017: "We
want to empower others to sell, to service, to make sure that other
people are more powerful than us. . . . We think, using our technology, we can make every company become Amazon."[1]

*Cross-border retail sales will become a major driver
of worldwide e-commerce growth*
As more of the emerging world's six billion shoppers buy smartphones and use them to shop, they are likely to begin their shopping
with online retailers who are local. But over time, as their incomes rise and they begin to seek new products and experiences,
they will begin to shop overseas after they realize that the world's

products are literally at their fingertips. The result will be a boom in cross-border retail sales, which have only just started.

Consider that during Alibaba's 2016 Singles' Day, shoppers in China bought products from retailers in more than two hundred countries and regions through cross-border transactions. This means that a family in rural China that wants to celebrate a special occasion might buy lobsters sent directly from Maine. Or an office worker in Kunming might buy a wedding dress from an online boutique based in France. Cross-border e-commerce has already arrived in China, making it possible for brands and entrepreneurs to sell into China directly, without setting up a local China operation. In fact, eMarketer estimated that cross-border sales into China would hit $85 billion by the end of 2016.[2]

As these cross-border sellers become more savvy about working through the customs paperwork and logistical challenges of cross-border fulfillment, they will pay more attention to other emerging markets, like India, where shoppers are quickly coming online. It's why a study by Accenture and AliResearch (Alibaba's research arm) estimates that B2C cross-border e-commerce volumes will surpass $1 trillion by 2020.[3]

However, as cross-border B2C transaction volumes rise, so will trade tensions between countries whose local retailers are adversely affected. After all, if a shopper in Mexico can get a better price on a product bought online from the United States or China and avoid local taxes, why wouldn't she go straight to Amazon or AliExpress for her purchase? In the recent political climate, with nationalism and protectionism on the rise around the world, a boom in cross-border e-commerce may also give rise to increased regulation designed to protect local jobs.

***The e-commerce boom will give rise to important
environmental challenges that emerging markets need
to manage responsibly***
It's easy to get excited about what e-commerce in emerging markets may bring. But no one should lose sight of the potential down-

sides and harmful effects, the greatest of which, in my view, is the potential for harm to the environment.

Nothing drove this home to me more than watching coverage of the 2015 Singles' Day Shopping Festival held by my former employer, Alibaba, in Beijing's Water Cube, once the venue for the swimming events of the 2008 Summer Olympics. As company officials and participants celebrated Alibaba smashing yet another record, air pollution was visible both within the venue and throughout the city. Even as China's orgy of online mass consumption was setting new records, people were walking Beijing's streets with face masks, protection from air quality deemed so unhealthy that parents were advised not to let their children play outside.

Yes—the benefits of e-commerce are great. And in a country like China, India, or Nigeria, it can provide a step up for a small entrepreneur's family, allowing them to buy basic necessities, such as enough protein to eat or books for their children's education. But simply replicating the mass consumerism of the West is not sustainable if these small entrepreneurs also want clean air and a healthy environment. Emerging markets should embrace e-commerce in a way that also considers the environmental impact to ensure that, as factories pump out more products and motorcycles whiz around town delivering packages, e-commerce's golden age doesn't lead to an environmental dark age.

NOTES

INTRODUCTION: A SHOPPING MALL IN EVERY POCKET

1. Goldman Sachs, "China E+Commerce: Shopping Re-imagined," February 28, 2017, 8; US Census Bureau, February 17, 2017, https://www.census.gov/retail/mrts/www/data/pdf/ec_current.pdf.
2. Unless otherwise specified, all dollar ($) values in the book are in US dollars.
3. Goldman Sachs, 3.

I: HOW THE WEST WAS WON

1. Boris Emmet and John E. Jeuck, *Catalogues and Counters: A History of Sears, Roebuck and Company* (Chicago and London: University of Chicago Press, 1950).
2. Ibid., 10.
3. Ibid.
4. Ibid., 11.
5. Ibid., 17.
6. Ibid., 20.
7. *Montgomery Ward & Co. Catalogue and Buyers' Guide 1895* (New York: Skyhorse Publishing, 2008).
8. Ibid.
9. Ibid., 1, 376.
10. Ibid., 2.
11. http://www.departmentstorehistory.net.
12. *Montgomery Ward & Co. Catalogue and Buyers' Guide*, Foreword, p. 1.
13. Robin Lewis and Michael Dart, *The New Rules of Retail* (New York: St. Martin's Press, 2014), 9.

14. Ibid., 16–17.
15. Sam Walton with John Huey, *Sam Walton: Made in America* (New York: Bantam Books, 1992), 29.
16. Ibid., 32–33.
17. Ibid., 63.
18. Ibid., 140–141, 276.
19. Ibid., 143.
20. Ibid., 116.
21. Ibid., 160.
22. Walmart 1995 Annual Report, http://corporate.walmart.com/our-story/our -history.
23. EBay company website.
24. *Business Week*, May 31, 1999.
25. "Montgomery Ward to Close Its Doors," *New York Times*, December 29, 2000; http://www.theforrester.com/2007/08/13/the-100-oldest-domains-on -the-internet/.

2: THE RISE OF E-COMMERCE IN CHINA

1. Goldman Sachs, "China E+Commerce: Shopping Re-Imagined" (Goldman Sachs Equity Research, February 28, 2017), 1.
2. eMarketer, "Worldwide Retail Ecommerce Sales: eMarketer Forecast for 2016," August 16, 2016, https://www.emarketer.com/Report/Worldwide -Retail-Ecommerce-Sales-eMarketer-Forecast-2016/2001849.
3. T. Talhelm, X. Zhang, S. Oishi, D. Duan, X. Lan, and S. Kitayama, "Large-Scale Psychological Differences Within China Explained by Rice versus Wheat Agriculture," *Science* 344, no. 6184 (May 9, 2014): 603–608.
4. "China's No. 1 Department Store," *New York Times*, November 28, 1982.
5. "Another China Net Pioneer Quits," CNN.com, August 10, 2001, http:// edition.cnn.com/2001/BUSINESS/asia/08/10/hk.dotcomdeparture/.
6. "JD.com Had a Big Quarter Thanks to China E-commerce Growth," *Business Insider*, May 12, 2016 (citing iResearch market share numbers).
7. Duncan Clark, *Alibaba* (New York: Harper-Collins, 2016), 147–149.
8. Stanford Graduate School of Business case study, "Taobao vs EBay China," January 4, 2010.
9. Kathrin Hille, "Lessons from an Early Failure," *Financial Times*, June 24, 2012.
10. Ibid.
11. Edward Tse, *China's Disruptors: How Alibaba, Xiaomi, Tencent, and Other Companies Are Changing the Rules of Business* (New York: Portfolio/ Penguin, 2015), 85.
12. eMarketer, "WeChat is China's Most Popular Chat App," June 9, 2016, https://www.emarketer.com/Article/WeChat-Chinas-Most-Popular-Chat -App/1014057.

3: THE GREAT MALL OF CHINA

1. "China's Online Shopping GMV Approached 5 Trillion Yuan in 2016," iResearch, February 14, 2017, http://www.iresearchchina.com/content/details7 _30708.html.

2. Boston Consulting Group and AliResearch Institute, "The New China Playbook: Young, Affluent, E-Savvy Consumers Will Fuel Growth," December 2015.

3. Catherine Cadell, "Alibaba Posts Record Singles' Day Sales, but Growth Slows," Reuters, November 11, 2016, http://www.reuters.com/article/us -alibaba-singlesday-idUSKBN13605X.

4. Gabriel Wildau and Leslie Hook, "China Mobile Payments Soar as US Clings to Plastic," *Financial Times*, February 14, 2017.

5. Selena Wang, "Alibaba's E-Commerce App Has a Social Network Facebook Would Love," *Bloomberg*, August 22, 2016.

6. Ibid.

7. Alissa Coram, "Move Over, Alibaba: Check Out This Other China E-Commerce Name," *Investor's Business Daily*, March 31, 2017.

8. Lulu Yilun Chen and Shai Oster, "China Startup 'Little Red Book' Said to Be Valued at $1 Billion," *Bloomberg*, March 30, 2016.

9. Frank Lavin, interview by author, April 14, 2016.

10. Ibid.

11. Twenty US dollars were worth about RMB133 as this book went to press.

12. Lavin interview.

13. Goldman Sachs, "China E+Commerce: Shopping Re-imagined," February 28, 2017, 8; eMarketer, "Worldwide Retail Ecommerce Sales: eMarketer Forecast for 2016" (eMarketer, August 2016).

14. "Amazon's Jeff Bezos Looks to the Future," *60 Minutes*, December 1, 2013, http://www.cbsnews.com/news/amazons-jeff-bezos-looks-to-the-future/.

15. McKinsey & Company, "China's eTail Revolution: Online Shopping as a Catalyst for Growth," March 2013.

16. Bain & Company, "China's E-commerce: The New Branding Game," 2015.

17. Boston Consulting Group and AliResearch Institute, "The New China Playbook: Young, Affluent, E-Savvy Consumers Will Fuel Growth," December 2015.

18. McKinsey & Company, "China's eTail Revolution."

19. Alizila Staff, "An introduction to Taobao Villages," Alizila, January 17, 2016, http://www.alizila.com/an-introduction-to-taobao-villages/.

20. Susan Wang, "Alibaba's Centers Now Reach 16,000 Villages," Alizila, May 26, 2016, http://www.alizila.com/alibabas-rural-service-centers-reach-16000 -villages/.

4: INDIA—THE NEXT MEGA-MARKET

1. Suryatapa Bhattacharya, "Flipkart to Deliver Using Mumbai's Dabbawalas," *Wall Street Journal*, April 10, 2015, http://blogs.wsj.com/indiarealtime/2015/04/10/flipkart-to-deliver-using-mumbais-dabbawalas/.
2. Mumbai history, http://www.mumbai.org.uk/history.html.
3. Mukul Kesavan, "Before the Change: When Austerity, Simplicity Ruled Everyday Middle Class Life," *Hindustan Times*, July 24, 2016, http://www.hindustantimes.com/india-news/before-the-change-when-austerity-and-simplicity-ruled-everyday-middle-class-life/story-PuanuEB9aMkrD4do qtzI4N.html.
4. Shovon Chowdhury, "Serving the Nation, One Bikini at a Time," *Indian Express*, July 24, 2016, http://indianexpress.com/article/lifestyle/life-style/serving-the-nation-one-bikini-at-a-time/.
5. "Best Decades Ever," *Times of India*, July 24, 2016, 15; Gaurav Choudhury, "25 Years of the Open Era: Reviewing India's Post-liberalisation Economy," *Hindustan Times*, July 24, 2016, http://www.hindustantimes.com/india-news/the-open-era-reviewing-india-s-post-liberalisation-economy/story-FteMwib4Jg6IHguI4LhGWM.html; Darrell M. West, John Villasenor, and Robin Lewis, "Inclusion in India: Unpacking the 2015 FDIP Report and Scorecard," Brookings Institution, September 9, 2015, https://www.brookings.edu/2015/09/09/inclusion-in-india-unpacking-the-2015-fdip-report-and-scorecard/.
6. Sapna Aggarwal, "India's Retail Market Expected to Double in Next 5 Years: Report," *Live Mint*, February 11, 2015, http://www.livemint.com/Industry/5Xu8P8GltZk8XEsz7Xk74O/Indian-retail-market-to-double-in-next-5-years-report.html.
7. Eric Bellman, "In India, a Retailer Finds Key to Success Is Clutter," *Wall Street Journal*, August 8, 2007.
8. Aggarwal, "India's Retail Market Expected to Double."
9. "FDI in Retail: I Will Set Walmart Stores on Fire, Threatens Uma Bharati," *Times of India*, November 25, 2011.
10. Aggarwal, "India's Retail Market Expected to Double."
11. Tadit Kundu, "Nearly Half of Indians Survived on Less than Rs38 a Day in 2011–12," *Live Mint*, April 21, 2016, http://www.livemint.com/Opinion/l1gVncveq4EYEn2zuzX4FL/Nearly-half-of-Indians-survived-on-less-than-Rs38-a-day-in-2.html.
12. Priya Virmani, "Note to India's Leaders: Your 150M Young People Are Calling for Change," *Guardian*, April 8, 2014, https://www.theguardian.com/commentisfree/2014/apr/08/india-leaders-young-people-change-2014-elections; PTI, "Per Capita Income This Year Seen Up 10% at Rs 7,378 a Month," *Economic Times* (India), February 9, 2015, http://articles.economictimes.indiatimes.com/2015-02-09/news/58967932_1_capita-income-constant-prices-central-statistics-office.

13. "India Rises to Second Spot on Global Business Optimism Index: Report," *Times of India*, November 6, 2016.

14. "India Market Report: India Internet Usage Stats and Telecommunications Market Report," Internet World Stats, page updated December 7, 2016, http://www.internetworldstats.com/asia/in.htm; "Indian PC Market Growth Falls for Two Consecutive Quarters: Expected to Crash to Half in the Year 2001," press release, Skoch Consultancy Services, March 7, 2001, http://www.skoch.in/images/stories/Press_Release_Pdf/indianpcmarketgrows.pdf.

15. "Arranged Marriage Is Not Forced Marriage," CNN, May 30, 2012, http://thecnnfreedomproject.blogs.cnn.com/2012/05/30/arranged-marriage-is-not-forced-marriage/.

16. "High-Growth Indian Online Matrimonial Matchmaking Market Beckons Investors," Frost & Sullivan press release, *BusinessWire India*, July 17, 2015, http://businesswireindia.com/news/news-details/high-growth-indian-online-matrimonial-matchmaking-market-beckons-investors/44523.

17. Niren Shah, phone interview by author, May 2, 2016.

5: INDIA'S E-COMMERCE GOLDEN ERA FINALLY ARRIVES

1. "Young Turks," CNBC, https://www.youtube.com/watch?v=9CUllBw3OsU.

2. Ibid.

3. Vikas Bajaj, "In India, Online Retailers Take a New Tack," *New York Times*, September 15, 2011, http://www.nytimes.com/2011/09/15/business/with-no-amazon-as-a-rival-flipkart-moves-fast-in-india.html.

4. Anusha Soni and Itika Sharma Punit, "Flipkart Raises $160 mn from New, Existing Investors," *Business Standard*, October 9, 2013, http://www.business-standard.com/article/companies/flipkart-raises-160-mn-from-new-existing-investors-113100900412_1.html.

5. Soni and Punit, "Flipkart Raises $160 mn from New, Existing Investors; Jubin Mehta, "Flipkart Launches Its Marketplace with 50 Sellers Onboard," *Yourstory*, April 6, 2013, https://yourstory.com/2013/04/flipkart-launches-a-marketplace-platform-onboards-50-sellers/; "Amazon.co.jp Launches Amazon Marketplace Enabling Third Party Buyers and Sellers to Trade Online," undated Amazon press release, http://phx.corporate-ir.net/phoenix.zhtml?c=176060&p=irol-newsArticle&ID=503055.

6. Alok Soni, "Everything You Wanted to Know about the Flipkart-Myntra Deal," *YourStory*, May 22, 2014, https://yourstory.com/2014/05/flipkart-myntra-acquisition/; Saritha Rai, "Online Retailers Hustle to Build an Alibaba in India, Take on Amazon," *Forbes*, May 22, 2014, http://www.forbes.com/sites/saritharai/2014/05/22/local-online-retailers-hustle-to-build-an-alibaba-in-india/#5e746f79145a.

7. Prince Thomas, "Who Will Be India's Alibaba, SnapDeal or Flipkart?" Forbesindia.com, May 28, 2014, http://www.forbesindia.com/blog/business-strategy/who-will-be-indias-alibaba-snapdeal-or-flipkart/.

8. NDTV, "Walk the Talk with the Snapdeal Founders Kunal Bahl and Rohit Bansal," April 1, 2016, http://www.ndtv.com/video/shows/walk-the-talk/walk-the-talk-with-snapdeal-founders-kunal-bahl-and-rohit-bansal-410161.
9. Ibid.
10. Ibid.
11. Kunal Bahl, interview by author, February 19, 2016, Delhi.
12. "Get to Know Snapdeal," Snapdeal.com, http://www.snapdeal.com/page/about-us.
13. Bahl interview by author.
14. PTI, "Invested $300 Million in Supply Chain, Logistics in 18 Months: Snapdeal," Economic Times (India), May 13, 2016, http://economictimes.indiatimes.com/industry/services/retail/invested-300-million-in-supply-chain-logistics-in-18-months-snapdeal/articleshow/52243823.cms.
15. Richa Maheshwari, "Ecommerce Majors Amazon, Flipkart Together Rented about 3.6 Million Square Feet Warehouse Space in 2015," Economic Times (India), January 29, 2016, http://economictimes.indiatimes.com/wealth/personal-finance-news/ecommerce-majors-amazon-flipkart-together-rented-about-3-6-million-square-feet-warehouse-space-in-2015/articleshow/50764978.cms.
16. "In an Industry First, Snapdeal Launches Multi-lingual Platform in 12 Languages and Brings Digital Commerce Closer to the Next 130 Million Indians," Snapdeal.com blog, December 15, 2015, http://blog.snapdeal.com/in-an-industry-first-snapdeal-launches-multi-lingual-platform-in-12-languages-and-brings-digital-commerce-closer-to-the-next-130-million-indians/.
17. Reuters, "Micromax Has Lost Nearly 50 Percent Market Share in One Year. Here's Why," DNA India, March 13, 2016, http://www.dnaindia.com/money/report-how-did-micromax-lose-nearly-half-of-its-market-share-in-one-year-2188696.
18. Shelley Singh, "How Ban on Discounts Have Changed Behaviour of Online Buyers," Economic Times (India), July 12, 2016, http://economictimes.indiatimes.com/industry/services/retail/how-ban-on-discounts-have-changed-behaviour-of-online-buyers/articleshow/53163899.cms.
19. Ratna Bhushan, "Maggi Ban Impact: Nestle India May Take 3 Years to Recover," Economic Times (India), February 24, 2016, http://economictimes.indiatimes.com/industry/cons-products/food/maggi-ban-impact-nestle-india-may-take-3-years-to-recover/articleshow/51114562.cms.
20. Vivienne Walt, "Amazon Invades India," Fortune, December 28, 2015.
21. Jason Dean, "Bezos Says Amazon Will Boost Investment in China," Wall Street Journal, June 6, 2007.
22. Dhanya Ann Thoppil, "India's Flipkart Raises $1 Billion in Fresh Funding," Wall Street Journal, July 29, 2014, http://www.wsj.com/articles/indias-flipkart-raises-1-billion-in-fresh-funding-1406641579.
23. "Amazon Goes One Up on Flipkart, to Invest $2 bn," Business Standard, July 31, 2014, http://www.business-standard.com/article/companies/now-amazon-announces-2-billion-investment-in-india-114073000379_1.html.

24. PTI, "Amazon to Increase Investment India to $5 billion," *The Hindu*, June 8, 2016, http://www.thehindu.com/business/Industry/amazon-to-increase -investment-india-to-5-billion/article8704018.ece.
25. Mihir Dalal, "Amazon Flags Regulatory Risk in India," *Live Mint*, October 31, 2014, http://www.livemint.com/Companies/9nBMMc6YYN3Mv-P2LxNojgO/Amazon-flags-regulatory-risk-in-India.html; "India Approves Foreign Investment in E-commerce Sector," Reuters, March 30, 2016, http://in.reuters.com/article/india-ecommerce-fdi-idINKCN0WV248.
26. Shilpa Phadnis, "Flipkart, Amazon Will Have to Downsize WS Retail, Cloudtail," *ET Tech* blog, *Economic Times*, April 1, 2016.
27. Madhav Chanchani, "Amazon India's Growth Threatens to Unsettle Ecommerce Firms Like Flipkart and Snapdeal," *Economic Times* (India), May 16, 2016, http://economictimes.indiatimes.com/industry/services/retail/amazon -indias-growth-threatens-to-unsettle-ecommerce-firms-like-flipkart-and -snapdeal/articleshow/52284757.cms; Alnoor Peermohamed, "Amazon Slashes Sellers' Fees to Take on Flipkart," *Business Standard*, June 17, 2016, http://www.business-standard.com/article/companies/amazon-slashes-seller -commissions-to-undercut-flipkart-snapdeal-116061600205_1.html.
28. Maheshwari, "Ecommerce Majors Amazon, Flipkart Together Rented."
29. Jeff Bezos, 2016 letter to Amazon shareholders, https://www.sec.gov/Archives /edgar/data/1018724/000119312516530910/d168744dex991.htm.
30. Jubin Mehta, "Paytm's Move into Mobile Commerce: A Zero Commission Marketplace," *YourStory*, April 25, 2015, https://yourstory.com/2015/04 /paytms-zero-commission-marketplace/.
31. Jai Vardhan, "Jack Ma's Alibaba Enters India by Buying 25% Stake in Paytm," *YourStory*, February 5, 2015, https://yourstory.com/2015/02/jack -mas-alibaba-enters-india-buying-25-stake-paytm/.
32. James Crabtree, "Vijay Sharma, Paytm: An Alibaba for India," *Financial Times*, November 18, 2015.
33. Vijay Shekar Sharma, phone interview by author, April 30, 2016.
34. Jai Vardhan, "Paytm Becomes the Largest Digital Commerce Company in India, Reports 350% Growth in 2013 over 2012," *YourStory*, May 7, 2014, https://yourstory.com/2014/05/paytm-digital-commerce/.
35. Bahl interview.
36. Richa Maheshwari, "Indian eCommerce Market to Grow Fastest Globally over 3 Years: Morgan Stanley," *Economic Times* (India), February 18, 2016, http://economictimes.indiatimes.com/industry/services/retail/indian -ecommerce-market-to-grow-fastest-globally-over-3-years-morgan-stanley /articleshow/51031652.cms.
37. Trefis Team, "Amazon Tops Indian E-Commerce Market in Web Traffic," *Forbes*, June 27, 2016, http://www.forbes.com/sites/greatspeculations/2016/06 /27/amazon-tops-indian-e-commerce-market-in-web-traffic/#1dc2285dc13b.
38. Richa Maheshwari, "E-commerce Boom in India Attracting Artisans, Entrepreneurs from Slums across the Country," *Economic Times* (India), February 19, 2016, http://economictimes.indiatimes.com/industry/services/retail/e

-commerce-boom-in-india-attracting-artisans-entrepreneurs-from-slums
-across-the-country/articleshow/51047812.cms.

39. EMarketer, "Worldwide Retail Ecommerce Sales," August 2016.

40. Sandeep Aggarwal, phone interview by author, March 29, 2016.

41. Ibid.

42. "Digital Payments Soar by Up to 300% after Demonitisation," *Times of India*, December 10, 2016.

43. Malavika Velayanikal, "What Are the Hottest Sectors for Venture Capital in India This Year? (INFOGRAPHIC)," *Tech in Asia*, October 22, 2015, https://www.techinasia.com/hottest-sectors-venture-capital-india-infographic.

44. IANS, "E-commerce to Invest $8 Billion in Infrastructure, Logistics in India: Study," *Economic Times* (India), June 29, 2016, http://economictimes.indiatimes.com/articleshow/52972911.cms?utm_source=contento finterest&utm_medium=text&utm_campaign=cppst; Emmanuel Amberber, "Investors Pump $9 Billion into Indian Startups in 2015—That's 50 Percent of the Past 5 Years' Total Deal Value," *YourStory*, December 31, 2015, https://yourstory.com/2015/12/indian-startups-raise-9billion-2015/.

6: SOUTHEAST ASIA

1. Milton Osborne, "What Is Southeast Asia?" in *Southeast Asia: An Introductory History* (New South Wales: Allen & Unwin, 2013).

2. Milton Osborne, *Southeast Asia: An Introductory History* (New South Wales: Allen & Unwin 2013), 1–17.

3. Sally McGrane, "3 Brothers, 4 Months, 1 Fortune in an Early Success in Germany," E-Commerce (special section), *New York Times*, September 22, 1999, https://partners.nytimes.com/library/tech/99/09/biztech/technology/22mcgr.html.

4. Thomas Ohr, "25 Things You Should Know about Oliver Samwer (CEO, Rocket Internet)," *EU-Startups*, August 19, 2014.

5. Max Finger and Oliver Samwer, *America's Most Successful Startups: Lessons for Entrepreneurs* (Weisbaden: Springer Fachmedian Wiesbaden GMBH, 1998), 18.

6. Ibid., 11.

7. Meg Whitman with Joan O'C. Hamilton, *The Power of Many: Values for Success in Business and in Life* (New York: Crown, 2010), 64–65.

8. Matt Cowan, "Inside the Clone Factory: The Story of the Samwer Brothers and Rocket Internet," *Wired*, March 2, 2012.

9. Andreas Winiarski, interview by author, October 5, 2015, Berlin.

10. Mike Butcher, "In Confidential Email Samwer Describes Online Furniture Strategy as a 'Blitzkrieg'," *TechCrunch*, December 22, 2011.

11. Christian Hardenberg, interview by author, May 19, 2016, Berlin.

12. Ibid.

13. Emma Thomasson and Chijoke Ohuocha, "Landing with a Bump? Germany's Rocket Falls Back to Earth," Reuters, June 29, 2016.

14. Hardenberg interview.
15. William Tanuwijaya, interview by author, May 13, 2016, Tokyo.
16. Ibid.
17. Ibid.
18. *CIA World Factbook*, https://www.cia.gov/library/publications/the-world-factbook/.
19. World Bank website, http://data.worldbank.org/indicator/NY.GDP.PCAP.CD?locations=CN-SG-MY-TH-ID.
20. "Southeast Asian Consumers Lead in Optimism Globally," *Insights*, Nielsen.com, July 28, 2015, http://www.nielsen.com/apac/en/insights/reports/2015/q2-2015-consumer-confidence-report.html.
21. Sheji Ho, phone interview by author, August 18, 2016.
22. Ibid.; eCommerce company presentation.
23. Ho interview.
24. Florian Hope, Sebastien Lamy, and Alessandro Cannarsi, "Can Southeast Asia Live Up to Its E-commerce Potential?" Bain & Company, 2016, 4.
25. Ibid., 3.
26. Sheji Ho, "Why Southeast Asia Is Leading the World's Most Disruptive Mobile Business Models," *TechCrunch*, September 8, 2015.
27. Judith Balea, "Here's How Much Startups Raised in Southeast Asia in 2015," *Tech in Asia*, January 4, 2016.
28. Shona, "Debit and Credit Card Usage in Asia," blog post, *Demystify Asia*, June 14, 2016, http://www.demystifyasia.com/creditdebit-card-adoption-asia/.
29. World Bank Logistics Performance Index, http://lpi.worldbank.org.

7: LATIN AMERICA

1. *Economist*, "A Century of Decline," February 15, 2014.
2. Ibid.
3. Ibid.
4. Ibid.
5. "MercadoLibre and Why South America Shouldn't Settle for Quick and Easy," *TechCrunch*, December 14, 2009.
6. Stelleo Tolda, interview by author, November 12, 2015.
7. Ibid.
8. Martinez-Jerez, Francisco de Asis, Joshua Bellin, and James Robert Dillon, "MercadoLibre.com," Harvard Business School Case 106-057, February 2006 (revised January 2007), 3.
9. Tolda interview.
10. Martinez-Jerez et al., "MercadoLibre.com," 3.
11. Tolda interview; Martinez-Jerez et al., "MercadoLibre.com."
12. "MercadoLibre and Why South America Shouldn't Settle."
13. Martinez-Jerez et al., "MercadoLibre.com," 8.
14. Tolda interview.

15. Ibid.
16. Sean Summers, interview by author, November 12, 2015, Buenos Aires.
17. MercadoLibre 2014 investor day presentation.
18. Tolda interview.
19. Anthony Harrup, "Mexican E-commerce Grows, but Requires Some Coaxing," *Wall Street Journal*, January 1, 2016.
20. Ibid.
21. Linio company presentation.
22. Summers interview.
23. Andreas Mjelde, interview by author, November 10, 2015, Mexico City.
24. Ibid.
25. Rebeca Dallal, MercadoLibre Case Study, https://www.slideshare.net/rebeca dallal/mercado-libre-54033523.
26. Mjelde interview.
27. Kimberly Weisul, "You Call This Diversity? A Disappointing Snapshot of Silicon Valley," *Inc.*, June 18, 2014.

8: AFRICA—THE FINAL FRONTIER

1. *African Powers for Retailing: New Horizons for Growth*, report (Deloitte & Touche, 2015), 5, http://www.demystifyasia.com/creditdebit-card-adoption -asia/.
2. Monique Verduyn, "BidorBuy: Andy Higgins," *Entrepreneur* (South Africa), July 2, 2010, http://www.entrepreneurmag.co.za/advice/success-stories/case -studies/bidorbuy-andy-higgins/.
3. *African Powers for Retailing*, 5.
4. "Why Does Kenya Lead the World in Mobile Money?" *Economist*, March 2, 2015.
5. Sim Shagaya, remarks at screening of *Crocodile in the Yangtze* (2012), January 14, 2014, Lagos, Nigeria.

9: SIX BILLION SHOPPERS

1. Nina Zipkin, "Jack Ma on Why Alibaba Isn't the Chinese Amazon," *Entrepreneur*, January 20, 2017, https://www.entrepreneur.com/article/288116.
2. "China Embraces Cross-Border Ecommerce," eMarketer, June 14, 2016, https://www.emarketer.com/Article/China-Embraces-Cross-Borders-Ecom merce/1014078.
3. Adam Najberg and Jim Erickson, "Cross-Border E-Commerce to Reach $1 Trillion in 2020," Alizila, June 11, 2015, http://www.alizila.com/cross-border -e-commerce-to-reach-1-trillion-in-2020/.

INDEX